Horizons

Mathematics 4

Book 2

Authors:

Cindi Mitchell & Lori Fowler

Editor:

Alan Christopherson

Graphic Design:

Chris Burkholder
Mark Aguilar
Lisa Kelly
JoAnn Cumming
John Charles Walker
Lisa Nelson
Annette Walker
Keith Piccolo
Robert Breen

Alpha Omega Publications, Inc.
Rock Rapids, IA

Media Credits:
Page 10: © TongRo Images Inc, iStock, Thinkstock; **page 203:** © Rost-9D, iStock, Thinkstock; **page 213:** © DAJ, iStock, Thinkstock

Horizons Mathematics 4, Student Workbook 2

804 N. 2nd Ave. E., Rock Rapids, IA 51246-1759

Printed in the United States of America
ISBN 978-1-58095-987-2

Telling Time

Sandra was assigned to make a class presentation on telling time. She made a poster to show how we measure time using a day and smaller units.

Telling Time

Units of Time

1 day	=	24 hours
1 hour	=	60 minutes
1 minute	=	60 seconds

The Clock

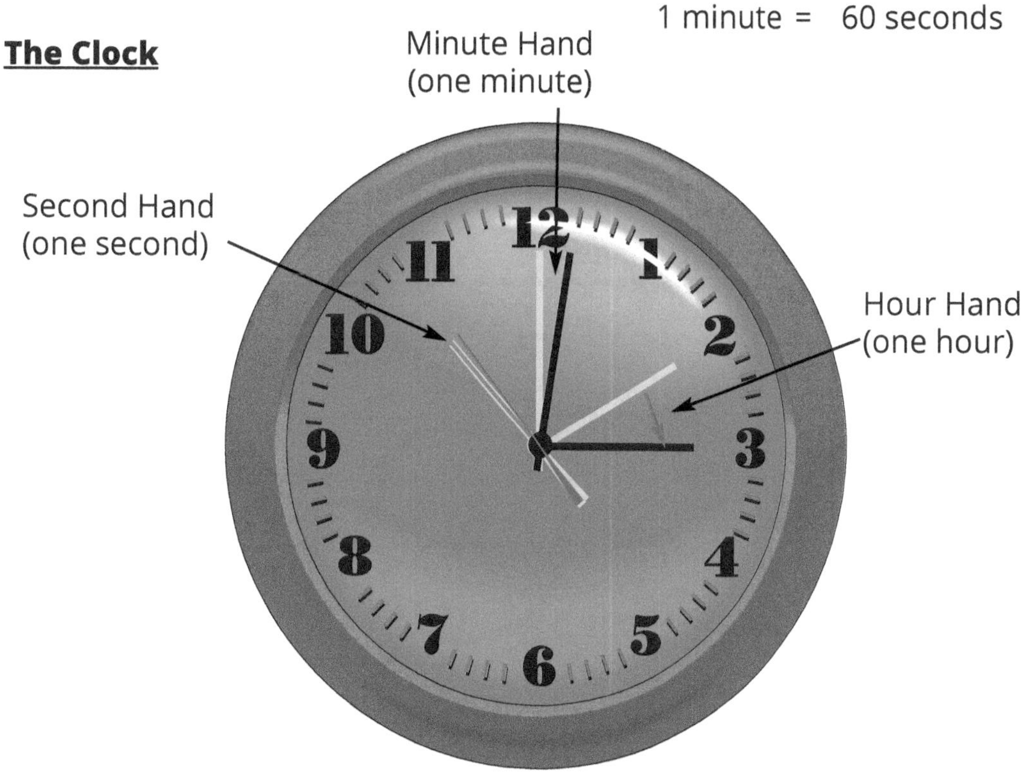

Minute Hand (one minute)

Second Hand (one second)

Hour Hand (one hour)

A given time may be read and stated in several different ways. The following are examples of times which may be stated different ways.

Read:

7:15	3:45	9:24
Seven fifteen or 15 minutes after 7 or a quarter after 7	Three forty-five or 45 minutes after 3 or a quarter until 4	Nine twenty-four or 24 minutes after 9

The reason time is often stated as "a quarter after," "a quarter before," or "half after" is because the clock face is a circle and minutes may be viewed as fractions of an hour. When the clock face is viewed as a fractional representation of minutes, 15 after is a quarter of the whole clock. 30 minutes is viewed as half of the clock face; half of an hour. Look at the diagram below.

12:15 or a quarter after 12

2:30 or half past 2

1 Write in the correct time.

______

______

______

______

______

______

2 Solve.

$3 + n = 5 + (2 \times 6)$

$7 + n = 8 + (3 \times 1)$

$n + 4 = 12 - (3 \times 2)$

3 Write in expanded form.

Three hundred thousand, forty-five =

Twenty-four million =

Sixty-five =

Nine million, eight hundred thousand =

Two billion =

4 Find the difference.

92 – 5 =	81 – 7 =	36 – 4 =
90 – 19 =	76 – 12 =	27 – 22 =

5 Multiply.

481	763	371	281	590
x 23	x 15	x 31	x 28	x 79

6 Fill in the blanks.

A ____________________ is 100 years.

______________ means Before Christ.

A ____________________ is 10 years.

__________ means *anno Domini* or *in the year of our Lord.*

A ____________________ is 1,000 years.

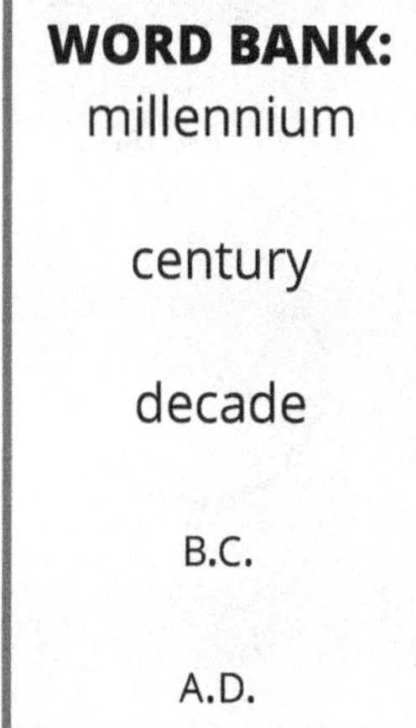

Telling Time

Kimberly went to bed at 12:45 after watching the late movie. Samantha ate an enchilada and taco dinner at 12:45.

12:45 P.M.

12:45 A.M.

How do we know what time of day these events occurred? Did Kimberly go to bed at 12:45 in the afternoon? Did Samantha eat at 12:45 at night? Probably not, but how could we know for sure? It is simple. **Times from 12:00 midnight up to noon are labeled A.M. Times from 12:00 noon up to midnight are labeled P.M.**

For example, we have labeled each of the following events and times as either A.M. or P.M.

Breakfast
7:15 A.M.

Dinner
6:30 P.M.

Sunday School
9:30 A.M.

Skydiving Lessons
4:30 P.M.

1 Write the time and label A.M. or P.M.

Starting School

Time: ______

Going to Bed

Time: ______

Ending the school day

Time: ______

Eating an early lunch

11:27

Time: ______

2 Match.

10 years	before Christ
100 years	millennium
B.C.	decade
A.D.	anno Domini
1,000 years	century

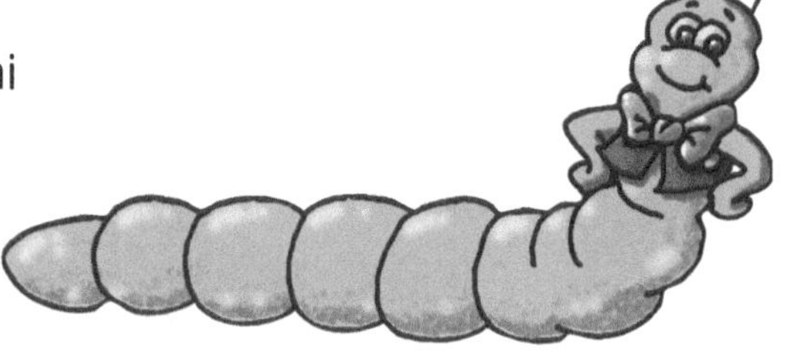

3 Order from largest to smallest.

6,729	6,808	6,333	6,395
______	______	______	______
9,867	9,291	9,365	9,567
______	______	______	______

4 Find the difference.

$\begin{array}{r} 754 \\ -\ 297 \\ \hline \end{array}$ $\begin{array}{r} 291 \\ -\ 123 \\ \hline \end{array}$ $\begin{array}{r} 170 \\ -\ 89 \\ \hline \end{array}$ $\begin{array}{r} 182 \\ -\ 125 \\ \hline \end{array}$ $\begin{array}{r} 395 \\ -\ 106 \\ \hline \end{array}$ $\begin{array}{r} 567 \\ -\ 307 \\ \hline \end{array}$

5 Solve.

$5 \times n = 45$ $9 \times n = 36$ $2 \times n = 18$ $4 \times n = 32$

6 Solve.

$9\overline{)56}$ $7\overline{)4}$ $6\overline{)9}$ $3\overline{)20}$ $7\overline{)46}$

Century

What is a century? A century is a time period of 100 years. We now live in the 21st Century. Look at the chart below. This chart shows all the dates and centuries up to the present.

1 A.D.	to	100 A.D.	-	1st century
101 A.D.	to	200 A.D.	-	2nd century
201 A.D.	to	300 A.D.	-	3rd century
301 A.D.	to	400 A.D.	-	4th century
401 A.D.	to	500 A.D.	-	5th century
501 A.D.	to	600 A.D.	-	6th century
↓				↓
1601 A.D.	to	1700 A.D.	-	17th century
1701 A.D.	to	1800 A.D.	-	18th century
1801 A.D.	to	1900 A.D.	-	19th century
1901 A.D.	to	2000 A.D.	-	20th century
2001 A.D.	to	2100 A.D.	-	21st century

If you look closely you will notice that the beginning digits of the year, 1996, and the beginning digits of the century, 20th century are one number off. This is an easy way to remember what century a year is in. Look at the first two digits of the year and then add one. For example: 1898 is in the 19th century, 1768 is in the 18th century, and 2012 is in the 21st century.

1 Tell the century for each year.

1594 = ____________ 1437 = ____________

1889 = ____________ 1776 = ____________

2001 = ____________ 987 = ____________

2 Tell the time. Label A.M. or P.M.

Breakfast

Late show

Football game

Bath time

________ ________ ________ ________

3 Order from smallest to largest.

4,070 6,080 9,050 4,406

________ ________ ________ ________

6,003 5,008 3,002 2,003

________ ________ ________ ________

4 Find the difference.

3,008	5,040	7,001	4,009	3,050
- 250	- 551	- 358	- 859	- 451

5 Divide.

$4\overline{)31}$ $8\overline{)5}$ $5\overline{)19}$ $6\overline{)9}$ $9\overline{)73}$ $3\overline{)16}$

6 Average.

17, 24, 34, 27, 18

43, 29, 38, 26, 19

18, 32, 29, 25

Time Conversions

Keri needed to record a 1 hour TV show for school. When she looked at her recording device, the space available was given in minutes, not hours. How many minutes of space would she need in order to record a one hour show?

This problem can easily be solved if Keri knows her time equivalents. The chart below shows these time equivalents.

1 minute	=	60 seconds
1 hour	=	60 minutes
1 day	=	24 hours

Keri would need at least 60 minutes of recording space in order to record her TV show.

How many minutes of space would be needed to record a 2 hour show? 120 minutes. If there are 60 minutes in 1 hour, then 60 minutes + 60 minutes = 120 minutes.

1 Match.

_____ 1 hour	A.	240 seconds
_____ 60 seconds	B.	2 days
_____ 24 hours	C.	60 minutes
_____ 48 hours	D.	2 hours
_____ 120 Minutes	E.	1 minute
_____ 4 minutes	F.	1 day

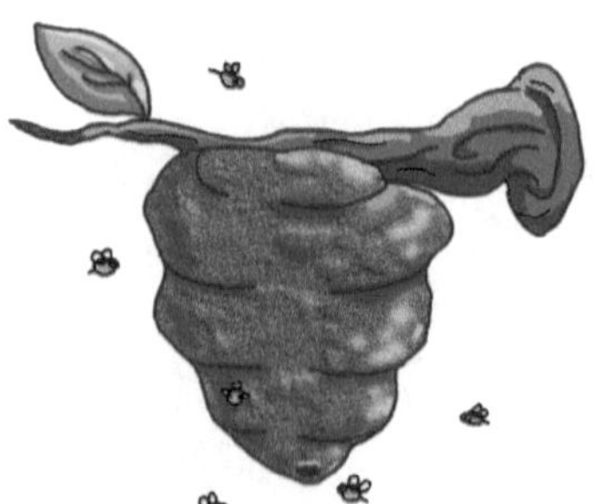

2 Draw in the time. Write an event which would occur at the specified time.

12:00 P.M.
____

8:30 A.M.
____

6:00 P.M.
____

9:00 A.M.
____

3 Write the time.

________A.M.

________P.M.

________A.M.

________P.M.

4 Divide.

$5\overline{)45}$ $6\overline{)48}$ $8\overline{)72}$ $2\overline{)12}$ $3\overline{)9}$

5 Divide.

$30\overline{)60}$ $10\overline{)80}$ $50\overline{)100}$ $20\overline{)40}$ $60\overline{)180}$

6 Follow the directions.

Find the sum of each vertical, horizontal, and diagonal row in the magic square below to reveal a magic number.

Construct a new magic square by dividing each number in the original square by 10. Write your answers in the grid provided.

What is the new magic number?

400	300	800
900	500	100
200	700	600

Magic number ______________

New magic number ___________

Elapsed Time

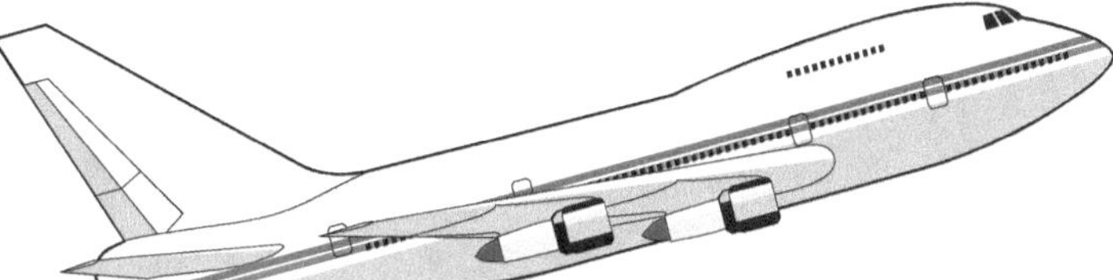

Current Time

Plane Destination	Departure Time
Big Sky, Montana	8:00
Denver, Colorado	8:20
Orlando, Florida	8:35
Atlanta, Georgia	8:45

In how many minutes will the plane leave for Orlando, Florida?

If it is now 7:45 (according to the clock), count by five to find the number of minutes from 7:45 to 8:35 when the Orlando plane leaves.

The plane bound for Orlando will leave in 50 minutes.

The plane bound for Big Sky, Montana stops 2 hours and 30 minutes into the flight for a connection in Dallas. What time will it be then? (Do not adjust for any time zone changes)

8:00	+	2 hours	+	30 minutes	=	10:30
(8:00)		(9:00, 10:00)		(10:30)		

These examples show how to calculate elapsed time, or the passing of time.

Find the elapsed time. Write the new time on the blank clock.

Add 2 hours	Add 10 min.	Add 30 min.	Add $1\frac{1}{2}$ hours	Add 45 min

Complete.

3 minutes = _______ seconds

3 days = _______ hours

5 hours = _______ minutes

30 minutes = _______ seconds

2 days = _______ hours

10 hours = _______ minutes

3 Label each activity either A.M. or P.M.

7:30	8:00	12:00
______	______	______

4 Color ONLY the squares which hold numbers that are divisible by 2, 3, 5, and 10 to reveal a hidden message.

11	13	23	41	97	73	23	1	7	17	31	53	89	79	67	43
79	13	67	29	79	11	13	29	53	67	19	7	31	59	71	29
31	17	65	83	55	16	47	14	18	41	3	37	25	1	12	5
7	67	85	13	45	61	53	6	61	23	15	97	50	51	4	37
91	23	90	19	35	32	31	80	24	47	18	71	60	13	2	20
37	1	10	53	27	29	59	71	90	1	9	7	12	19	53	15
44	66	20	41	24	18	37	70	5	11	3	4	8	67	10	30
67	49	77	7	61	43	77	1	29	91	19	61	59	31	41	23

5 Divide.

$40\overline{)80}$ $20\overline{)60}$ $20\overline{)100}$ $70\overline{)140}$ $10\overline{)120}$

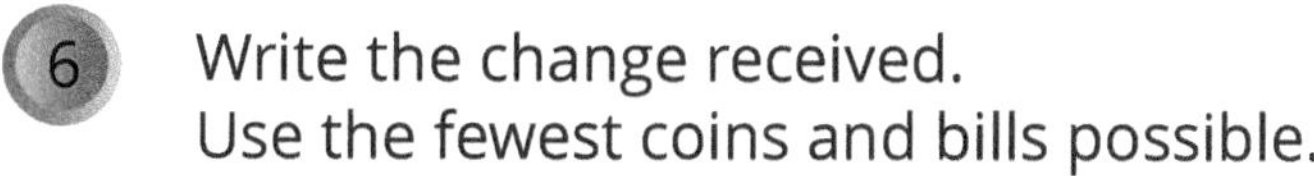

6 Write the change received.
Use the fewest coins and bills possible.

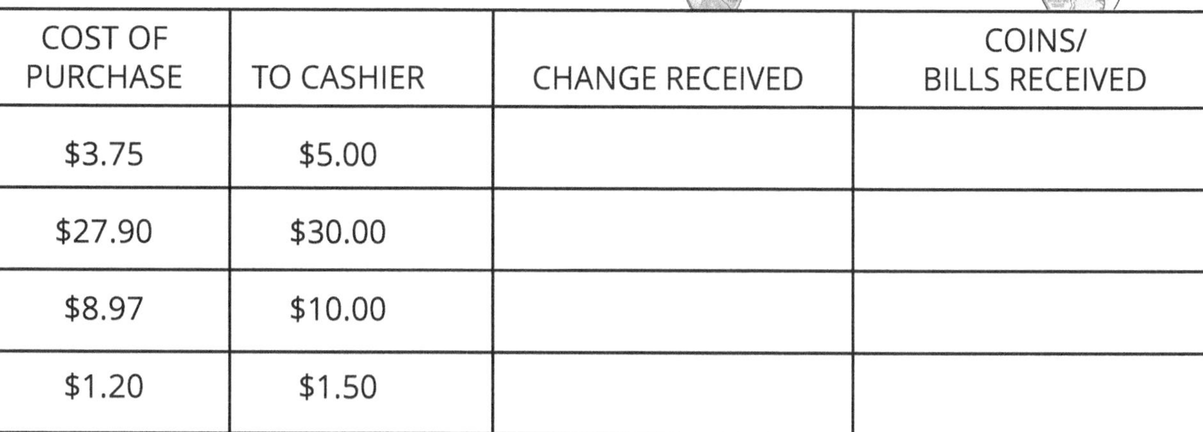

COST OF PURCHASE	TO CASHIER	CHANGE RECEIVED	COINS/ BILLS RECEIVED
\$3.75	\$5.00		
\$27.90	\$30.00		
\$8.97	\$10.00		
\$1.20	\$1.50		

Calendar Conversions

"Thirty days have September, April,
June, and November.
And just for fun, all the rest have 31,
except February.
February alone doesn't hold the line.
For three years it has 28,
and in the fourth year, 29."

Almost everyone has heard this familiar poem. It is used to help us remember which months have 30 days and which ones have 31. There are other calendar units which we also need to remember.

CALENDAR UNITS

1 year	= 365 days	10 years	= 1 decade
1 leap year	= 366 days	100 years	= 1 century
1 year	= 52 weeks	1,000 years	= 1 millennium
1 year	= 12 months	1 week	= 7 days
		1 month	= 30 or 31 days (except February)

SEPTEMBER

S	M	T	W	T	F	S
					1	2
3	4	5	6	7	8	9
10	11	12	13	14	15	16
17	18	19	20	21	22	23
24	25	26	27	28	29	30

1 Use the calendar and calendar units chart on the previous page to answer these questions.

If Labor Day is the first Monday in September, what date is that?

How many school days are there in September if school starts on the fifth of the month?

Some school years have 187 days. How many full weeks is that?

How many weeks are there in a decade?

How many months are there in a century?

How many weeks are there in 49 days?

Which is more, 369 days or one leap year?

Which is more, 27 hours or 2 days?

2 Use the rule to find each missing time.

Rule: Add 1 hour and 15 minutes.

Input	Output
2:15	
1:30	
5:45	

Rule: Subtract 20 minutes.

Input	Output
3:00	
7:35	
9:20	

3 Complete.

300 seconds = ______ minutes

28 hours = ______ whole days and ______ hours

4 hours = ______ minutes

480 minutes = ______ hours

4 Name the century.

1245 = ____________

1523 = ____________

1975 = ____________

278 = ____________

5 Divide.

$23\overline{)150}$ $32\overline{)155}$ $40\overline{)261}$ $45\overline{)135}$

6 Write the change received.
Use the fewest coins and bills possible.

COST OF PURCHASE	TO CASHIER	CHANGE RECEIVED	COINS/ BILLS RECEIVED
$2.15	$5.00		
$17.19	$20.00		
$45.55	$50.55		
$245.53	$250.03		

Time Zones

Lori lives in Georgia. Her friend Cindi lives in Arizona.
Cindi needs to call Lori before she leaves for work at 9:00 A.M. (Georgia time).
At what time in Arizona must Cindi make the call?

Alaska

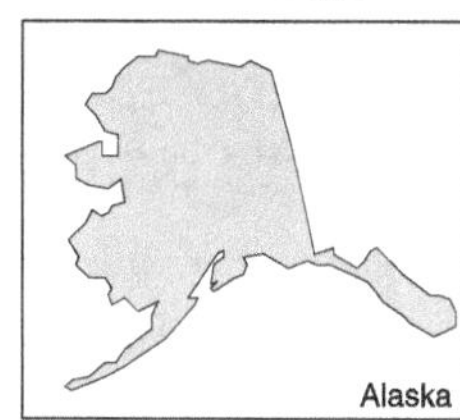

There are 24 different time zones in the world.
The diagram below shows the different time zones that effect the United States. There are 6 of them.
As you travel from east to west, subtract one hour for each time zone. This means that at 9:00 A.M. in Georgia, which is in the Eastern time zone, it is 7:00 A.M. in Arizona.
If you were traveling from west to east, then you would add an hour for each time zone.

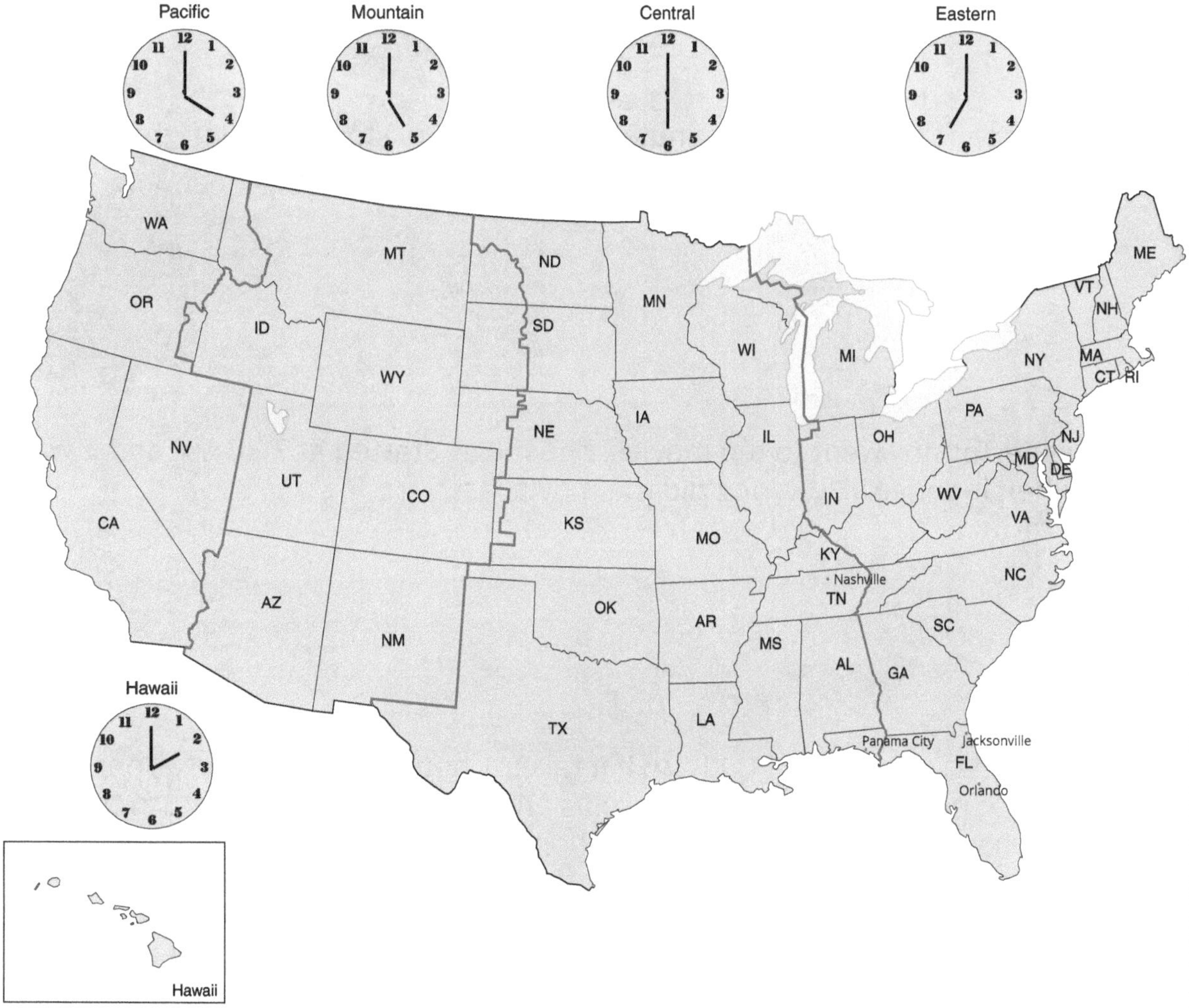

Pacific Mountain Central Eastern

Hawaii

Hawaii

1 Use the map to answer these questions.

When it is 3:00 P.M. in Las Vegas, Nevada, what time is it in the following places:

New York, New York? ______ Nashville, Tenn.? ______

When it is 10:30 A.M. in Boston, Mass., what time is it in the following places:

Orlando, Fla.? ______ Dallas, Texas ? ______ Denver, Colorado? ______

2 Solve.

Brett watched three TV shows which lasted a total of 1 hour and 30 minutes. If he started watching TV at 3:30, what time did he finish watching these programs?

Charles spent 1 hour and 10 minutes at the grocery store. If he left the store at 5:00, what time was it when he began his grocery shopping?

Alice and Tommy went to the movies. The movie started at 7:30 P.M. and it was 9:45 P.M. when it ended. How long did the movie last?

Chet's airplane leaves at 11:00 A.M. If it takes 1 hour to drive to the airport, 45 minutes to park and check luggage, plus another 15 minutes to return the rental car, at what time will he need to leave home in order to be on the plane by 10:45?

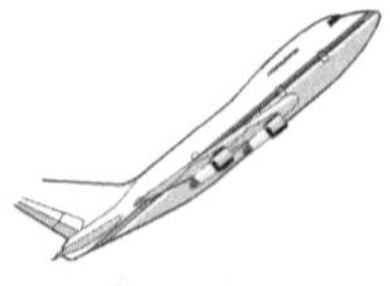

3 Solve.

If a dog is 156 months old, how many years old is it?

If a decade is 10 years, how many weeks are there in a decade?

Lori is 360 months old. How many years is this?

How many weeks are there in a century?

4 Complete.

15 minutes = _____ seconds

5 hours = _____ minutes

72 hours = _____ days

1,020 seconds = _____ minutes

5 Complete.

57,893,456,120

_____ is in the thousands' place.

_____ is in the hundreds' place.

_____ is in the millions' place.

_____ is in the hundred thousands' place.

_____ is in the ten millions' place.

_____ is in the ten billions' place.

6 Solve.

$n - 2 = 14$ $n - 10 = 20$ $n - 8 = 24$ $n - 7 = 9$

Logical Reasoning

Problem solving is an everyday skill. This lesson will focus on logical thinking to solve a problem. When presented with a problem, begin with the information which is already given to you in the original problem. Work from there to figure out any additional information which will help you solve the problem. Look at the example below.

There are three houses on Cal's street. One is a blue house, one is a white house, and one is a brick house. One house has roses planted in the front yard. Another house has green shutters, and the other house has a white picket fence around it. Read the clues below and try to figure out which item (rose bushes, green shutters, or picket fence) belongs to which house (blue, white, or brick).

Strategies to solve a problem logically.

1. Draw a grid to solve this problem.
2. List the choices across the top and sides of the grid.
3. Read the clues given and mark out the options which could not be paired together.
4. By process of elimination the answers should be unraveled.

	Blue House	White House	Brick House
Rose Bushes	YES	NO	NO
Green Shutters	NO	YES	NO
Picket Fence	NO	NO	YES

Clues:

1. The first house has the picket fence around it.
2. The third house is blue.
3. The second house has green shutters.
4. The white house is between the blue house and the brick house.

Strategy after reading clues:

1. Since you know that the first house has the picket fence, the blue house cannot have a picket fence around it because it is the third house. Write NO in the box where blue house and picket fence intersect to eliminate that pairing.

2. Read your clues again. You know that the second house has green shutters, and you know that the white house is between the brick house and the blue house. This means that the white house must be the second house and therefore have green shutters. Indicate that the white house has green shutters by writing YES in the box where these two categories intersect. Also write NO in the box where the brick house and the green shutters intersect.

3. You know that the blue house cannot have a picket fence. You also know that the white house is the second house, so it does not have a picket fence, and you can write NO where those boxes intersect. Finally, by process of elimination, you now only have one choice left. The brick house must have the picket fence.

4. By process of elimination, the blue house must have the rose bushes. This means that you may now write NO in the boxes where rose bushes intersect with the white house and the brick house.

This is a typical problem solving problem commonly called a logic problem.

1 Solve.

On the shelf in the cabinet are four types of soup; chicken noodle, tomato, vegetable, and clam chowder.

Read the clues below to determine what order they are in going from the right to the left.

	Chicken Noodle	Tomato	Vegetable	Clam Chowder
1st				
2nd				
3rd				
4th				

Clues:
1. The chowder is next to the tomato soup.
2. The chicken noodle is next to the vegetable.
3. The tomato is last in line.
4. The vegetable soup is next to the chowder.

2 Solve.

If it is 3:00 P.M. in California, what time is it in the following cities:

Anchorage, Alaska? ________ Philadelphia, Penn.? ________ Santa Fe, NM.? ________

Name the time zones where these cities are located:

Time Zone: ________ ________ ________

If it is 5:00 A.M. in Jacksonville, Florida, what time is it in the following cities:

Panama City, FL.? ________ Minneapolis, MN.? ________ Honolulu, Hawaii? ________

(Hint: Florida has 2 time zones.)

Name the time zones where these cities are located:

Time Zone: ________ ________ ________

3 Complete.

Which month is 5 months before July? ____________

In what month do we celebrate Christmas? ____________

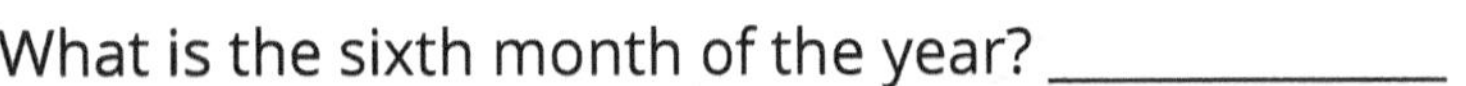

What is the sixth month of the year? ____________

Which month is 9 months after November?____________

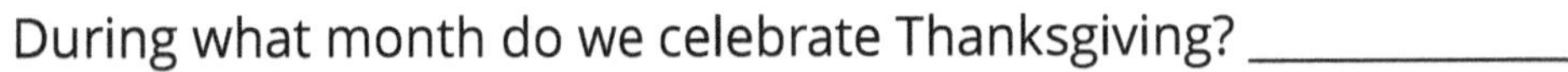

During what month do we celebrate Thanksgiving? ____________

4 Solve.

$n - 6 = 12 - 4$ $n - 4 = 11 - 2$ $n - 9 = 15 - 5$ $n - 4 = 10$

Logical Reasoning

To work backward in order to arrive at a solution is a problem solving strategy for solving non-routine word problems. Some problems can be solved more easily by applying this strategy. It is called working backward.

Try this. Kimberly asked her dad how old he was. He replied "If you add 10 years to my age and then tripled that number, you get 165. Can you figure it out?

Making a flowchart can aid in this backward process.

Age ? → +10 → x 3 → 165.

Remember that adding and subtracting undo each other, and multiplying and dividing undo each other.

Work backward.

165 ÷ 3 – 10 = 45

Kimberly's father is 45 years old.

1 Write in standard form.

(1 x 100,000,000) + (4 x 10,000,000) + (6 x 1,000,000) + (3 x 100,000) + (5 x 10,000) + (6 x 1,000) + (0 x 100) + (2 x 10) + (9 x 1) = ______________

(2 x 100,000) + (8 x 10,000) + (7 x 1,000) + (5 x 100) + (4 x 10) + (2 x 1) =

____

2 Write in expanded form.

186 =

4,235 =

71,235 =

3 Multiply.

$$\begin{array}{r} 258 \\ \times\ 19 \\ \hline \end{array} \qquad \begin{array}{r} 369 \\ \times\ 21 \\ \hline \end{array} \qquad \begin{array}{r} 642 \\ \times\ 32 \\ \hline \end{array} \qquad \begin{array}{r} 798 \\ \times\ 45 \\ \hline \end{array}$$

4 Add.

$\frac{1}{5} + \frac{2}{5} =$ $\qquad$ $\frac{3}{20} + \frac{9}{20} =$

$\frac{4}{10} + \frac{5}{10} =$ $\qquad$ $\frac{8}{11} + \frac{3}{11} =$

5 Write < or >.

378,615 _____ 378,915 $\qquad$ 249,076 _____ 295,076 $\qquad$ 537,298 _____ 537,289

713,028 _____ 613,928 $\qquad$ 816,439 _____ 864,139 $\qquad$ 451,289 _____ 415,289

6 Complete.

6,915,327,486

Name the place values of all the prime numbers in the number written above.

_______________ _______________

_______________ _______________

Name the place values of all the composite numbers in the number written above.

_______________ _______________

_______________ _______________ _______________

Use the table to answer the questions.

Site	Visitation Hours
Dinosaur Exhibit	9:00 A.M. – 5:00 P.M.
Art Museum	10:00 A.M. – 5:30 P.M.
Archives Building	10:00 A.M. – 4:00 P.M.

Catherine arrived at the Archives Building 30 minutes before it opened. What time was it?

Mr. Smith's class left school at 8:30 to go to the Dinosaur Exhibit. If it takes the school bus 45 minutes to get there, what time will they arrive?

Doug arrived at the Art Museum at 4:00 P.M. He put enough money in the parking meter to last 2 hours. Will he be able to stay at the museum until it closes?

Geometric Terms

Points, Lines, Segments, Rays

A **point** shows an exact location. It is named by a capital letter. (• K)

A **line** goes on and on in both directions. ($\overleftrightarrow{DE}$)

A **line segment** is part of a line. It has two endpoints. ($\overline{LM}$)

A **ray** is part of a line. It has one endpoint and goes on and on in one direction. ($\overrightarrow{UV}$)

Intersecting, Parallel, and Perpendicular Lines

Intersecting lines cross each other, or intersect. 

Parallel lines run next to each other the same distance apart. 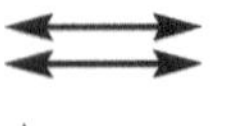

Perpendicular lines form right angles where they intersect.

Geometry Terms	Geometry in Pictures	Geometry in Symbols	Geometry in Words
Point	•K	K	Point K
Line	D E	$\overleftrightarrow{DE}$	Line DE
Line Segment	S T	$\overline{ST}$	Line Segment
Ray	X Y	$\overrightarrow{XY}$	Ray XY Always name the endpoint first.
Intersecting Lines	l m	l intersects m	Line l intersects line m.
Parallel Lines	x y	$x \parallel y$	Line x is parallel to line y.
Perpendicular Lines	b a	$a \perp b$	Line a is perpendicular to line b.

1 Write the name of each figure using symbols. Name it using words.

1. • H

2. A B

3. R S

4. B C

5. • G

2 Use //, ⊥, or *intersects* to write a statement in symbols about the pairs of lines.

1. 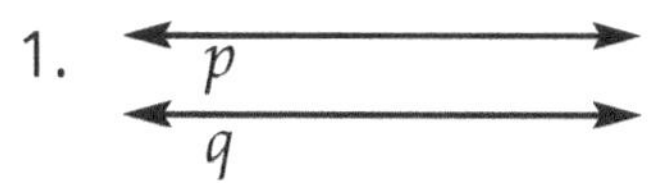

2. 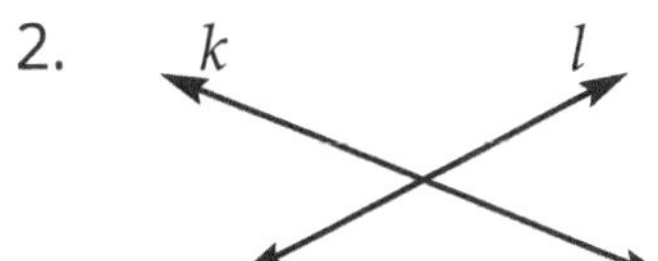

3. 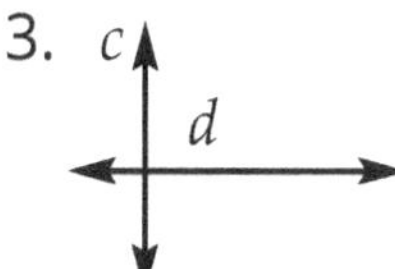

3 Solve.

1. If Amy multiplies her cat's age by 6 and subtracts 12, she gets 6. How old is her cat?

2. Susan had five more flowers than Dawn. When you subtract 2 from the number Susan has, you get 11. How many flowers does Dawn have?

4 Find the sum.

39	89	42	87	90
+ 39	+ 37	+ 58	+ 95	+ 88

5 Write the standard form.

1. 40,000 + 900 + 2 __________
2. 300,000 + 300 + 50 + 2 __________
3. 45 thousand __________
4. 1 million __________
5. 470 billion __________

6

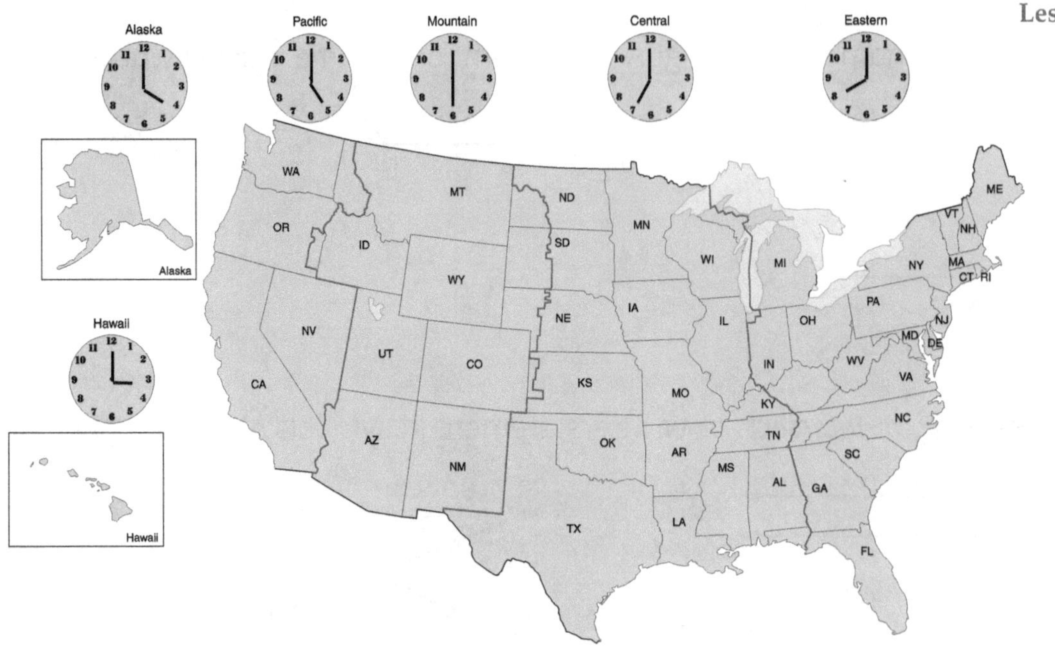

1. Suppose it is 3:00 Eastern Time, what time is it in:
   - Central Time? ____________
   - Mountain Time? ____________
   - Pacific Time? ____________
   - Hawaii Time? ____________
2. Suppose it is 8:00 in California, what time is it in:
   - Eastern Time? ____________
   - Mountain Time? ____________
   - Hawaii Time? ____________
   - Alaska Time? ____________

7

1 year = 365 days   1 year = 52 weeks

1 year = 12 months   1 week = 7 days

1. How many years is a century? ____________
2. How many years is a decade? ____________
3. How many days in a decade? ____________
4. How many weeks in a decade? ____________
5. Paul is 3,650 days old. How many years old is Paul? ____________
6. Theodore is 468 weeks old. How many years old is Theodore? ____________
7. The baby kitten is 56 days old. How many weeks old is the kitten? ____________

1 Find the quotient. 5 pts. total for this exercise.

7)$45.64   4)$3.56   3)$9.27   12)$15.60   18)$56.52

2 Estimate by rounding 1 and 2 digit numbers to the 10's and three digit numbers to the 100's. 5 pts. total for this exercise.

8)454   24)396   83)431   12)689   18)782

3 Solve. 3 pts. total for this exercise.

Suzanne had 32 tennis balls to divide among 8 players.
How many tennis balls did each player get?

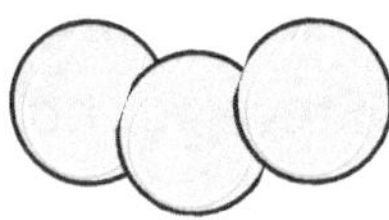

Karen had 88 pennies. She wanted to divide them between two people.
How many pennies would each person get?

Pauline had $8.15 to buy suckers.
If each sucker costs 5¢, how many suckers can she buy?

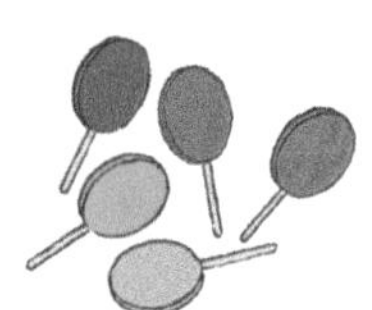

4 Solve. 2 pts. total for this exercise.

The ice cream shop has the following flavors of ice cream: chocolate, vanilla, strawberry. These are the following kind of cones: waffle or cake. If each cone can have two dips of ice cream, how many different combinations can one make? Name them.

Jim is choosing a new bike. He can get the following colors: red, black, gold. He can get the following decals: racer, mountaineer, space age. If each bike can have one color choice and one decal choice, how many combinations can one make?

5 Match. 5 pts. total for this exercise.

B.C.	1,000 years
A.D.	Before Christ
decade	100 years
century	Anno Domini-in the year of our Lord
millennium	10 years

6 Draw hands on the clock to represent the following times. 6 pts.

quarter after one | half past four | quarter to eleven

twenty minutes after two | forty-five minutes after six | one forty-five

7 Write A.M. or P.M. 4 pts. total for this exercise.

Pamela at breakfast at 7:00 _______.

Steve got home from school at 3:30 _______.

Doris wanted to watch her favorite television show right after dinner at 7:00 _______.

Morning church services are at 9:30 _______ every Sunday.

8 Beside each date write the century. 6 pts. total for this exercise.

1911	____________	1217	____________
277	____________	1841	____________
13	____________	678	____________

9 Match. 4 pts. total for this exercise.

60 minutes	2 days
60 seconds	1 hour
24 hours	1 day
48 hours	1 minute

10 Look at the initial time. Add the elapsed time and state the new time. 4 pts.

Initial Time	Elapsed Time	New Time
3:45	20 minutes	
7:15	45 minutes	
2:02	32 minutes	
6:11	60 minutes	

Angles

An **angle** is two rays that share a common end point.

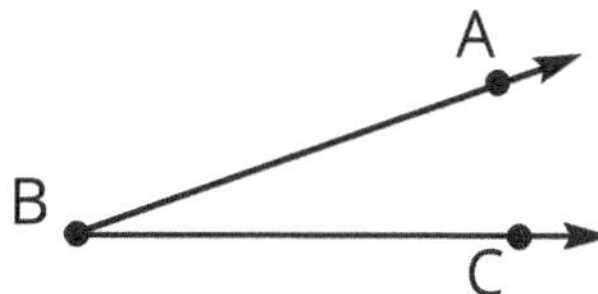

The rays $\overrightarrow{BA}$ and $\overrightarrow{BC}$ are called sides.
Point B, the common end point of the two rays is called the vertex of the angle.
The angle can be referred to as: ∠ABC, ∠ B, or ∠CBA.
There are three kinds of angles.

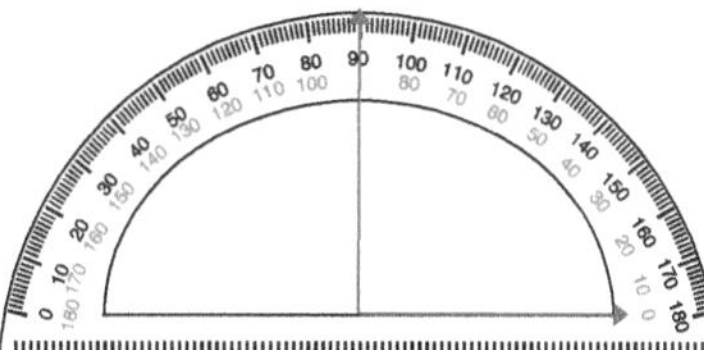

A **right angle**.
It measures 90°.

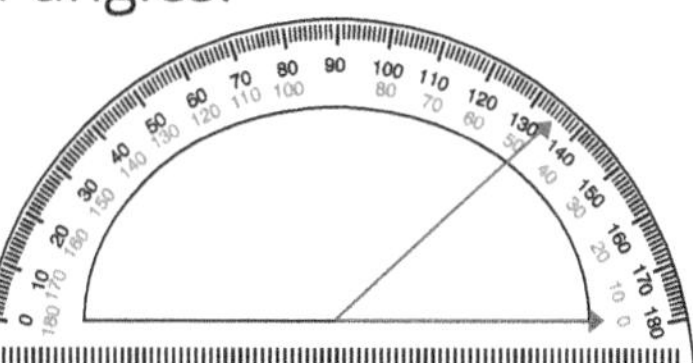

An **acute angle**.
It measures less than 90°.

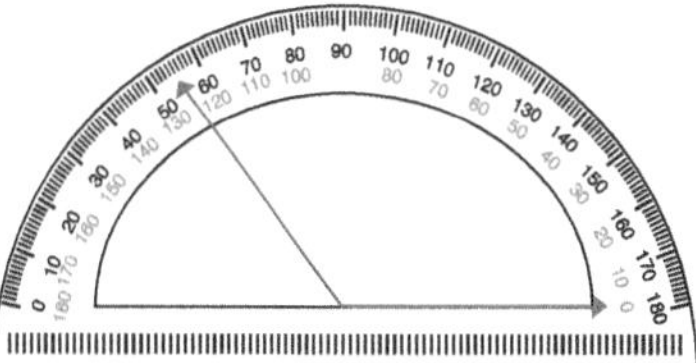

An **obtuse angle**.
It measures greater than 90°.

1

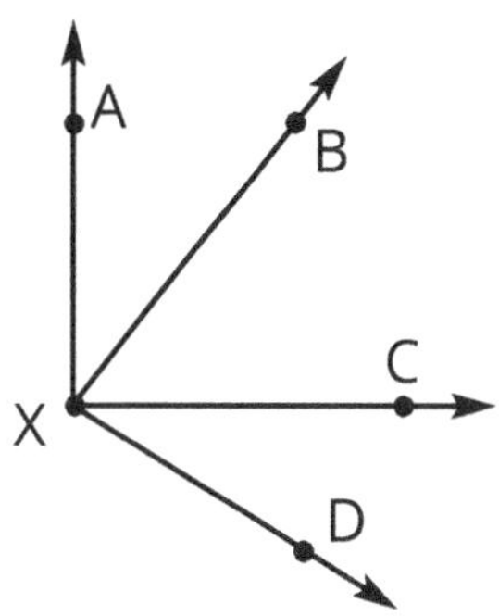

1. Using symbols name at least 4 different angles found in the diagram above.

   Define each as right, acute, or obtuse.

2. Find ∠AXC. Give one other name for this angle. ____________________

3. What is the vertex of ∠AXC ? ____________________

4. What are the sides of ∠AXC ? ____________________

2 Find each sum.

489	634	902	420	244	987
+ 139	+ 190	+ 329	+ 309	+ 899	+ 293

3

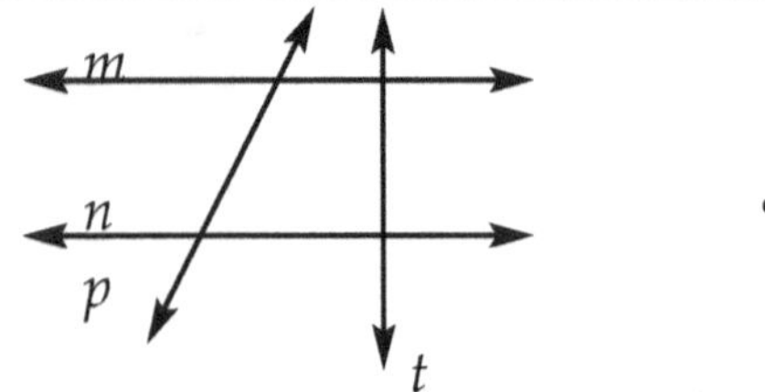

•G

1. Name a pair of parallel lines. ____________________
2. Name a point. ____________________
3. Name a pair of perpendicular lines. ____________________
4. Name a pair of intersecting lines. ____________________
5. Will line p and line t eventually intersect if they are extended? __________

4 Write the name of each figure using symbols.

•W

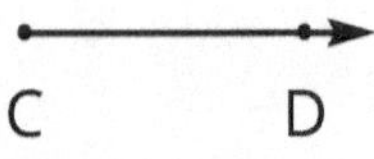

A B

________ ________ ________ ________

5 Find each product. Place the answers from least to greatest in the lines below and read the message.

265	890	605	320
x 34	x 47	x 47	x 40
= O	= T	= E	= R

967	477	627
x 21	x 13	x 49
= R	= C	= C

______ ______ ______ ______ ______ ______ ______

___ ___ ___ ___ ___ ___ ___

6 Solve.

Pauline bought some doughnuts. She gave half of them to her friends and has 12 left. How many did she have originally?

You have soccer at 7:30 P.M. You have 30 minutes of homework and 45 minutes of chores. When is the latest you can begin your homework and chores?

7 Solve these problems.

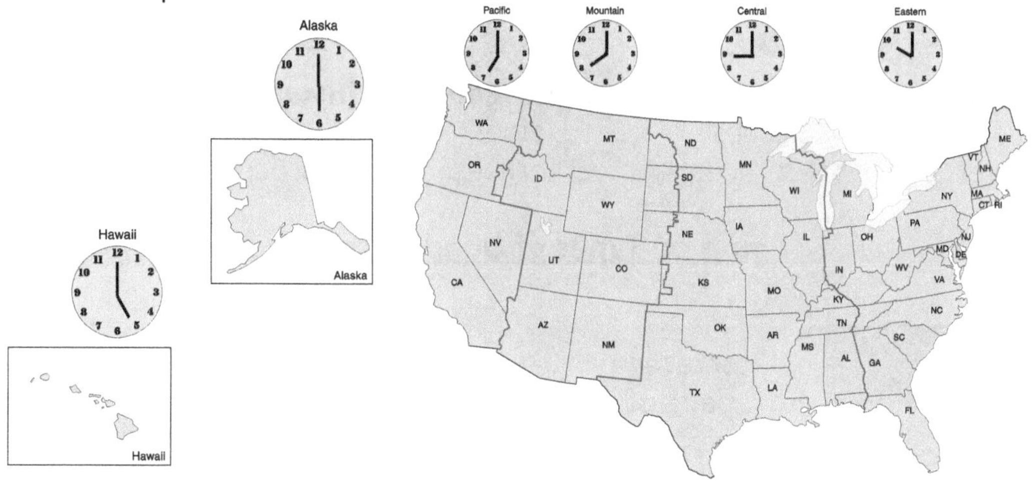

1. It is 4:00 P.M. in Dallas, Texas. What time is it in Phoenix, Arizona?

2. Paul wants to call his grandmother in Washington State and wish her a happy birthday at 6:00 A.M. her time. He lives in Baltimore, Maryland. What time should he make his call?

3. Jeremy is flying from Seattle, Washington to Atlanta, Georgia. He will leave at 10:00 A.M. and it will take him 6 hours. What time will it be in Atlanta when he arrives?

4. When it is 6:00 P.M. in Indianapolis, Indiana, what time is it in Los Angeles, California?

Identifying Polygons

Polygons are closed plane figures with three or more straight sides.

A **vertex** is formed where two sides meet.

Regular polygons have all sides the same length and angles the same measure. The hexagon is a regular polygon.

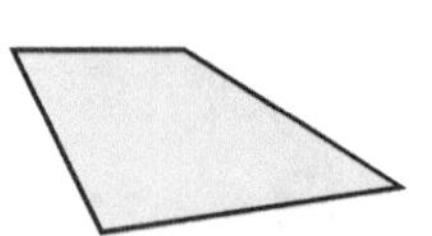

quadrilateral
4 sides
4 vertices

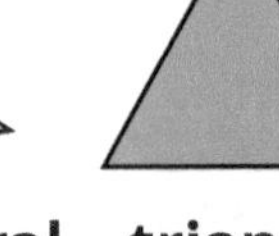

triangle
3 sides
3 vertices

pentagon
5 sides
5 vertices

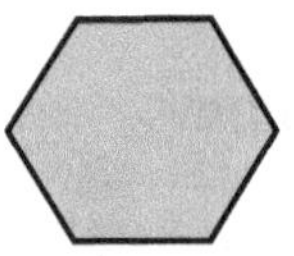

hexagon
6 sides
6 vertices

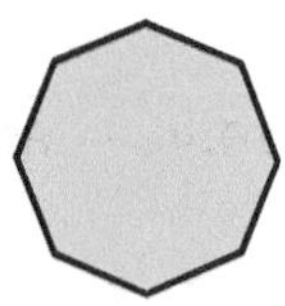

octagon
8 sides
8 vertices

Common Types of Quadrilaterals

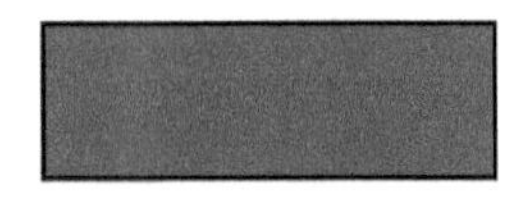

Rectangle
2 pairs of sides equal.

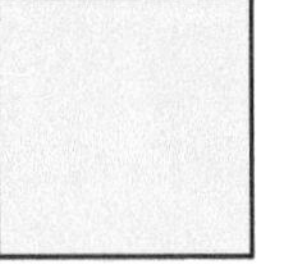

Square
All sides the same length.

Parallelogram
Two pairs of sides the same length.
Two pairs of parallel sides.

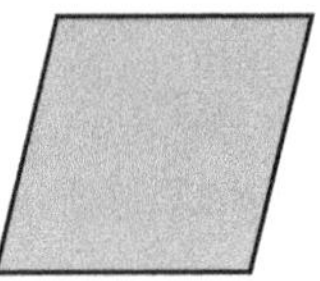

Rhombus
All sides the same length.

Trapezoid
One pair of parallel sides.

1 Glue toothpicks on construction paper to make the following shapes: pentagon, triangle, hexagon, quadrilateral, and octagon. Label each figure.

2

1. How many sides does a pentagon have? ______
2. How many sides does a quadrilateral have? ______
3. Are all quadrilaterals rectangles? Explain. ______
______
4. Are all rectangles quadrilaterals? Explain. ______
______
5. Draw a quadrilateral that is not a square or rectangle. ______
6. Is a circle a polygon? Explain. ______
______
7. Draw an example of a regular polygon.
8. What quadrilateral is a regular polygon? ______
9. Draw the five types of quadrilaterals we have studied. Place the correct name under each.

3 Average.

62, 29, 19, 30 ______ 16, 18, 36, 26 ______ 30, 57, 33 ______

94, 86 ______

4 Draw and label the angles as described.

Right Angle	Acute Angle	Obtuse Angle
Label ∠ TRS	Label ∠ JKL	Label ∠ CDE

5 Connect the term and matching picture.

Term	Picture
1. point	a. • D
2. intersecting lines	b.
3. line	c.
4. line segment	d.
5. ray	e.
6. parallel	f.
7. perpendicular lines	g.

6 Solve.

Jane spent $2.25 at a candy store. She bought gummi bears for $1.50, gumballs for 40 cents and a giant sour ball. How much did the giant sour ball cost?

Colleen spent $4.75 for a notebook and 40 cents for an eraser. She had 85 cents left over. How much did her mother give her?

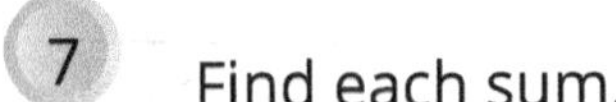

7 Find each sum.

25	47	65	52
13	90	43	28
47	33	15	55
+ 35	+ 42	+ 37	+ 65

Congruent and Similar

Congruent figures have the same exact size and shape.
Similar figures have the same shape, but not necessarily the same size.

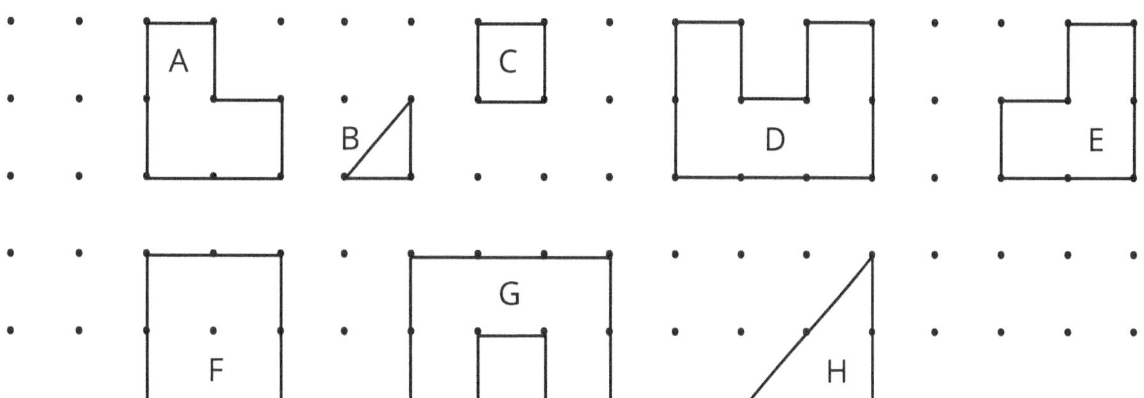

Shapes A and E are congruent. Can you name another congruent pair?
Did you choose the two congruent shapes D and G?

Shapes C and F are similar. They have the same shape, but F is four times bigger than C.

What other shapes are similar? Did you choose the similar triangles B and H?

1 Beside each shape, draw a congruent figure and a similar figure.

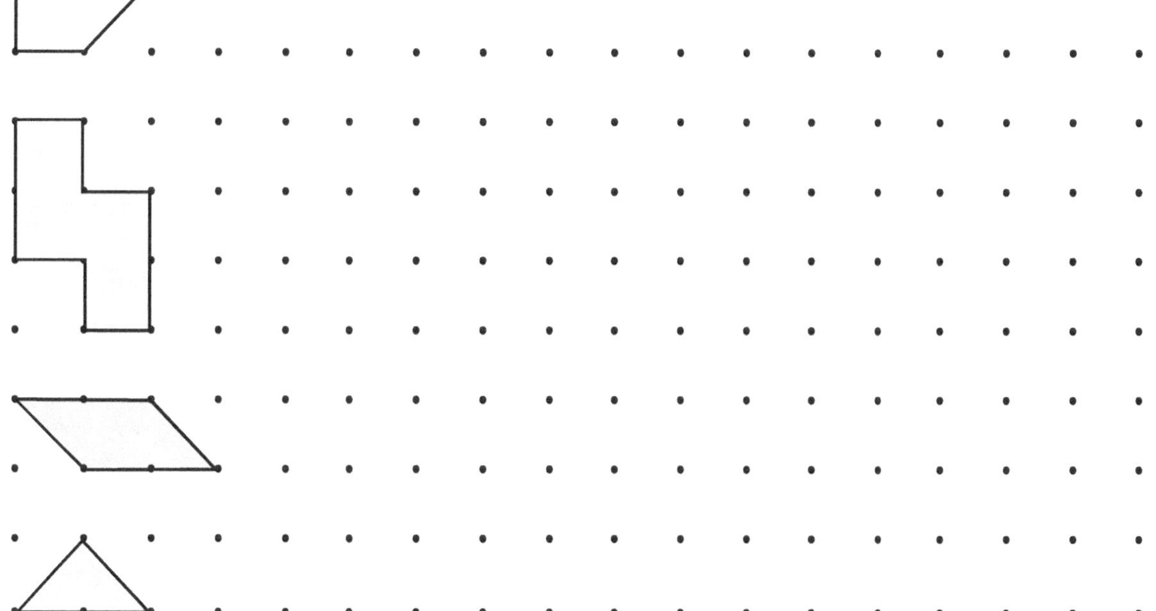

2 Write the name of the figure on the line. Choose from the following: octagon, triangle, quadrilateral, pentagon, and hexagon.

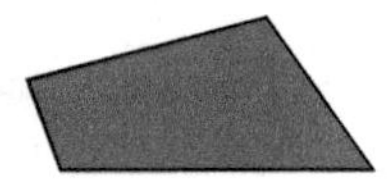 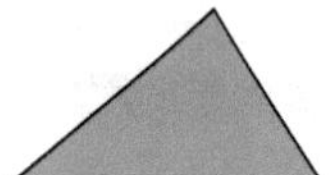  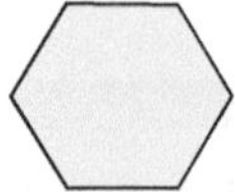 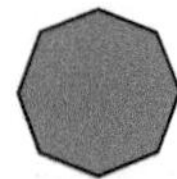

__________ __________ __________ __________ __________

3

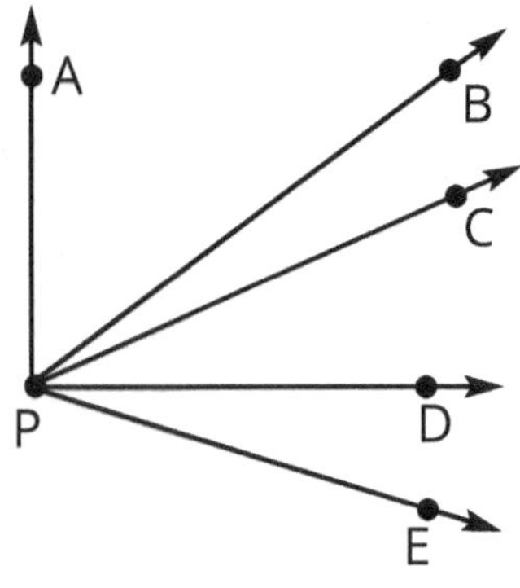

1. Name all of the acute angles. ________________
2. Name the right angle. ________________
3. Name an obtuse angle. ________________
4. Find ∠ APE. Give one other name for this angle.
   ____
5. Draw a line parallel to $\overrightarrow{PE}$. Label it ST.
6. Place a point between the two sides of ∠ APB. Label it X.

4 Draw and label the geometric terms as described.

Point Label B	Line Label AB	Line Segment Label RS
Ray Label UV	Intersecting Lines Label one line *e* and one line *f*.	Parallel Lines Label one line *c* and one line *d*.

5 Find the difference.

493	845	902	630	312
- 106	- 809	- 398	- 404	- 293

6 Find the quotient.

$7\overline{)48}$ $5\overline{)49}$ $9\overline{)77}$ $6\overline{)37}$ $8\overline{)34}$ $4\overline{)35}$

7 Match the quadrilaterals with the correct term.

 __________

 __________

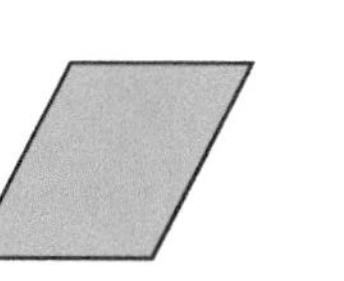 __________

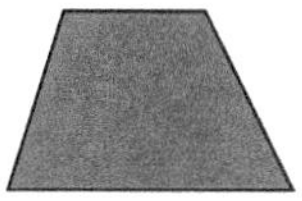

____

 __________

a. square

b. parallelogram

c. rectangle

d. trapezoid

e. rhombus

Symmetry

A line of symmetry divides a figure into two congruent parts. Some shapes have more than one line of symmetry.

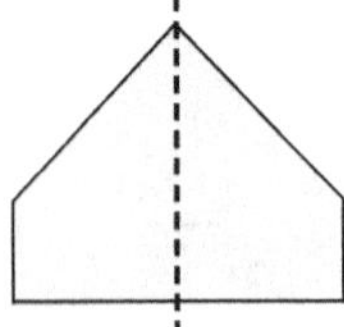
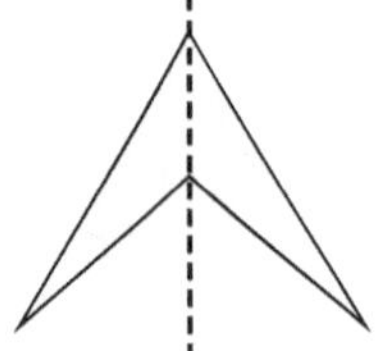
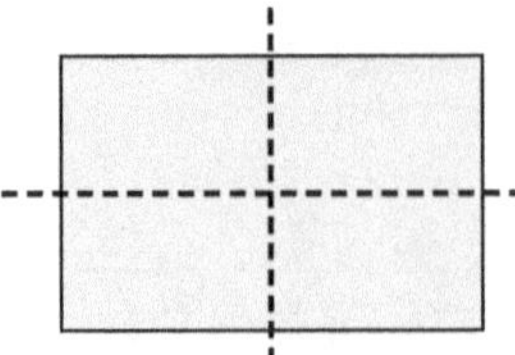
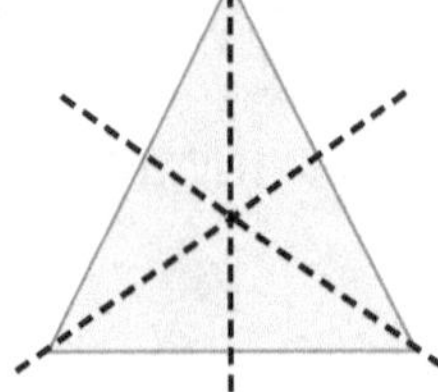

To determine if the three figures below are symmetrical, trace their shapes on a blank piece of paper. Cut the figures out. Fold them down the middle. If the halves are exactly alike, they are symmetrical. Which of the figures below are symmetrical?

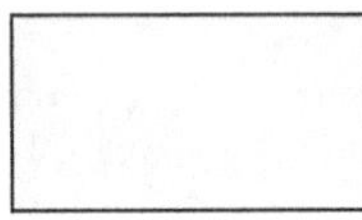
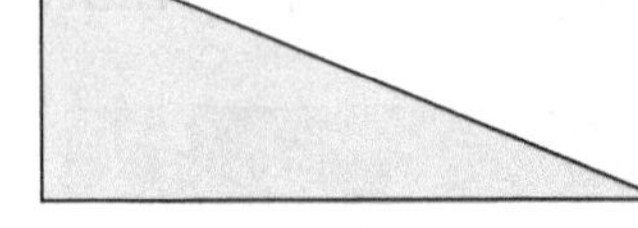

If you chose the circle and rectangle, you were correct.
The triangle is not symmetrical.

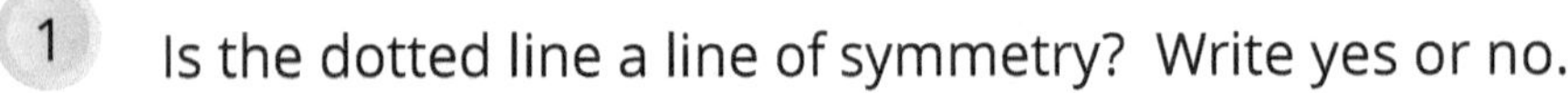

1 Is the dotted line a line of symmetry? Write yes or no.

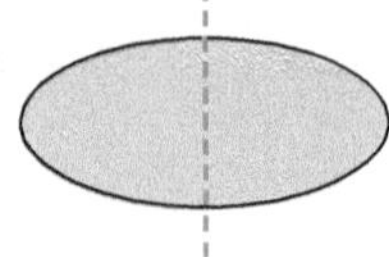
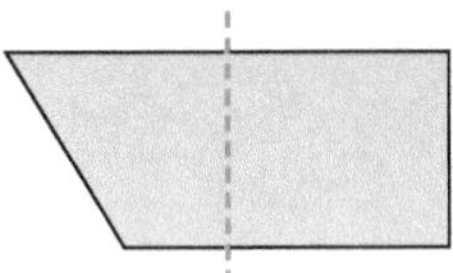

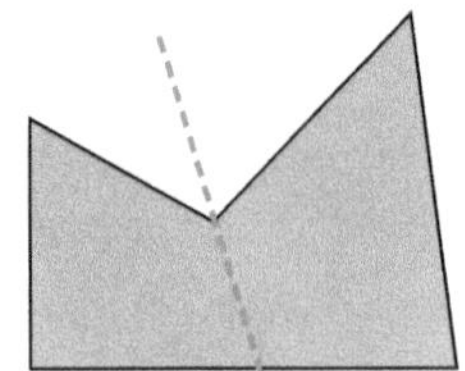

__________ __________ __________ __________

Draw a line of symmetry in each figure.

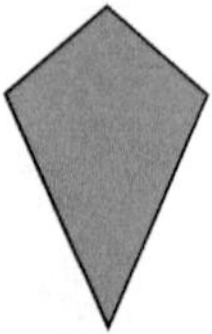
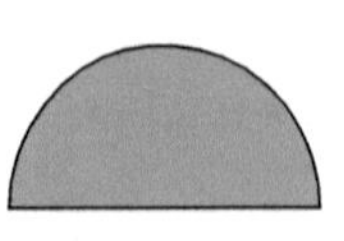
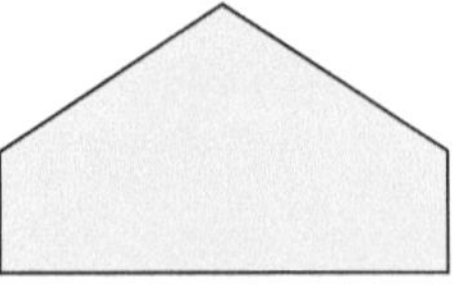
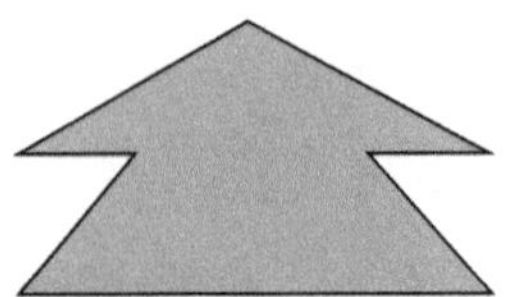

How many lines of symmetry does each figure have?

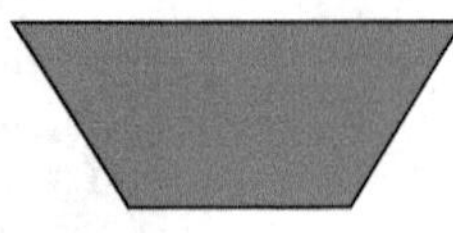

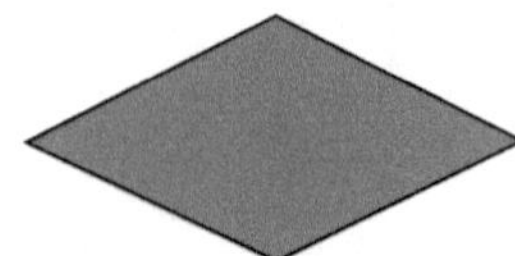

_____ _____ _____ _____

2 Draw a line to match the name of the figure with its number of sides.

triangle	4 sides
octagon	3 sides
decagon	5 sides
quadrilateral	6 sides
hexagon	10 sides
pentagon	8 sides

3 Solve using the angles given.

A B C D

E F G

1. Which angles are obtuse? ____________________
2. Which angles are acute? ____________________
3. Which angles are right angles? ____________________
4. Which angles are congruent? ____________________

4

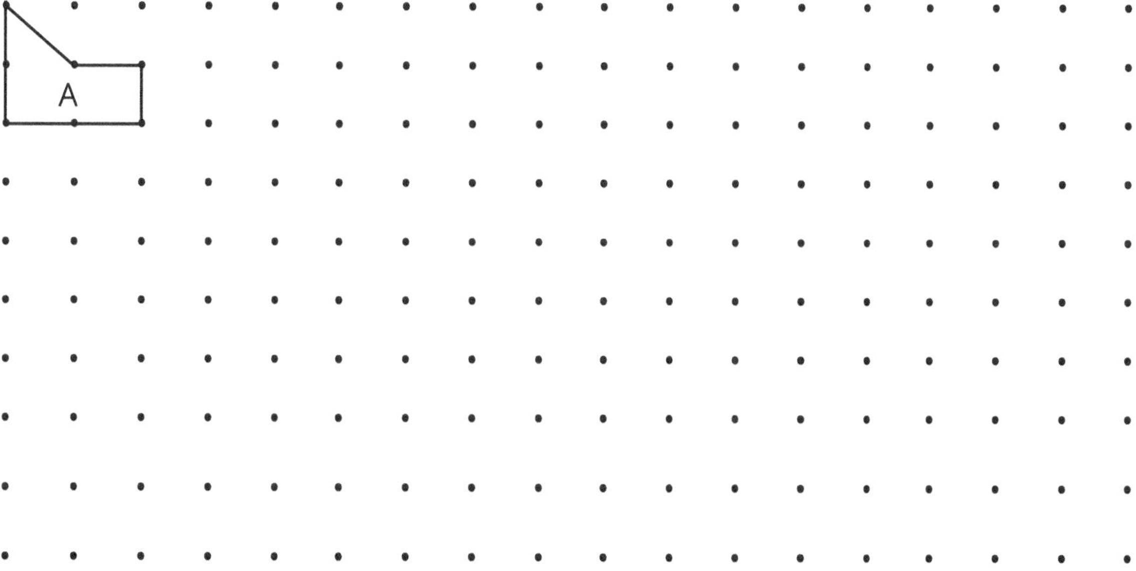

Use the dotted grid to answer the questions.
1. Draw a figure congruent to figure A.
2. Draw a figure similar to figure A.
3. Draw a figure twice as large as figure A.
4. Draw two congruent triangles.

5 Find the quotient.

$3\overline{)10}$ $\quad$ $9\overline{)27}$ $\quad$ $6\overline{)33}$ $\quad$ $9\overline{)49}$ $\quad$ $8\overline{)77}$

6 Choose the correct answer.

A.M. | 21st century | 7 days | decade
1st century | 24 hours | midnight | century
P.M. | 20th century | 60 minutes | millennium

1. A ______________ is a period of 1,000 years.
2. A __________ is a period of one hundred years.
3. There are ________ in a week.
4. There are ________ in a day.
5. One hour equals ___________.
6. The year 92 was in the ____________.
7. The year 1998 is in the ____________.
8. The year 2000 will begin the ____________.
9. John went to bed at 8:00 ___. (A.M., P.M.)
10. Another name for 12:00 at night is ____________.
11. A __________ is a period of ten years.
12. We refer to 10:00 in the morning as 10:00 ____. (A.M., P.M.)

7 A quadrilateral has four sides and four angles.
The square pictured has sides $\overline{DE}$, $\overline{EF}$, $\overline{FG}$, and $\overline{GD}$.
It has four angles ∠ D, ∠ E, ∠ F, and ∠ G. All the sides and angles are equal.

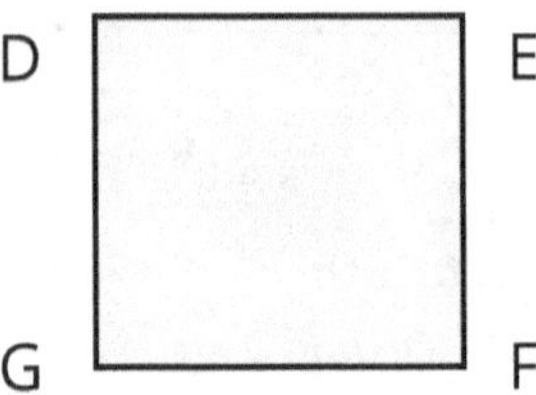

Draw and label these quadrilaterals.

Rhombus Label ABCD	Rectangle Label UVWX	Trapezoid Label STUV	Parallelogram Label LMNO

Circles

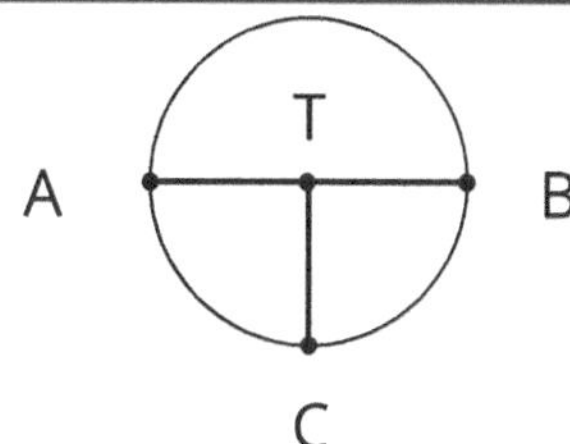

Identify a circle by the letter in the center of the circle. Point T is in the center of the circle, so the circle above is circle T.

A **radius** is a line segment from the center to any point on the circle. Name the three radii. Did you name $\overline{AT}$, $\overline{TB}$, and $\overline{TC}$? $\overline{TA}$, $\overline{BT}$, and $\overline{CT}$ would also be correct.

A **diameter** is a line segment with two points on the circle which passes through the center of the circle.

$\overline{AB}$ is the diameter of circle T.

The diameter is double the length of the radius. The radius is the diameter divided by 2. Give the diameter or radius of each circle.

34 m

a. diameter = _____ b. radius = _____ c. diameter = _____ d. radius = _____

1

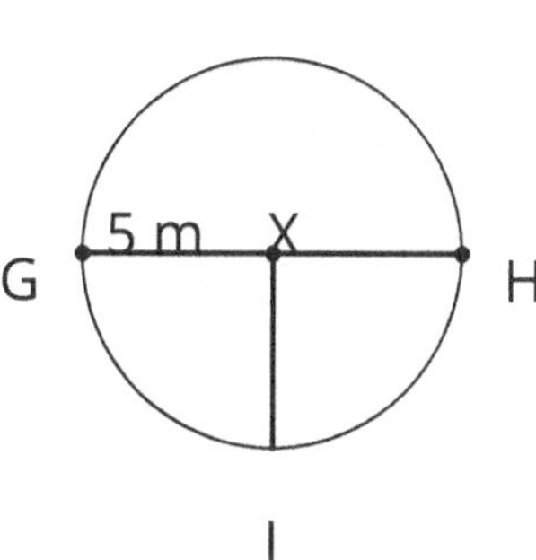

Name the circle above. ____________________

Name the 3 radii. ____________________

Name the diameter. ____________________

If the radius is 5 m, what is the diameter? ____________________

Are all the radii the same length? Explain. ____________________

____

2. Which of these letters of the alphabet are symmetrical? A B C D E F G H I J K

____

3. Draw similar figures to the ones given.

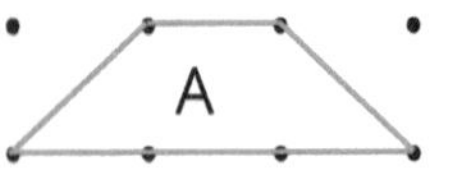

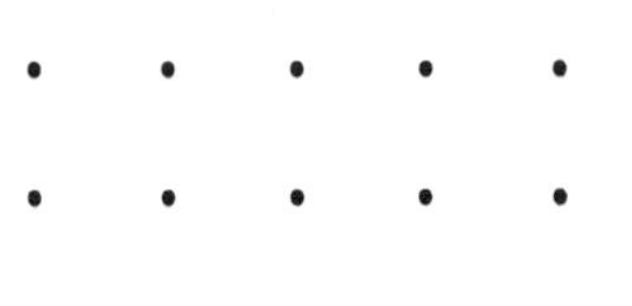

C

Figure A is a ______________________________.

Figure B is a ______________________________.

Figure C is a ______________________________.

4. Match.

1. 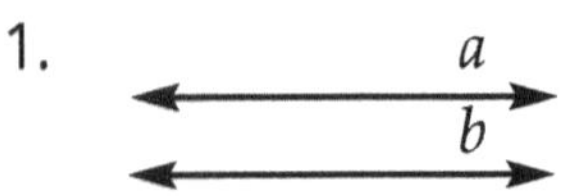

2. 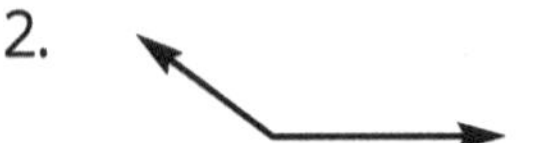

3. 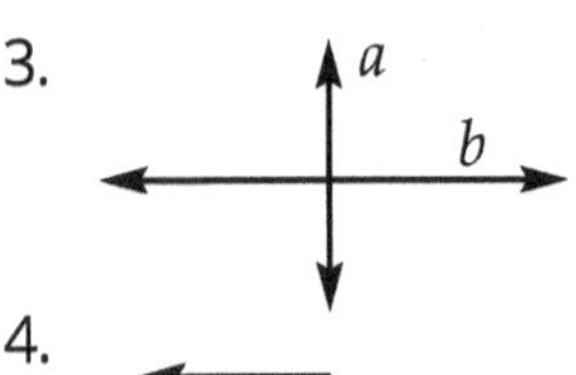

4.

5. 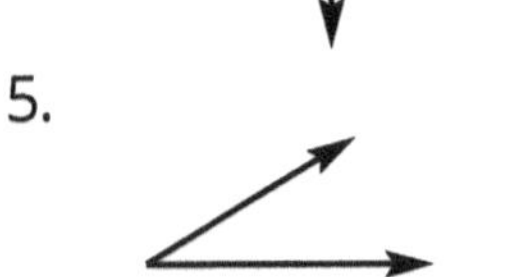

6. 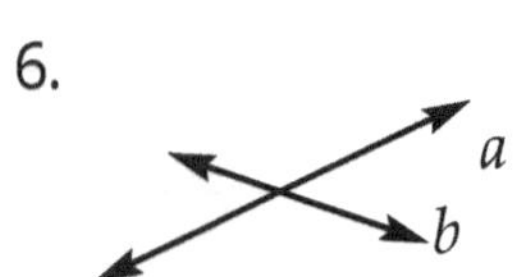

a. line *a* intersects line *b*

b. acute angle

c. $a \parallel b$

d. obtuse angle

e. $a \perp b$

f. right angle

5 Draw the following figures.

Octagon	Pentagon	Triangle	Hexagon	Quadrilateral

6 Find the quotient.

$8\overline{)80}$ $3\overline{)60}$ $7\overline{)280}$ $6\overline{)360}$ $9\overline{)918}$

7 Match.

1. A.M. a. in the year of the Lord
2. P.M. b. decade
3. A.D. c. century
4. B.C. d. before Christ
5. 10 e. 12:00 midnight to 12:00 noon
6. 100 f. millennium
7. 1,000 g. 12:00 noon to 12:00 midnight

Space Figures

Many solid figures have faces, edges, and vertices.

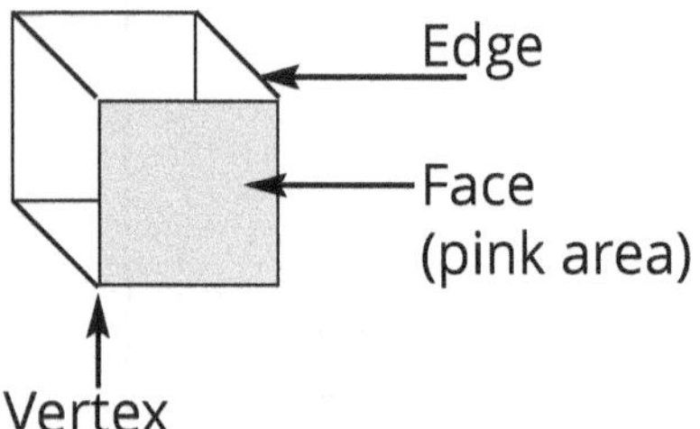

The cube has 6 faces.
It has 12 edges.
It has 8 vertices.

Five types of space figures.

Cones	Cylinder	Pyramids	Spheres	Prisms
1. A base that is not a polygon. 2. Curved sides.	1. Two parallel bases that are not polygons. 2. Curved sides.	1. One polygon base. 2. All faces are triangles that meet at a point.	1. All points are the same distance from the center.	1. Two parallel polygon bases. 2. All other faces are rectangles.

1 Give the number of faces, edges and vertices.

Triangular Prism	Rectangular Prism	Pentagonal Prism
Faces__ Edges__ Vertices __	Faces__ Edges__ Vertices __	Faces__ Edges__ Vertices __
Triangular Pyramid	**Rectangular Pyramid**	**Hexagonal Pyramid**
Faces__ Edges__ Vertices __	Faces__ Edges__ Vertices __	Faces__ Edges__ Vertices __

2 Draw a picture of a cone, sphere, and cylinder.

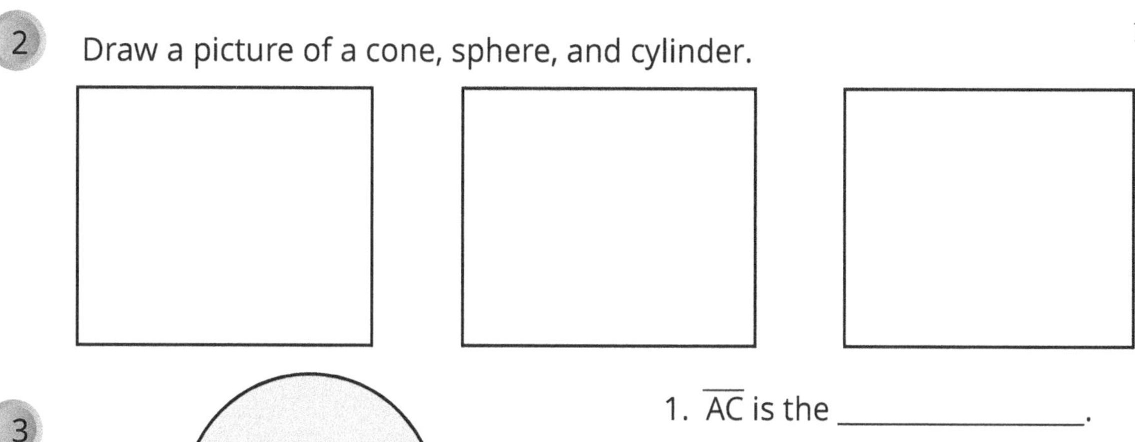

3

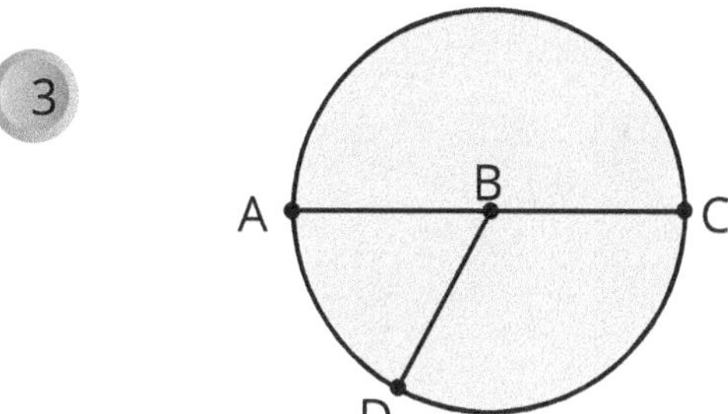

1. $\overline{AC}$ is the ________________.
2. $\overline{AB}$ = _____ and _____.
3. If $\overline{AC}$ is 10 m, what is the length of $\overline{BD}$?

   ____
4. $\overline{BC}$ is one of the ________________.

4 Draw two lines of symmetry for each figure. Label the figures with the following terms: triangle, rectangle, oval, hexagon, octagon, decagon, diamond, rhombus, square, pentagon.

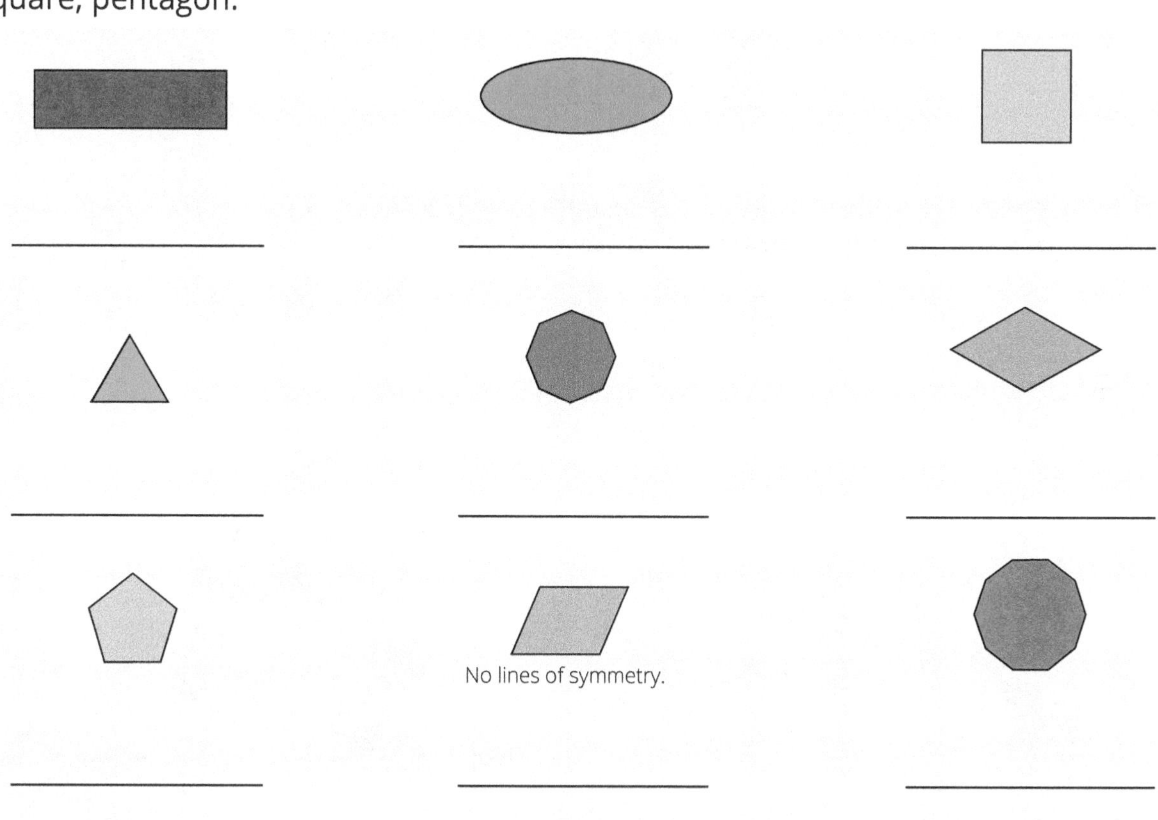

5 Draw a congruent and a similar figure.

6 Round each number to the nearest 10.

47 _____ 88 _____ 21 _____ 75 _____ 99 _____

7 Test each number to see if it is divisible by 2, 5,10, or 3.
Circle the correct responses.

715 is divisible by	2	5	10	3
400 is divisible by	2	5	10	3
711 is divisible by	2	5	10	3
669 is divisible by	2	5	10	3
940 is divisible by	2	5	10	3

Perimeter

Joshua and Andrew decided to jog around the perimeter of the park. How far did they jog?

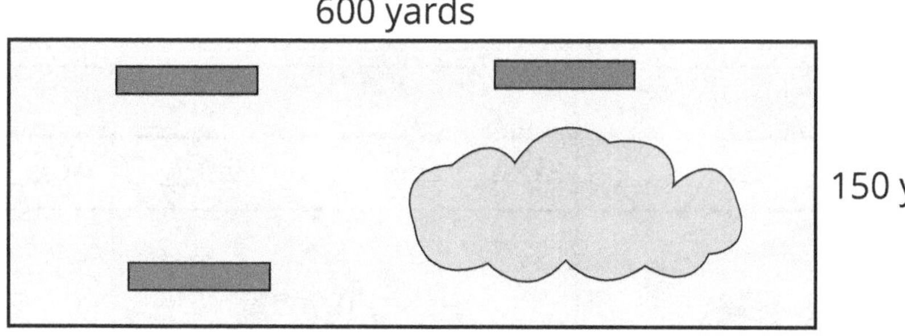

To find the perimeter of the park, we must add the measure of the sides.

$$\begin{array}{r} 600 \\ 600 \\ 150 \\ +\ 150 \\ \hline 1{,}500 \text{ yards} \end{array}$$

1 Find the perimeter of these regions.

1. Audry walked around the park. How far did she walk? If a mile is 1,760 yards, did she walk a mile?

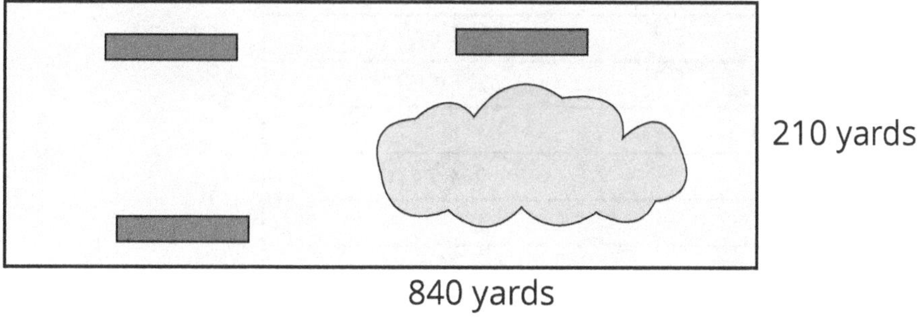

2. The Smiths' backyard is rectangular. If the width is 235 m and the length is 193 m, what does the perimeter of the yard measure?

3. The school playground has six sides. What does the perimeter measure?

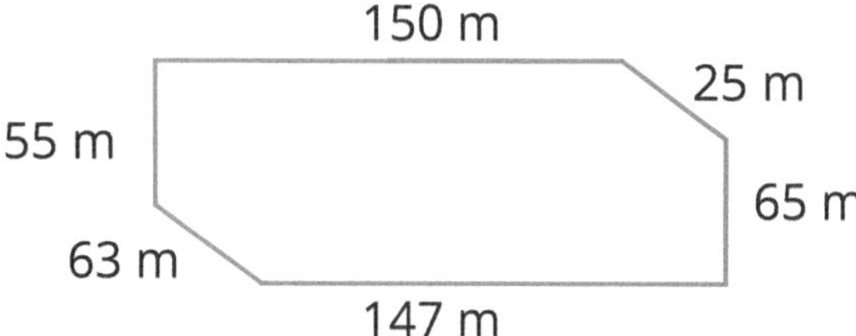

4. Andrea is planting a triangular flower garden. The sides each measure 38 inches. What is the perimeter?

2 Give the number of faces, edges, and vertices.

Faces___ Edges___ Vertices ___	Faces___ Edges___ Vertices ___	Faces___ Edges___ Vertices ___

3 What is the diameter of the circle with the given radius? What is the radius of the circle with the given diameter?

Radius	Diameter
3 cm	
18 cm	
	54 cm
	28 cm
72 cm	
	136 cm
103 cm	
	226 cm

4 Draw a symmetrical shape.

5 Round each number to the nearest hundred.

679 ________ 952 ________ 3,578 ________ 398,711 ________

401 ________ 329 ________ 7,999 ________ 931,001 ________

6 Find your way through the maze by following the prime numbers.

FINISH ↓

12	45	72	5	80	14	4	12
30	35	10	13	11	3	6	4
15	36	42	6	4	7	63	60
23	2	3	13	29	41	49	18
7	12	81	4	9	30	44	14

START ↑

7 Solve the equations and check.

$n \div 9 = 4$ x x Check:	$n \div 5 = 7$ x x Check:	$n \div 8 = 8$ x x Check:
$n \div 2 = 5$ x x Check:	$n \div 8 = 2$ x x Check:	$n \div 7 = 7$ x x Check:

Area

The hall is 8 m long and 2 m wide. What is the area of the hall?

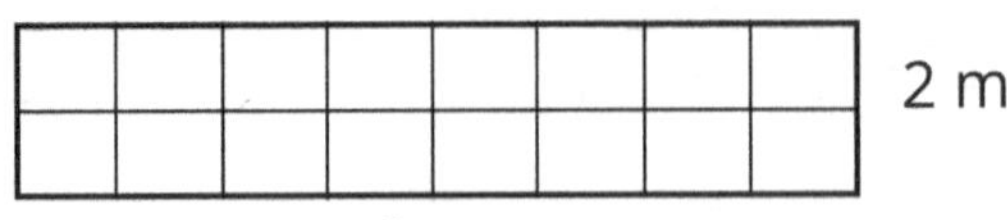

You can find the area by counting the number of squares.
There are 16 square units.

You can use a formula to compute area.

Area = Length x Width
A = L x W
A = 8 m x 2 m
A = 16 square units ($16\ m^2$)

1. Find the area of each region.

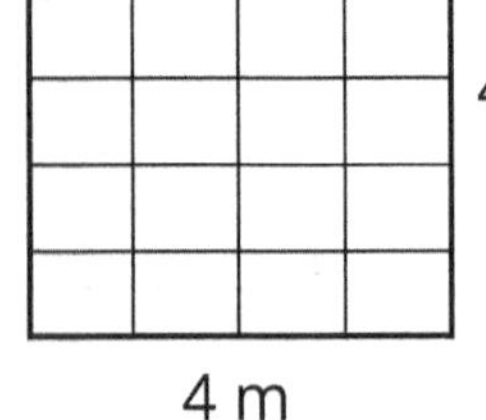

______

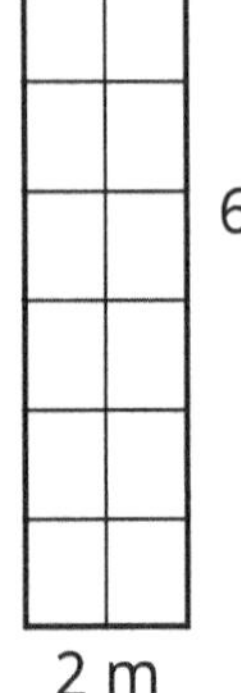

______

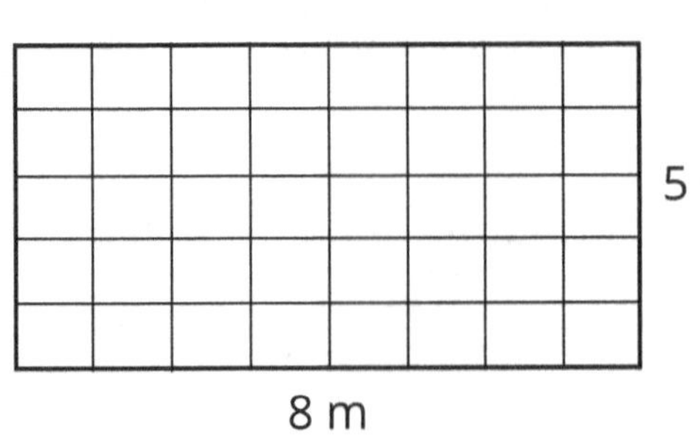

______

2. Find the perimeter of each polygon. The problems marked with an asterisk (*) are more difficult to solve.

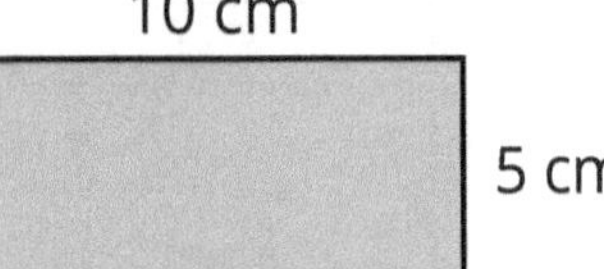

______

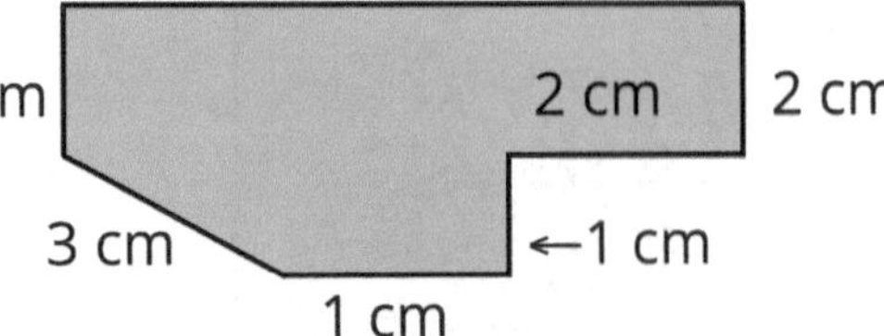

______

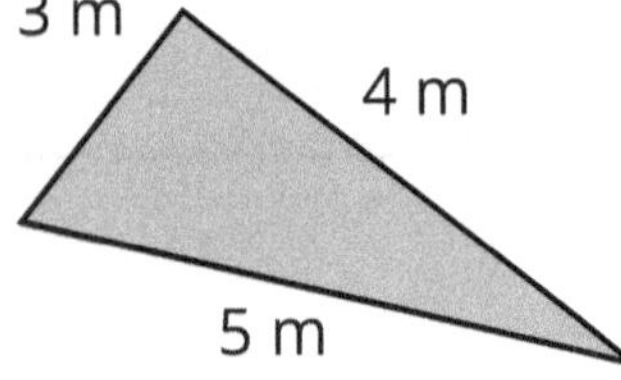

______

2 m

8 m

______

A triangle has a perimeter of 15 m. Two sides are 6 m each, what is the measure of the third side?

*A square has a perimeter of 16 cm. One side is 4 cm, what do the other three sides measure?

*A parallelogram has a perimeter of 30 m. If one side is 10 m, what is the measure of the other three sides?

3 Draw an example of each type of space figure.

Cone	Cylinder	Pyramid	Sphere	Prism

4

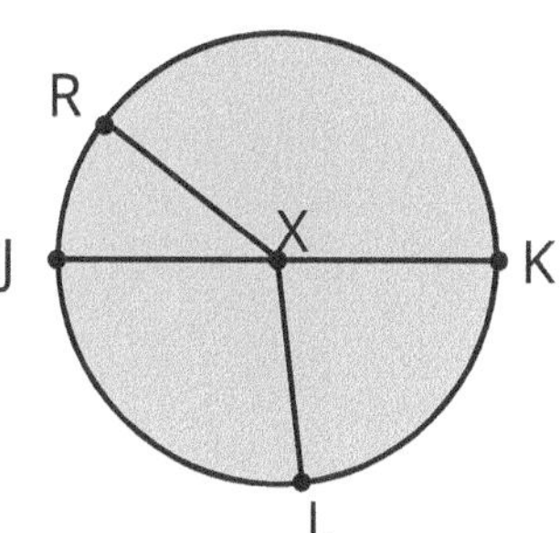

Name the 4 radii. ______________________________

Name the circle. ____________

Name the diameter. ___________

If the diameter is 142 cm, what is the radius? __________

Draw a line above the circle parallel to $\overline{JK}$. Label the line AB.

Draw a point outside of the circle. Label it point V.

Draw a point inside the circle. Label it point Y.

5 Round each number to the nearest 100.

356 ________ 7,901 ________

897,255 ________ 302,097 ________

6 Solve the equations and check.

$n + 61 = 137$	$n + 38 = 126$	$n + 47 = 198$
$-\quad -$	$-\quad -$	$-\quad -$
Check:	Check:	Check:

7 Find the quotient.

$43\overline{)333}$ $48\overline{)304}$ $90\overline{)457}$ $57\overline{)230}$

$52\overline{)438}$

Volume

Volume is the number of cubic units a figure contains.

You can find the volume by counting the number of cubic units.
There are 24 cubic units.

You can use a formula to compute volume.

Volume = Length x Width x Height

V = L x W x H

V = 4 x 3 x 2

V = 24 cubic units

A cubic unit can be measured in cubic millimeters (mm^3), cubic centimeters (cm^3), or cubic meters (m^3).

When finding volume be sure and label the problem in cubic units.

1 Find the volume of each figure.

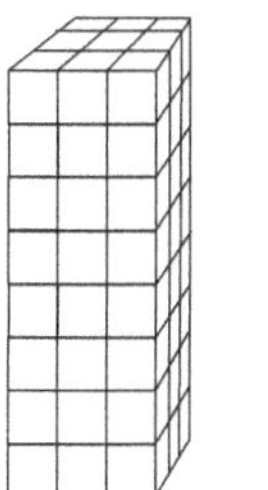

cm

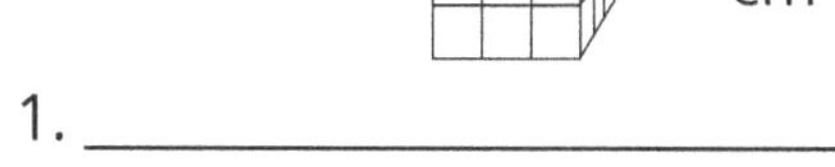

1. ______________________

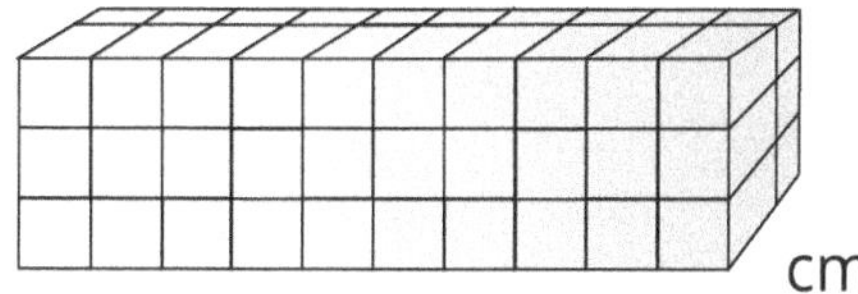

cm

2. ______________________

cm

3. ______________________

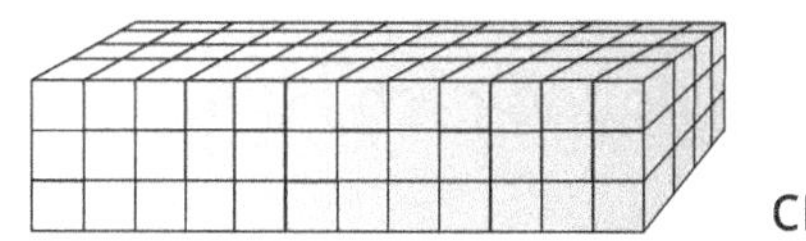

cm

4. ______________________

2 Use the correct symbol for cubic units.

6 cubic centimeters ____________ 7 cubic millimeters ____________

16 cubic meters ____________ 37 cubic meters ____________

13 cubic centimeters ____________ 78 cubic millimeters ____________

3 Find the missing length, width, perimeter, and/or area of the polygons.

Polygon	Square	Square	Rectangle	Rectangle
Length	4 cm	8 m	9 m	12 cm
Width	4 cm		3 m	4 cm
Perimeter				
Area	16 cm^2		27 m^2	

4 Give the number of faces, edges and vertices.

Cube	Rectangular Prism	Pentagonal Prism
Faces___ Edges___ Vertices ___	Faces___ Edges___ Vertices ___	Faces___ Edges___ Vertices ___

5 Round each number to the nearest 100.

648 ________ 98,312 ________ 809,021 ________ 1,897,955 ________

6 Solve the equations and check.

$n + 20 = 1{,}074$ $-\quad -$ Check:	$n + 328 = 1{,}206$ $-\quad -$ Check:	$n + 479 = 983$ $-\quad -$ Check:

7 Average.

16 + 17 + 19 + 36 = ____

37 + 28 + 33 + 42 = ____

42 + 127 + 125 + 130 = _____

136 + 114 + 140 = _____

8 Find the quotient.

67 ⟌ 129   60 ⟌ 331   82 ⟌ 741   71 ⟌ 636

42 ⟌ 392   92 ⟌ 841   65 ⟌ 571   33 ⟌ 254

Fractions–Parts of a Whole

The chocolate cake was cut into 8 equal pieces. 7 pieces were eaten. What part of the cake was eaten?

We use a fraction to answer this question.

$\frac{7}{8}$ ← NUMERATOR - This number shows the parts eaten.
← DENOMINATOR - This number shows the total number of parts.

Seven-eighths of the cake was eaten.

1 Name the numerator and denominator.

$\frac{4}{7}$ ______ ______ $\frac{7}{8}$ ______ ______ $\frac{10}{13}$ ______ ______ $\frac{34}{37}$ ______ ______

Complete the fraction for the shaded part.

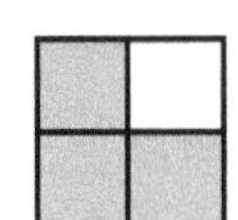

$\frac{\_\_}{2}$ $\frac{\_\_}{4}$

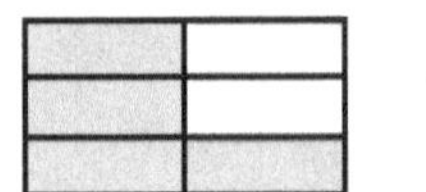

$\frac{\_\_}{6}$

2 Find the volume of each figure.

1. 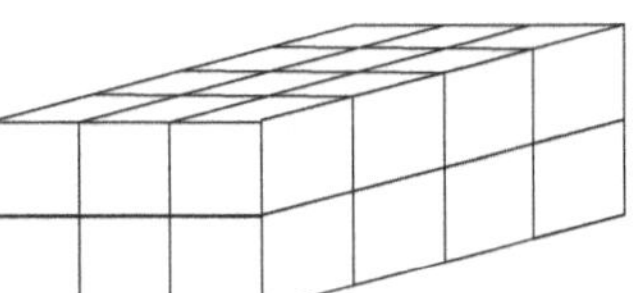 ______ cm

2. 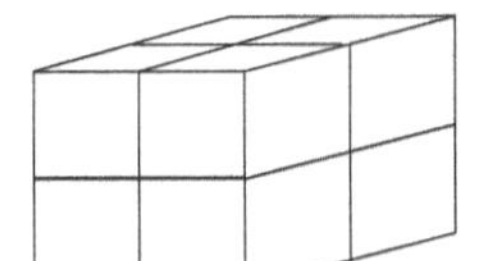 ______ cm

3. 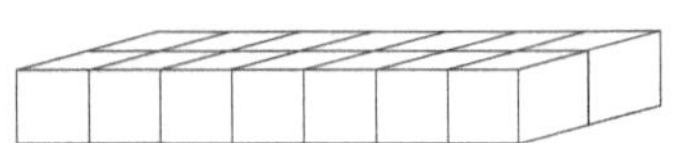 ______ cm

4. ______ cm

3 Find the perimeter and area of each figure.

36 cm × 12 cm

perimeter ________ cm

area ____________ cm^2

8 cm × 8 cm

perimeter ________ cm

area ____________ cm^2

4 Shade the numbers indicated by place value. The first one has been done for you. Can you identify the Christian symbols?

ten thousands, hundred thousands	6	7	8	3	9	7	6	4	8
thousands, millions	3	4	6	0	7	8	9	0	9
ten millions, hundreds, ones	7	6	4	4	8	8	6	0	9
hundred millions, tens	6	5	6	0	0	7	8	8	8
ten millions, hundreds, ones	4	2	4	6	0	1	6	3	8
thousands, millions	8	2	1	3	0	1	5	4	7
ten thousands, hundred thousands	6	2	2	5	0	3	6	6	6
blank	7	8	4	5	8	1	2	8	1
hundred thousand	6	6	0	7	6	2	1	9	1
hundred thousand	5	7	8	9	1	3	8	0	1
ten thousands, hundred thousands, millions	3	7	7	8	4	2	9	8	1
hundred thousands	2	0	6	7	6	1	6	9	5
hundred thousands	9	0	5	9	3	3	0	6	7
hundred thousands	7	0	3	9	2	5	6	8	4
hundred thousands	1	0	8	0	1	6	4	5	5

5 Circle the correct answer. Place the letter next to the correct answer in the boxes below to complete the passage: "**Cast your _______ upon the Lord.**" **Ps. 55:22.**
The number below each box corresponds to the problem number. The first one has been done for you.

1. Round 2,359 to the nearest hundred.
   2,300 A
   2,400 B
   2,450 C

2. Round 68,902 to the nearest hundred.
   69,000 E
   68,800 S
   68,900 U

3. Round 754 to the nearest hundred.
   750 S
   700 G
   800 R

4. Round 769,832 to the nearest hundred.
   769,800 D
   769,900 O
   769,930 T

5. Round 5,283 to the nearest hundred.
   5,000 U
   5,300 E
   5,200 M

6. Round 989 to the nearest hundred.
   900 E
   990 B
   1,000 N

Cast your 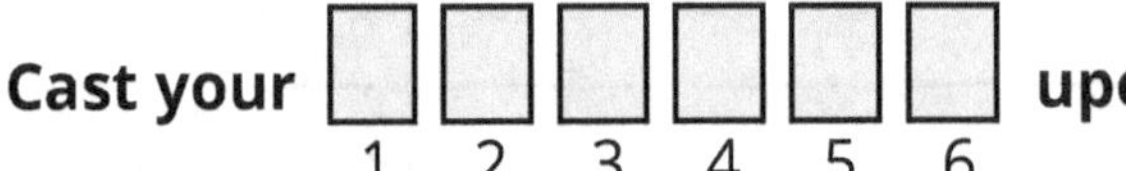 **upon the Lord. Ps. 55:22**

1 2 3 4 5 6

6 Find each product.

$$\begin{array}{r} 354 \\ \times\ 31 \\ \hline \end{array} \qquad \begin{array}{r} 374 \\ \times\ 80 \\ \hline \end{array} \qquad \begin{array}{r} 908 \\ \times\ 54 \\ \hline \end{array}$$

$$\begin{array}{r} 253 \\ \times\ 27 \\ \hline \end{array} \qquad \begin{array}{r} 419 \\ \times\ 84 \\ \hline \end{array}$$

Test 10

46 points total Lessons 86-95

1 a. Jan is going to leave for Camp Hope the third Friday of January. What will be the date?

b. Jan will stay at camp two nights and return home the following day. What will be the date?

c. Steven will begin selling popcorn on January 2. He may sell for one week. What is the last day he can sell popcorn?

JANUARY

S	M	T	W	T	F	S
			1	2	3	4
5	6	7	8	9	10	11
12	13	14	15	16	17	18
19	20	21	22	23	24	25
26	27	28	29	30	31	

d. Pete has a science project due January 22. He found out about the project January 1. How many days does he have to work on it? How many weeks?

e. It is January 10, and Susan wants to make reservations to see an art exhibit. The exhibit is open every Wednesday. She must make the reservation two full weeks in advance. If Susan wants to go to the art show in January, what is the only possible date she can go?

6 pts. total for above exercise.

2

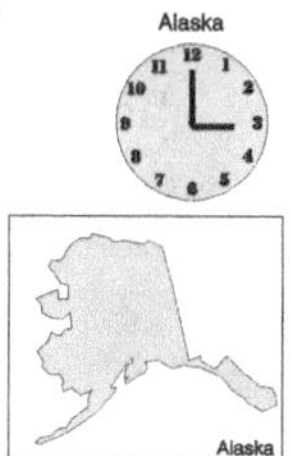

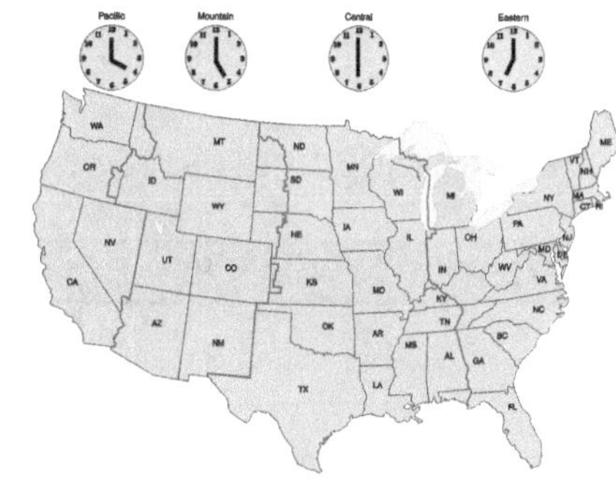

It is 9:00 in Arizona. What are the times in the following time zones? 4 pts. for this exercise.

Central Time ______ Eastern Time ______ Pacific Time ______ Hawaii Time ______

3 Use a chart to solve the logic problem. 1 pt. for this exercise.

Paula, Steven, Carrie, and Floyd are sitting around a table. Carrie is sitting across from Paula. Paula is sitting at Steven's right. Where is each person sitting?

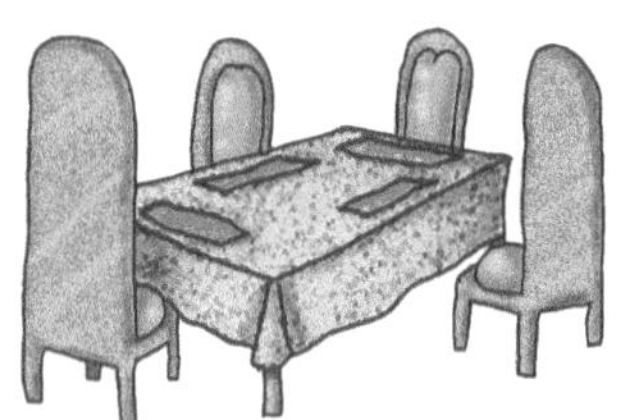

4 Use the problem solving strategy, work backwards, to solve this problem. 1 pt.

Steve asked Paul how many trading cards he collected. Paul said, "If you add 4 to the amount and double it, you get 228."

5 Write the name of each figure using symbols. Name it using words. 8 pts.

1. 

2. 

3. 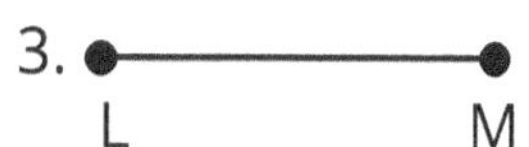

4. 

__________ __________ __________ __________

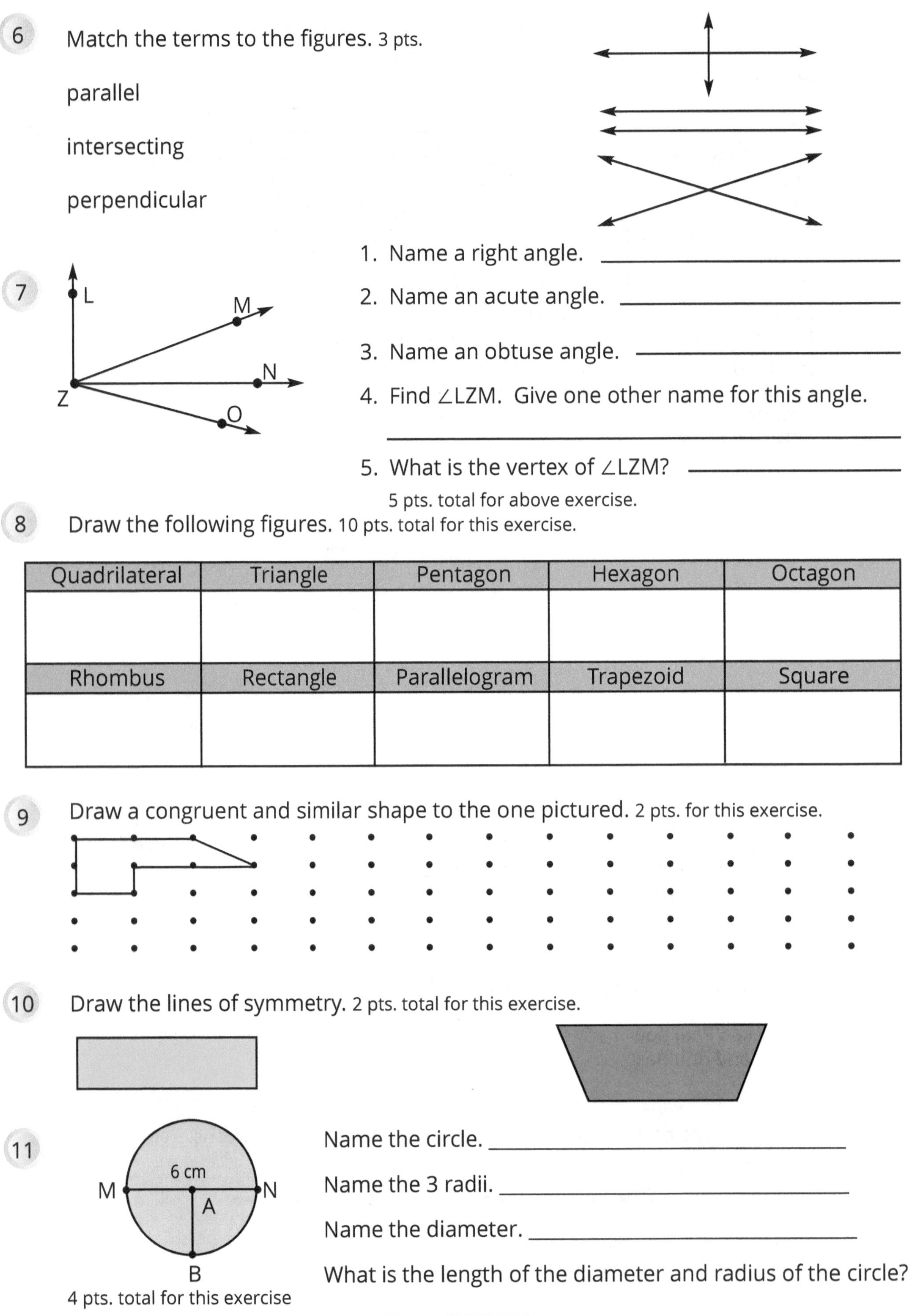

6 Match the terms to the figures. 3 pts.

parallel

intersecting

perpendicular

7

1. Name a right angle. ______________
2. Name an acute angle. ______________
3. Name an obtuse angle. ______________
4. Find ∠LZM. Give one other name for this angle.

   ____
5. What is the vertex of ∠LZM? ______________

5 pts. total for above exercise.

8 Draw the following figures. 10 pts. total for this exercise.

Quadrilateral	Triangle	Pentagon	Hexagon	Octagon
Rhombus	**Rectangle**	**Parallelogram**	**Trapezoid**	**Square**

9 Draw a congruent and similar shape to the one pictured. 2 pts. for this exercise.

10 Draw the lines of symmetry. 2 pts. total for this exercise.

11

4 pts. total for this exercise

Name the circle. ______________

Name the 3 radii. ______________

Name the diameter. ______________

What is the length of the diameter and radius of the circle?

____

Naming Fractions

Write the word name for the following fractions:

$\frac{1}{4}$	$\frac{7}{9}$	$\frac{6}{11}$	$\frac{8}{13}$
one-fourth	seven-ninths	six-elevenths	eight-thirteenths

Write the fractions for the following word names:

zero-fifths	one-half	two-thirds	six-sevenths
$\frac{0}{5}$	$\frac{1}{2}$	$\frac{2}{3}$	$\frac{6}{7}$

1 Write the word name for each fraction.

$\frac{3}{4}$ ____________ $\frac{5}{5}$ ____________ $\frac{4}{7}$ ____________ $\frac{6}{13}$ ____________ $\frac{0}{8}$ ____________

Write the fraction for each word name.

two-fifths ____ one-eighth ____ seven-tenths ____ eight-sixteenths ____

2 Give the fraction of the region shaded.

3 Find the volume of each figure.

1. 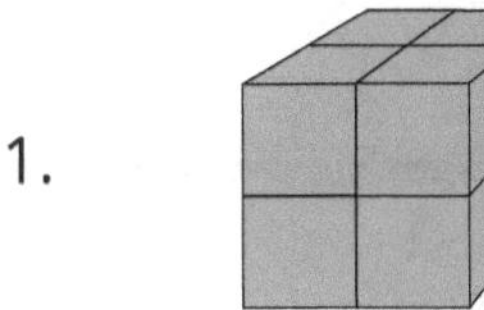

____

2. 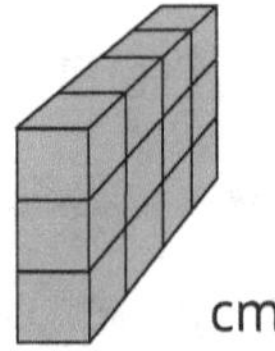

____

3. 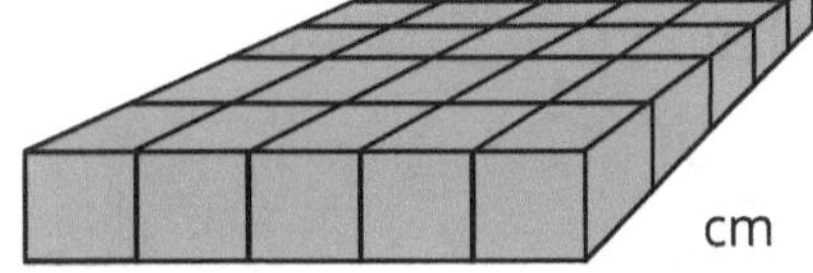

____

4. 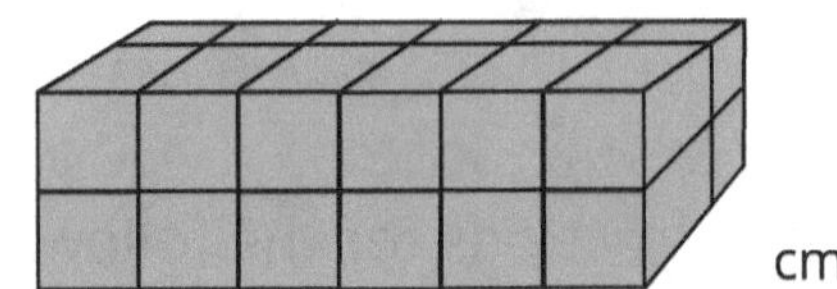

____

4 Use the clues to find the mystery number.

___ ___ ___ , ___ ___ ___ , ___ ___ ___ , ___ ___ ___

a. The number in the hundreds' place is 5.

b. The number in the tens' place is 0.

c. The number in the ten millions' and hundred millions' are the same.

d. The number in the ones' place is odd and less than 2.

e. The number in the ones' place plus the number in the hundreds' place is equal to the number in the hundred billions' place.

f. The number in the ten billions' place is one less than the number in the hundred billions' place.

g. The number in the billions' place is 9.

h. The number in the ten thousands' place and hundred thousands' place are equal to the number in the tens' place.

i. The number in the thousands' place is 2.

j. The number in the millions' place is the number in the billions' place minus 2.

k. The number in the ten millions' place is even and greater than 7.

5 Circle the correct answer. Place the letter next to the correct answer in the boxes below to complete the passage: **"Thy word is a lamp unto my feet, and a _____ unto my path."** (Ps.119:105) The number below each line corresponds to the problem number.

1. Round 27,439 to the nearest thousand.

   27,000 **L**
   27,400 **M**
   28,000 **N**

2. Round 134,987 to the nearest thousand.

   134,900 **E**
   134,000 **S**
   135,000 **I**

3. Round 1,892 to the nearest thousand.

   1,900 **H**
   2,000 **G**
   1,000 **R**

4. Round 9,984 to the nearest thousand.

   10,000 **H**
   9,900 **I**
   9,000 **J**

5. Round 15,209 to the nearest thousand.

   15,200 **U**
   15,000 **T**
   16,000 **M**

"Thy word is a lamp unto my feet, and a ___ ___ ___ ___ ___ **unto my path."** Ps.119:105

1 2 3 4 5

6 Multiply.

390	207	198	265	382
x 35	x 41	x 37	x 93	x 72

Fractions of Sets

Alice is making a flower arrangement for her mother's birthday. Of the 6 flowers, how many are red?

$\frac{2}{6}$ Number of red flowers / Total number of flowers **Two-sixths of the flowers are red.**

We can also write how many of the 6 flowers are yellow.

$\frac{4}{6}$ Number of yellow flowers / Total number of flowers **Four-sixths of the flowers are yellow.**

1 What fraction of each set is in the box?

1.

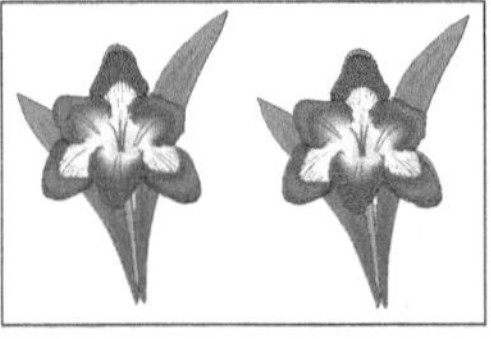

____

2.

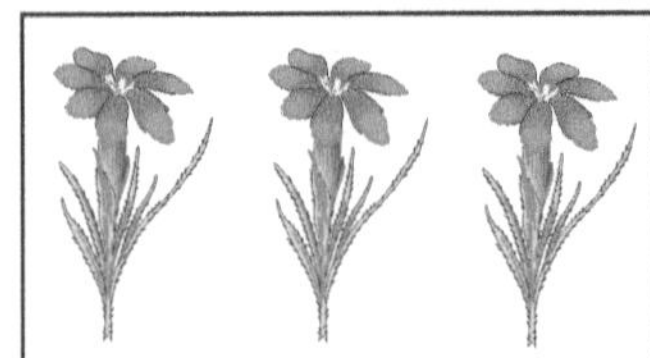

____

3.

____

4.

____

2 Write the word name for the following fractions.

$\frac{1}{2}$ ______________

$\frac{6}{7}$ ______________

$\frac{8}{10}$ ______________

$\frac{12}{13}$ ______________

3 Write the fraction for each word name.

three-fourths	seven-sevenths	three-sixteenths	zero-tenths
______	______	______	______

4 Give the fraction of the shaded region.

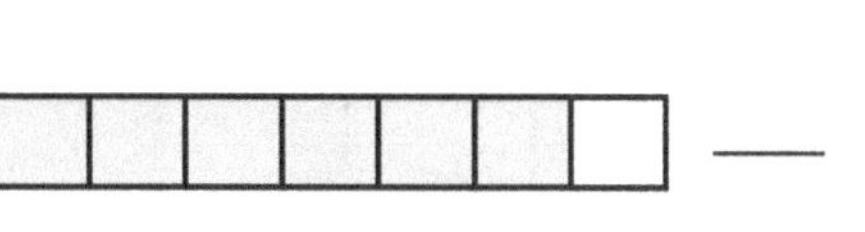 ___ 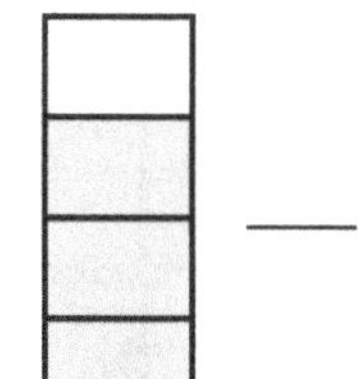 ___ 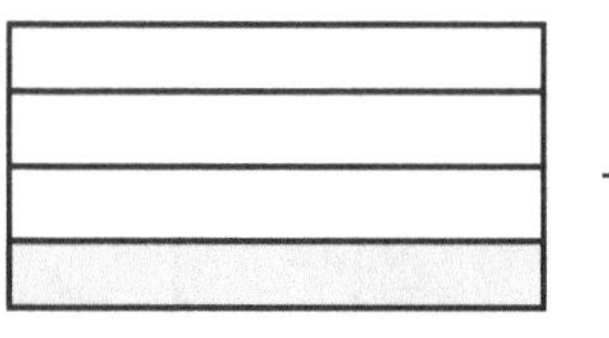 ___

5 Solve the equations and check.

$6 \times n = 42$	$n \times 8 = 64$	$6 \times n = 24$
______	______	______
Check:	Check:	Check:

6 Write each number in expanded form.

722,980 ______________________

3,904 ______________________

24,001 ______________________

539 ______________________

7 Complete the crossword puzzle.

1	2	3			4			5	6
7								8	
9					10				
11			12	13			14		
	15						16		
			17			18			
	19								

Across

1. five hundred twenty-seven thousand, nine hundred one
5. twenty-eight
7. one hundred eighty-two
8. seventeen
9. two hundred thirty-two
10. sixty-three thousand, four hundred fifty-two
11. six hundred ten thousand, eight hundred fifty-seven
14. seven hundred twenty-nine
15. seven thousand, four hundred ninety
16. three hundred eighty-three
17. twenty-two
18. six thousand, four hundred seventeen
19. eight hundred eighteen thousand, three hundred sixty- seven

Down

1. five thousand, one hundred twenty-six
2. twenty-eight thousand, three hundred seventeen
3. seventy-two thousand, two hundred four
4. one thousand, two hundred sixty-seven
5. two hundred fifteen thousand, two hundred eighty-one
6. eight hundred seventy-two thousand, nine hundred thirty-seven
12. eight thousand, nine hundred twenty-eight
13. five thousand, twenty-three
18. sixty-seven

Equivalent Fractions

$\frac{1}{2}$, $\frac{2}{4}$, and $\frac{3}{6}$ are all different ways to express the same number.

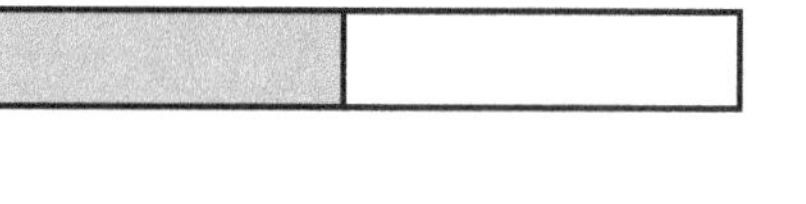

$\frac{1}{2}$

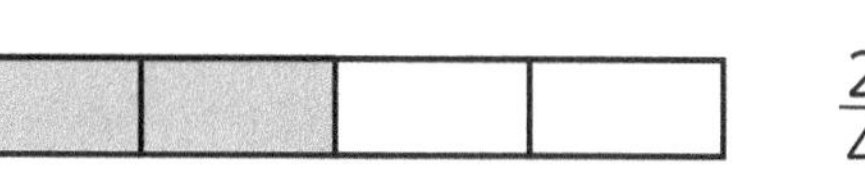

$\frac{2}{4}$

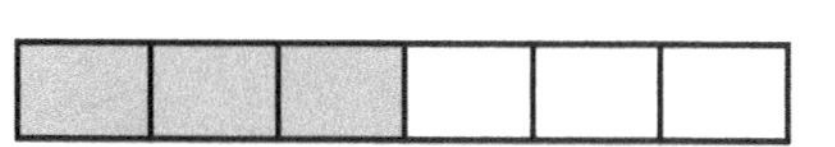

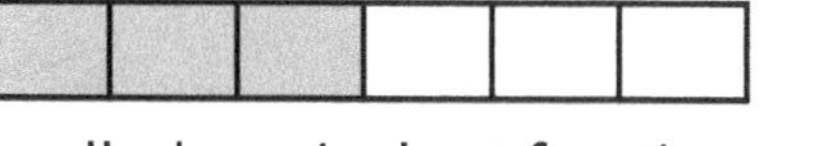

$\frac{3}{6}$

They are called equivalent fractions.

Equivalent fractions can be found by multiplying the numerator and denominator of a fraction by the same number.

$$\frac{1}{2} = \frac{1 \times 2}{2 \times 2} = \frac{2}{4} \qquad \frac{1}{2} = \frac{1 \times 3}{2 \times 3} = \frac{3}{6}$$

1 Find the equivalent fractions.

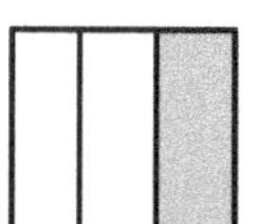 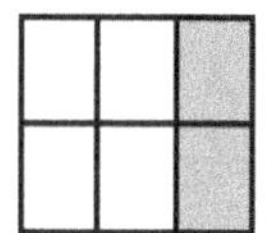 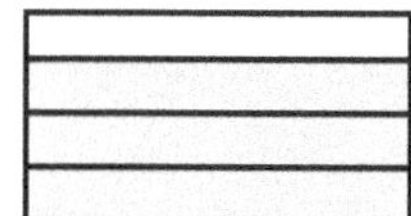 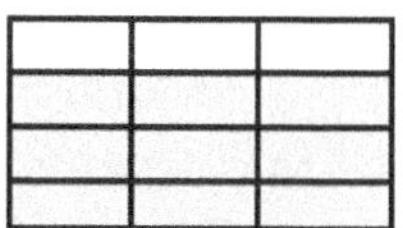 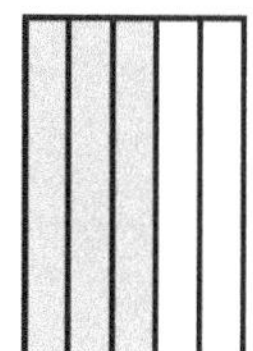 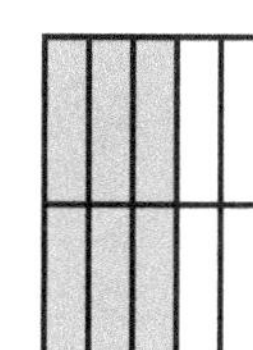

$\frac{1}{3} = \frac{1 \times 2}{3 \times 2} = \_\_$ $\qquad$ $\frac{3}{4} = \frac{3 \times 3}{4 \times 3} = \_\_$ $\qquad$ $\frac{3}{5} = \frac{3 \times 2}{5 \times 2} = \_\_$

$\frac{3}{7} = \frac{3 \times 3}{7 \times 3} = \_\_$ $\qquad$ $\frac{2}{6} = \frac{2 \times 4}{6 \times 4} = \_\_$ $\qquad$ $\frac{4}{9} = \frac{4 \times 4}{9 \times 4} = \_\_$

Give the missing numerator.

$\frac{2}{7} = \frac{\_\_}{14}$ $\qquad$ $\frac{5}{8} = \frac{\_\_}{40}$ $\qquad$ $\frac{1}{10} = \frac{\_\_}{20}$ $\qquad$ $\frac{3}{9} = \frac{\_\_}{81}$ $\qquad$ $\frac{4}{9} = \frac{\_\_}{36}$

2 What fraction of each set is shaded?

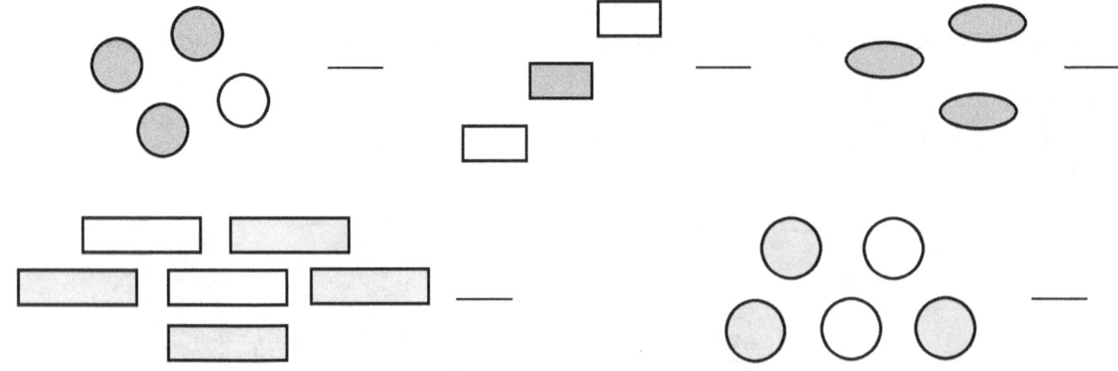

3 Write the word name for the following fractions.

$\frac{1}{7}$ $\frac{16}{17}$ $\frac{9}{10}$ $\frac{12}{12}$

4 Write the fraction for each word name.

three-fifths seven-seventeenths three-sixteenths eight-tenths

5 Give the fraction of the region shaded. Label with the terms denominator and numerator.

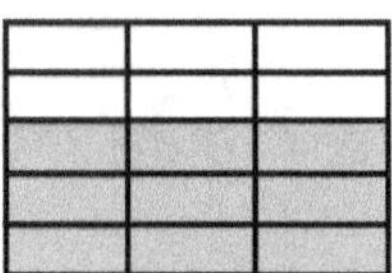

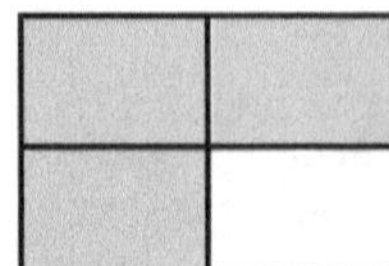

6 Solve the puzzle by placing the numbers in standard form in the appropriate boxes. There is only one right solution.

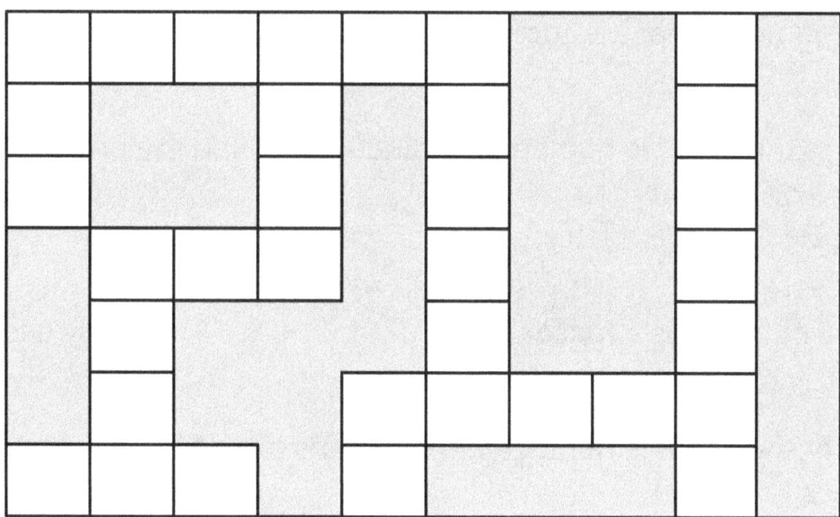

1. 700,000
2. three hundred thirty-two
3. 30 + 7
4. 500 + 10 + 2
5. 564,567
6. 5,000 + 600 + 60 + 7
7. seven hundred eighty-seven
8. thirty thousand, two hundred four
9. 7,643
10. 3,590,042

7 Find the quotient.

$7\overline{)47}$ $6\overline{)38}$ $8\overline{)64}$ $9\overline{)77}$ $4\overline{)15}$ $6\overline{)49}$

Greatest Common Factor

Factors are numbers that are combined in the multiplication process to obtain a product.

What are all of the possible number combinations to find the product 16?

1 x 16 = 16
2 x 8 = 16
4 x 4 = 16

Each of those numbers is a **factor** of 16: 1, 2, 4, 8, 16 (We only use each number above once.)

What are all of the possible number combinations to find the product 4?

1 x 4 = 4
2 x 2 = 4

Each of those numbers is a **factor** of 4: 1, 2, 4

What is the **greatest common factor** of the two numbers 16 and 4?
Both numbers share the **common factors** 1, 2, and 4.
The **greatest common factor** is 4.

Find the greatest common factor of 10 and 12.

10: 1, 2, 5, 10
12: 1, 2, 3, 4, 6, 12
common factors: 1, 2
greatest common factor: 2

1 Find the common factors and greatest common factors for each pair of numbers.

8:
20:

common factors:
greatest common factor:

13:
15:

common factors:
greatest common factor:

42:
28:

common factors:
greatest common factor:

15:
12:

common factors:
greatest common factor:

10:
20:

common factors:
greatest common factor:

16:
24:

common factors:
greatest common factor:

2 Complete these problems.

$\frac{1}{7} = \frac{1 \times 2}{7 \times 2} =$ $\frac{2}{9} = \frac{2 \times 3}{9 \times 3} =$ $\frac{4}{5} = \frac{4 \times 2}{5 \times 2} =$

$\frac{5}{8} = \frac{5 \times 4}{8 \times 4} =$ $\frac{3}{7} = \frac{3 \times 6}{7 \times 6} =$ $\frac{4}{9} = \frac{4 \times 5}{9 \times 5} =$

3 Give the missing numerator.

$\frac{6}{9} = \frac{\quad}{18}$ $\frac{5}{7} = \frac{\quad}{49}$ $\frac{8}{9} = \frac{\quad}{81}$ $\frac{3}{12} = \frac{\quad}{24}$ $\frac{1}{7} = \frac{\quad}{21}$

4 Match the word fractions and number fractions.

two-fifths	$\frac{6}{15}$
eight-thirteenths	$\frac{2}{5}$
seven-nineteenths	$\frac{1}{4}$
one-fourth	$\frac{2}{8}$
two-eighths	$\frac{7}{19}$
six-fifteenths	$\frac{8}{13}$

5 Shade the part named by the fraction.

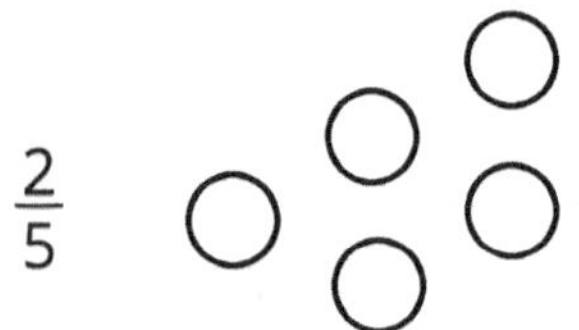

$\frac{2}{5}$ $\frac{4}{7}$ $\frac{1}{3}$

6 Order the numbers from least to greatest. If the order is correct, the letter beside each number will complete the verse:
"The Lord is far from the wicked, but he heareth the prayer of the __________ ."
Proverbs 15:29

21	**R**	1,010	**E**	551	**H**
120,000	**S**	515	**G**	12,000	**U**
514	**I**	1,001	**T**	1,021	**O**

1.____________________ ___ 6.____________________ ___

2.____________________ ___ 7.____________________ ___

3.____________________ ___ 8.____________________ ___

4.____________________ ___ 9.____________________ ___

5.____________________ ___

7 Find the difference.

2061	4102	7002	3021	1004
- 1921	- 3891	- 1234	- 1242	- 926

8 Find the quotient.

9)89 4)18 6)38 7)47 8)64

Lowest-Terms Fractions

15 out of 20 students voted for Stephen for class President.

Write $\frac{15}{20}$ in lowest terms.

A fraction is in lowest terms if the greatest common factor of both the numerator and denominator is 1.
Find the common factors and greatest common factor of 15 and 20.

15: 1, 3, 5, 15
20: 1, 2, 4, 5, 10, 20
common factors: 1, 5
greatest common factor: 5

METHOD ONE **Greatest Common Factor.** To write a fraction in lowest terms, divide the numerator and denominator by their greatest common factor.

$\frac{15 \div 5}{20 \div 5} = \frac{3}{4}$ $\frac{3}{4}$ of the students voted for Stephen for President.

METHOD TWO **Repeated Division By a Common Factor**

Write $\frac{24}{40}$ in lowest terms.

$\frac{24 \div 2}{40 \div 2} = \frac{12}{20}$ $\frac{12 \div 4}{20 \div 4} = \frac{3}{5}$

1 Write each fraction in lowest terms.

$\frac{10}{20} =$ $\frac{15}{25} =$ $\frac{4}{16} =$ $\frac{6}{24} =$ $\frac{14}{35} =$

$\frac{3}{12} =$ $\frac{12}{20} =$ $\frac{18}{81} =$ $\frac{75}{100} =$ $\frac{90}{100} =$

2 Give the missing numerator or denominator.

$\frac{3}{4} = \frac{}{16}$ $\frac{5}{7} = \frac{25}{}$ $\frac{1}{9} = \frac{}{72}$ $\frac{13}{12} = \frac{26}{}$ $\frac{8}{11} = \frac{}{33}$

3 Find the common factors and greatest common factors for each pair of numbers.

6:
9:

common factors:
greatest common factor:

15:
35:

common factors:
greatest common factor:

5:
25:

common factors:
greatest common factor:

24:
18:

common factors:
greatest common factor:

8:
24:

common factors:
greatest common factor:

16:
40:

common factors:
greatest common factor:

4 Write a fraction to name each point. The first one has been done for you.

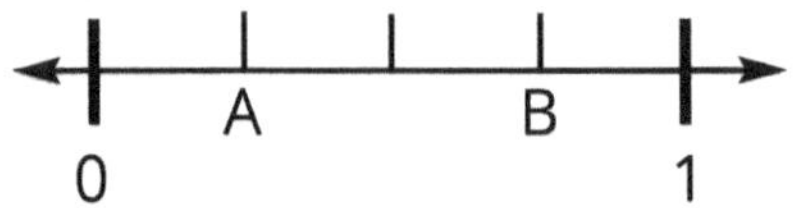

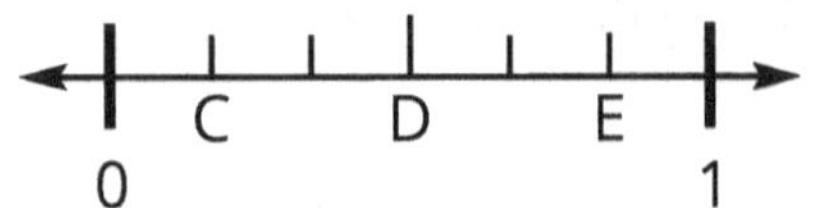

A. $\frac{1}{4}$ C. _____ E. _____

B. _____ D. _____

5 Write the numbers in order from greatest to least.

298,000,745 23 802,000,908 10,000,000 32 29,800
1,000,000 802,000,990 80,200,908 2,980,000 2,980 840

1. ____________________ 7. ____________________

2. ____________________ 8. ____________________

3. ____________________ 9. ____________________

4. ____________________ 10. ____________________

5. ____________________ 11. ____________________

6. ____________________ 12. ____________________

Solve each problem. Find the quotient in the picture below and color it as indicated.

9)81	_______	Tan
8)64	_______	Almond
6)31	_______	Yellow
8)40	_______	Gray
4)16	_______	Almond
7)49	_______	Lt. Blue
6)12	_______	Desert Sand
9)44	_______	Red
7)42	_______	Brown
6)45	_______	D. Blue
6)56	_______	Green
6)39	_______	Orange
6)28	_______	Black
6)18	_______	Orange

Comparing and Ordering Fractions

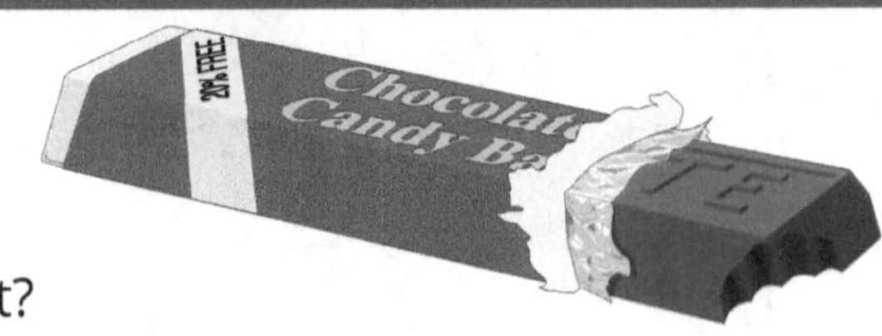

John ate $\frac{1}{4}$ of a candy bar.

Thomas ate $\frac{3}{4}$ of a candy bar. Who ate the most?

When we compare fractions with the same denominator, it is easy to decide which fraction is the largest. It is the one with the largest numerator, as shown by these pictures.

$\frac{1}{4}$ 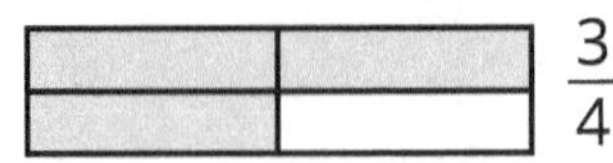 $\frac{3}{4}$

Thomas ate the most candy. $\frac{3}{4} > \frac{1}{4}$

Sam walked for $\frac{1}{3}$ of an hour. Paul walked for $\frac{2}{4}$ of an hour. Who walked the longest? We can compare using a number line.

Paul walked the longest. $\frac{2}{4} > \frac{1}{3}$

Renaming. We can compare fractions by renaming them as like fractions.

$$\frac{2 \times 3}{4 \times 3} = \frac{6}{12} \qquad \frac{1 \times 4}{3 \times 4} = \frac{4}{12}$$

We can see that $\frac{6}{12} > \frac{4}{12}$ or $\frac{2}{4} > \frac{1}{3}$

Cross Product. This can be used **AFTER** there is a thorough understanding of the methods above. Cross multiply 2 x 4 to get the first product. Cross multiply 3 x 3 to get the second product. They must be multiplied in this order for every pair of fractions being compared.

Compare $\frac{2}{3}$ ⤨ $\frac{3}{4}$ 2 x 4 = 8
3 x 3 = 9

Since the second product is larger, the second fraction is larger. $\frac{2}{3} < \frac{3}{4}$

1 Compare with the correct sign. (>, <, =)

$\frac{3}{8}$ ___ $\frac{7}{8}$ $\frac{4}{12}$ ___ $\frac{2}{12}$ $\frac{6}{14}$ ___ $\frac{7}{14}$ $\frac{8}{42}$ ___ $\frac{14}{42}$

$\frac{1}{3}$ ___ $\frac{2}{6}$ $\frac{2}{3}$ ___ $\frac{3}{4}$ $\frac{7}{12}$ ___ $\frac{2}{3}$ $\frac{4}{5}$ ___ $\frac{5}{6}$

$\frac{5}{9}$ ___ $\frac{2}{5}$ $\frac{3}{6}$ ___ $\frac{1}{2}$ $\frac{4}{5}$ ___ $\frac{6}{8}$ $\frac{7}{8}$ ___ $\frac{6}{9}$

2 Write each fraction in lowest terms. Match your answer with the fraction below. Place the appropriate letter on the line and read the mystery message.

1. $\frac{5}{10}$ = ___ **W**
2. $\frac{15}{20}$ = ___ **D**
3. $\frac{18}{20}$ = ___ **R**
4. $\frac{12}{15}$ = ___ **A**
5. $\frac{5}{125}$ = ___ **I**
6. $\frac{8}{14}$ = ___ **C**
7. $\frac{3}{9}$ = ___ **O**
8. $\frac{6}{21}$ = ___ **N**
9. $\frac{24}{36}$ = ___ **T**
10. $\frac{14}{16}$ = ___ **Z**
11. $\frac{4}{18}$ = ___ **F**

___ ___ ___ ___ ___ ___ ___ ___

$\frac{2}{9}$ $\frac{9}{10}$ $\frac{4}{5}$ $\frac{4}{7}$ $\frac{2}{3}$ $\frac{1}{25}$ $\frac{1}{3}$ $\frac{2}{7}$

___ ___ ___ ___ ___ ___

$\frac{1}{2}$ $\frac{1}{25}$ $\frac{7}{8}$ $\frac{4}{5}$ $\frac{9}{10}$ $\frac{3}{4}$

3 Find the common factors and greatest common factors for each pair of numbers.

14:
28:
common factors:
greatest common factor:

12:
18:
common factors:
greatest common factor:

45:
81:
common factors:
greatest common factor:

11:
18:
common factors:
greatest common factor:

4:
12:
common factors:
greatest common factor:

18:
27:
common factors:
greatest common factor:

4 Look at the fraction in the center of the daisy. Find the fractions in the box that are equivalent to that fraction. Place those equivalent fractions in the petals. The first one has been done for you.

$\frac{50}{100}$	$\frac{6}{12}$	$\frac{5}{15}$	$\frac{10}{30}$	$\frac{10}{60}$	$\frac{16}{24}$	$\frac{4}{8}$	$\frac{10}{15}$	$\frac{4}{12}$	$\frac{2}{6}$
$\frac{3}{9}$	$\frac{5}{30}$	$\frac{20}{30}$	$\frac{3}{6}$	$\frac{8}{12}$	$\frac{4}{6}$	$\frac{2}{12}$	$\frac{10}{20}$	$\frac{3}{18}$	$\frac{4}{24}$

5 Shade the prime numbers to find your way through the maze.

↓ END

7	33	29	3	11	6	8	10	12	4	2	12	2
11	3	23	4	7	2	31	23	3	19	17	18	10
12	16	12	14	60	50	30	25	14	12	19	16	26
14	80	8	4	50	20	25	40	22	10	3	20	24
2	4	40	30	12	70	55	4	21	6	43	11	2
4	21	8	6	25	24	20	18	20	6	8	4	3

START ↑

6 Test each number to see if it is divisible by 2, 5, 10, or 3. Circle the correct responses. The first one has been done for you.

45 is divisible by	2	(5)	10	(3)
81 is divisible by	2	5	10	3
800 is divisible by	2	5	10	3
6,412 is divisible by	2	5	10	3
7,200 is divisible by	2	5	10	3

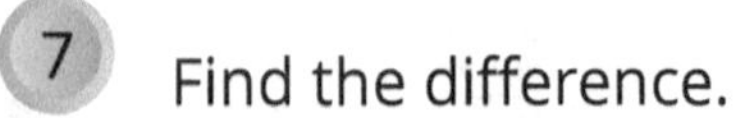

7 Find the difference.

249	490	201	982	375
- 199	- 393	- 47	- 195	- 186

Mixed Numbers

Joan had 4 small loaves of bread. She sliced each loaf into 5 pieces. 18 slices were eaten. What fraction of the bread was eaten?

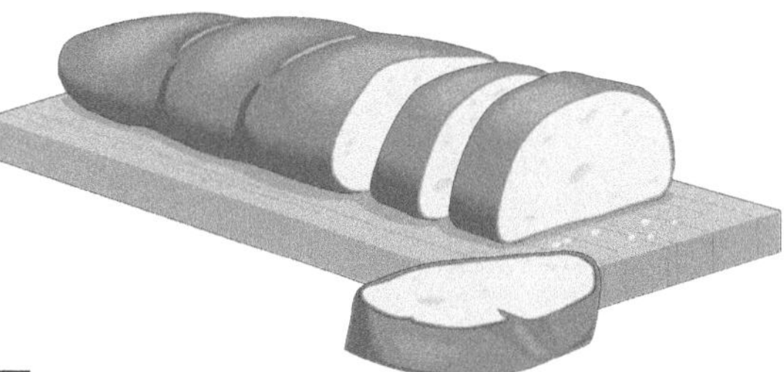

 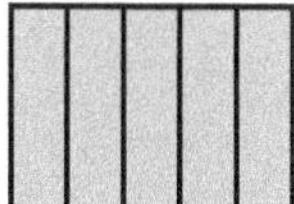  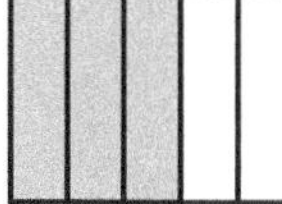

Altogether, three and three-fifths of the bread was eaten.

We can also write this mixed number as an improper fraction. The number of slices eaten is the numerator, and the number of slices in each loaf is the denominator.

MIXED NUMBER		**IMPROPER FRACTION**
$3\frac{3}{5}$	=	$\frac{18}{5}$

Change the number $8\frac{2}{3}$ into an improper fraction. You can use the method above by drawing a picture, or follow these simple steps.

1. Multiply the whole number by the denominator in the fraction. **8 x 3 = 24**
2. Add the numerator of the fraction to the product in step one. **24 + 2 = 26**
3. The sum is the numerator of the mixed fraction. The denominator remains the same. $\mathbf{\frac{26}{3}}$

MIXED NUMBER		**IMPROPER FRACTION**
$8\frac{2}{3}$	=	$\frac{26}{3}$

(8 x 3) + 2 = 26

1 Name each mixed fraction.

1.  ________

2.  ________

3. 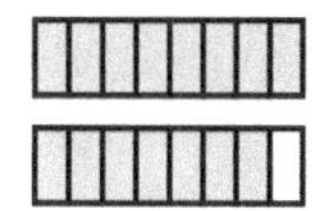 ________

Change each mixed fraction to an improper fraction.

$1\frac{3}{5}$ = ________ $3\frac{6}{7}$ = ________ $7\frac{2}{8}$ = ________ $2\frac{5}{6}$ = ________

$6\frac{8}{9}$ = ______ $5\frac{7}{9}$ = ______ $4\frac{1}{3}$ = ______ $8\frac{5}{8}$ = ______

2 Compare with the correct sign. (>, <, =)

$\frac{3}{12}$ ___ $\frac{7}{12}$ $\frac{4}{15}$ ___ $\frac{2}{15}$ $\frac{11}{11}$ ___ $\frac{7}{11}$ $\frac{5}{9}$ ___ $\frac{3}{4}$

$\frac{4}{8}$ ___ $\frac{5}{12}$ $\frac{2}{10}$ ___ $\frac{1}{5}$ $\frac{7}{8}$ ___ $\frac{4}{24}$ $\frac{1}{8}$ ___ $\frac{2}{15}$

3 Shade the fractions that are in lowest terms to find your way through the maze. You may move diagonally, if a horizontal or vertical move cannot be made.

Finish↓

$\frac{2}{11}$	$\frac{2}{6}$	$\frac{3}{9}$	$\frac{6}{12}$	$\frac{10}{20}$	$\frac{2}{4}$	
$\frac{1}{8}$	$\frac{6}{7}$	$\frac{4}{5}$	$\frac{2}{7}$	$\frac{1}{6}$	$\frac{12}{16}$	
$\frac{8}{16}$	$\frac{3}{6}$	$\frac{2}{8}$	$\frac{2}{6}$	$\frac{2}{3}$	$\frac{2}{4}$	
$\frac{9}{12}$	$\frac{7}{14}$	$\frac{6}{18}$	$\frac{4}{12}$	$\frac{7}{14}$	$\frac{1}{3}$	←Start

4 Find the missing numerators in the answer box. Place the letter next to the answer on the lines provided to complete the scripture: **"You shall see the son of man coming in the clouds of _____ with power and great glory."** Matthew 24:30

9 **N**	16 **E**	14 **E**
5 **H**	6 **V**	12 **A**

$\frac{1}{3} = \frac{\quad}{15}$ ___ $\frac{4}{7} = \frac{\quad}{28}$ ___ $\frac{3}{8} = \frac{\quad}{32}$ ___ $\frac{1}{6} = \frac{\quad}{36}$ ___

$\frac{2}{5} = \frac{\quad}{35}$ ___ $\frac{3}{11} = \frac{\quad}{33}$ ___

5 Solve the equations and check.

$n + 45 = 89$ $- \quad -$ Check:	$n + 87 = 190$ $- \quad -$ Check:	$n + 78 = 643$ $- \quad -$ Check:

Solve the equations and check.

$n \div 3 = 5$ $\underline{\times \quad\; \times}$ Check:	$n \div 9 = 4$ $\underline{\times \quad\; \times}$ Check:	$n \div 9 = 9$ $\underline{\times \quad\; \times}$ Check:

7 Choose the word from the answer box that defines each picture. Write the word on the line.

square pentagon hexagon rectangle triangle
octagon decagon trapezoid rhombus

______ ______ ______

______ ______ ______

______ ______ ______

Improper Fractions

John has $\frac{7}{2}$ of the total apples. How many apples would he have using a mixed fraction?

John would have $3\frac{1}{2}$ apples.

You can change any improper fraction into a mixed fraction by following these simple steps.

IMPROPER FRACTION		**MIXED NUMBER**
$\mathbf{\frac{7}{2}}$	=	$\mathbf{3\frac{1}{2}}$

1. Divide the numerator by the denominator. $2\overline{)7}$ quotient 3, -6, remainder 1

2. The quotient is the whole number. 3
3. Write the remainder over the divisor as the fractional part. $\frac{1}{2}$
4. Write a mixed number. $3\frac{1}{2}$

1 Change each improper fraction to a whole number or mixed fraction. Reduce the answer to lowest terms.

$\frac{19}{5}$ = ________ $\frac{16}{4}$ = ________ $\frac{23}{6}$ = ________ $\frac{17}{2}$ = ________

$\frac{27}{4}$ = ________ $\frac{33}{9}$ = ________ $\frac{12}{2}$ = ________ $\frac{13}{10}$ = ________

$\frac{25}{5}$ = ________ $\frac{10}{3}$ = ________ $\frac{18}{4}$ = ________ $\frac{48}{10}$ = ________

2 Draw a pictorial representation of each mixed fraction. Next to the drawing, write the improper fraction.

$1\frac{3}{4}$	$2\frac{3}{7}$
$1\frac{7}{8}$	$3\frac{1}{6}$

3 Compare with the correct sign. (>, <, =)

$\frac{4}{12}$ ___ $\frac{1}{12}$ $\frac{4}{25}$ ___ $\frac{2}{25}$ $\frac{1}{2}$ ___ $\frac{2}{4}$ $\frac{5}{8}$ ___ $\frac{3}{4}$

$\frac{6}{13}$ ___ $\frac{5}{15}$ $\frac{1}{9}$ ___ $\frac{4}{36}$ $\frac{1}{3}$ ___ $\frac{3}{9}$ $\frac{3}{12}$ ___ $\frac{5}{7}$

4 Reduce the fractions to lowest terms. Find the solution in the answer box. Place the corresponding letter on the line to answer the following riddle:
What does a baby corn call its father?

$\frac{5}{12}$ **N** $\frac{4}{9}$ **R** $\frac{1}{10}$ **P** $\frac{2}{3}$ **P** $\frac{1}{4}$ **O** $\frac{1}{3}$ **O** $\frac{1}{9}$ **C**

$\frac{8}{12}$ = ___ ___ $\frac{3}{12}$ = ___ ___ $\frac{2}{20}$ = ___ ___

$\frac{5}{45}$ = ___ ___ $\frac{8}{24}$ = ___ ___ $\frac{16}{36}$ = ___ ___ $\frac{25}{60}$ = ___ ___

___ ___ ___ ___ ___ ___ ___

5 Round each number to the nearest hundred.

1,869 ____________ 2,476 ____________ 9,010 ____________

557 ____________ 204 ____________ 960 ____________

6 Solve the equations and check.

$n + 395 = 8{,}908$ $-\quad -$	$n + 895 = 1{,}900$ $-\quad -$	$n + 708 = 1{,}603$ $-\quad -$
Check:	Check:	Check:

7 Find the average.

1. 16, 15, 20 ________
2. 42, 48, 57 ________
3. 113, 112, 150, 125 ________
4. 259, 364, 424, 381 ________

8 Choose the word from the answer box that defines each picture. Write the word on the line.

rectangular pyramid	triangular pyramid	cone
sphere	cylinder	hexagonal pyramid

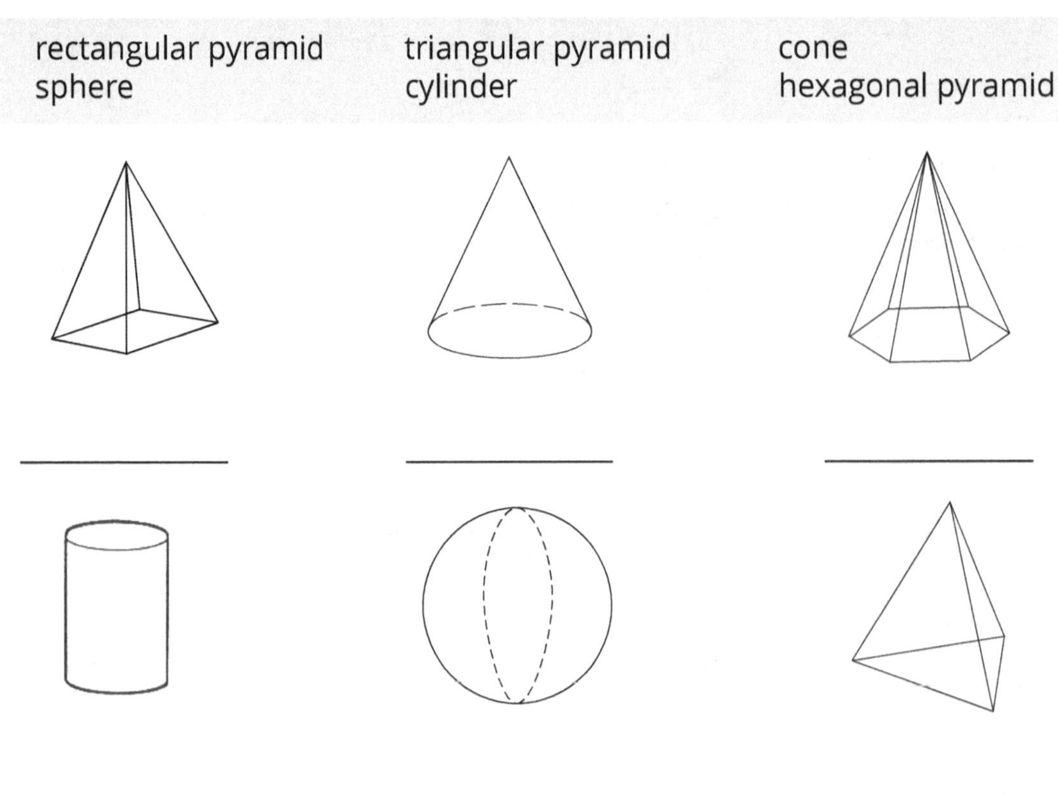

Problem Solving–Make It Simpler

Some problems contain large numbers, fractions, or decimals that make the problem difficult to solve. It is often helpful to make a simpler problem and figure out how to solve it. Then solve the problem using the actual numbers.

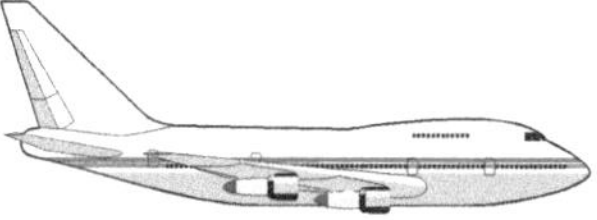

Christi flew from Maryland to Arizona to see her sister. The cost of the flight was $347.95. She got a rental car at the airport at the cost of $74.28.
How much did Christi spend in all?

This problem uses decimals and large numbers. Try this simpler version to get started with a solution.

MAKE IT SIMPLER	**USE ACTUALS**
$300 (cost of flight)	$347.95
+ 74 (cost of car)	+ 74.28
$374 (total cost)	$422.23

Use simpler numbers to write a number sentence for the problem. Then solve the problem with the actual numbers.

1. The bake sales were a huge success. The spring sale brought profits of $89.45. The winter sale netted $112.85. What was the total profit for the two sales?

2. Suzanne bought toys for $837.19. She sold the toys at the church fundraiser for $1,345.76. How much profit did she make?

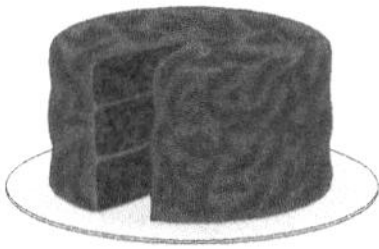

3. Sean needed to sell 83 bumper stickers by Friday to win a soccer ball. Monday he sold 37. Tuesday and Wednesday he sold a total of 14 over the two days. Thursday he sold 5. How many did he have to sell Friday to make his goal?

4. Jeff worked at the soda fountain for $3\frac{1}{2}$ hours. Mike worked for the next $3\frac{1}{2}$ hours. The shop was open 8 hours. How many hours were left over?

5. Pauline delivers newspapers. She gets $3.75 for every 30 papers she delivers. How much will she get for delivering 120 papers?

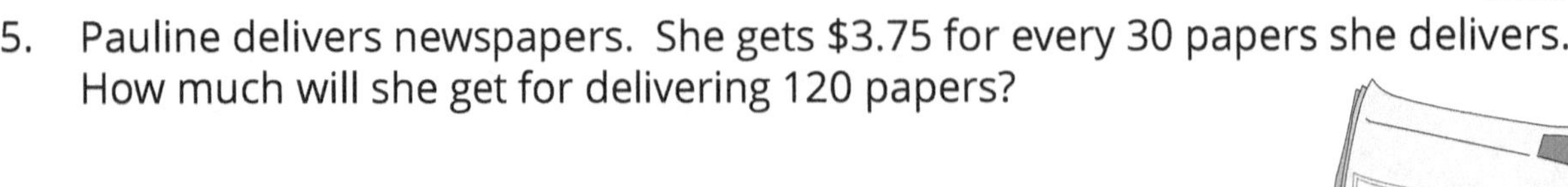

2 Change each improper fraction to a mixed number or whole number. Reduce the answers to lowest terms.

$\frac{21}{5}$ = ______ $\frac{18}{4}$ = ______ $\frac{24}{3}$ = ______ $\frac{4}{2}$ = ______

$\frac{27}{8}$ = ______ $\frac{86}{9}$ = ______ $\frac{7}{2}$ = ______ $\frac{18}{7}$ = ______

3 Change each mixed fraction to an improper fraction.

$1\frac{4}{9}$ = ______ $2\frac{1}{7}$ = ______ $5\frac{2}{3}$ = ______ $3\frac{5}{8}$ = ______

$4\frac{2}{9}$ = ______ $8\frac{4}{5}$ = ______ $2\frac{3}{6}$ = ______ $9\frac{3}{7}$ = ______

4 Compare with the correct sign. (>, <, =)

$\frac{3}{4}$ ____ $\frac{4}{4}$ $\frac{4}{12}$ ____ $\frac{1}{3}$ $\frac{2}{3}$ ____ $\frac{5}{6}$ $\frac{9}{12}$ ____ $\frac{3}{4}$

$\frac{5}{6}$ ____ $\frac{1}{3}$ $\frac{3}{5}$ ____ $\frac{6}{15}$ $\frac{4}{5}$ ____ $\frac{2}{20}$ $\frac{4}{5}$ ____ $\frac{5}{7}$

5 Draw the lines of symmetry.

  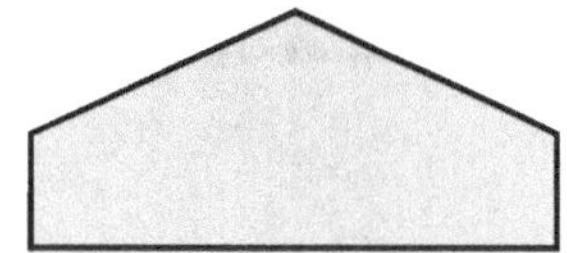 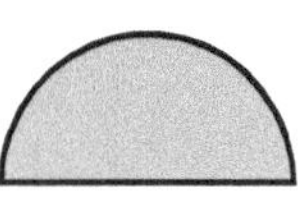

Draw a figure with two lines of symmetry. Draw a figure with no lines of symmetry.

6 Divide to get the quotient. Find the quotient in the answer box to solve the riddle:
What kind of shoes can you make from banana skins?

____ ____ ____ ____ ____ ____ ____ ____
1 2 3 4 5 6 7 8

100 r 8 **R**	119 r 6 **S**	775 r 5 **L**	109 r 56 **E**
255 r 12 **I**	136 r 22 **P**	315 r 2 **S**	140 r 3 **P**

1. 20)6302 ________ 2. 11)8530 ________ 3. 16)4092 ________

4. 54)7563 ________ 5. 42)5734 ________ 6. 72)7904 ________

7. 27)2708 ________ 8. 46)5480 ________

Addition with Like Fractions

Susan made a cherry cheesecake and cut it into eight pieces. The family ate $\frac{5}{8}$ of the cheesecake after dinner. She and a friend ate $\frac{2}{8}$ of the cheesecake for a snack. How much was eaten?

$$\frac{5}{8} + \frac{2}{8} = \frac{7}{8}$$

When you add fractions with like denominators, add the numerators and keep the denominator the same.

Try this one. Sam eats $\frac{3}{8}$ of a large piece of pizza. His dad eats the same amount. How much will they eat?

$$\frac{3}{8} + \frac{3}{8} = \frac{6}{8}$$

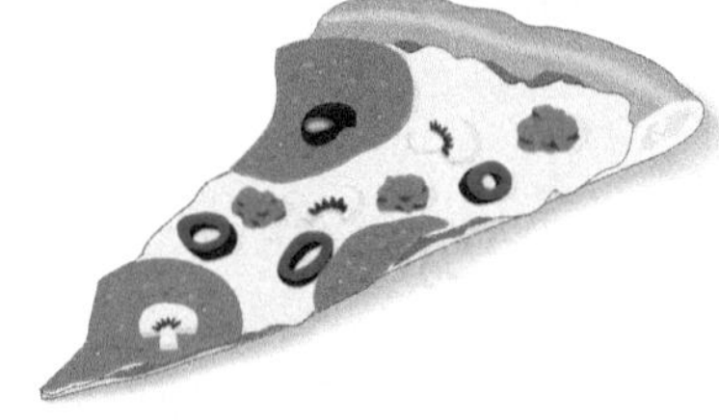

Be sure to change $\frac{6}{8}$ to lowest terms.

$$\frac{6}{8} \frac{\div 2}{\div 2} = \frac{3}{4}$$

1 Find the sum. Make sure the answer is in lowest terms.

$\frac{1}{7} + \frac{2}{7} =$ $\quad$ $\frac{2}{9} + \frac{3}{9} =$ $\quad$ $\frac{4}{12} + \frac{4}{12} =$ $\quad$ $\frac{1}{6} + \frac{3}{6} =$

$\frac{3}{15} + \frac{2}{15} =$ $\quad$ $\frac{4}{5} + \frac{1}{5} =$ $\quad$ $\frac{4}{12} + \frac{2}{12} =$ $\quad$ $\frac{1}{3} + \frac{2}{3} =$

$\frac{6}{8} + \frac{1}{8} =$ $\quad$ $\frac{7}{10} + \frac{2}{10} =$ $\quad$ $\frac{4}{11} + \frac{5}{11} =$ $\quad$ $\frac{6}{18} + \frac{7}{18} =$

2 Use simpler numbers to write a number sentence for the problem. Then solve the problem with the actual numbers.

1. Pam collected $18.79 for her trip to Chicago from a bake sale. She received $39.49 from calendar sales. If she needs $87.95 to pay for the trip, how much more must she earn?

2. Timothy is required to practice piano for 30 minutes a day. If he practiced from 6:47 to 7:21, did he practice long enough?

3. The movie started at 8:07 and played until 10:13. How long was the movie?

4. Stephen collects $35.00 a month from his paper route. His goal is to save $350.00 after one year. Is that possible? Explain.

3 Change each improper fraction to a mixed number or whole number. Reduce the answers to lowest terms.

$\frac{15}{5}$ = ________ $\frac{18}{5}$ = ________ $\frac{21}{3}$ = ________ $\frac{4}{3}$ = ________

$\frac{13}{8}$ = ________ $\frac{88}{9}$ = ________ $\frac{17}{3}$ = ________ $\frac{75}{9}$ = ________

4 Change each mixed fraction to an improper fraction.

$1\frac{2}{3}$ = ________ $7\frac{1}{8}$ = ________ $4\frac{2}{4}$ = ________ $8\frac{5}{9}$ = ________

$7\frac{2}{10}$ = ________ $5\frac{1}{5}$ = ________ $12\frac{3}{5}$ = ________ $4\frac{7}{7}$ = ________

5 Solve. You'll need scrap paper for the calculations. Find the answer in the table to the right. Circle each answer and read the solution to the riddle:
What should you make a frying pan for its birthday?

Problem		
3,052 ÷ 28 =	P	632
15,800 ÷ 25 =	L	110
3,922 ÷ 37 =	A	109
1,127 ÷ 49 =	N	28
6,171 ÷ 51 =	S	25
1,876 ÷ 67 =	C	23
1,131 ÷ 13 =	R	15
	A	87
	K	121
	S	112
	E	106

_____ _____ _____ _____ _____ _____ _____

6 Draw the other half of the symmetrical figures.

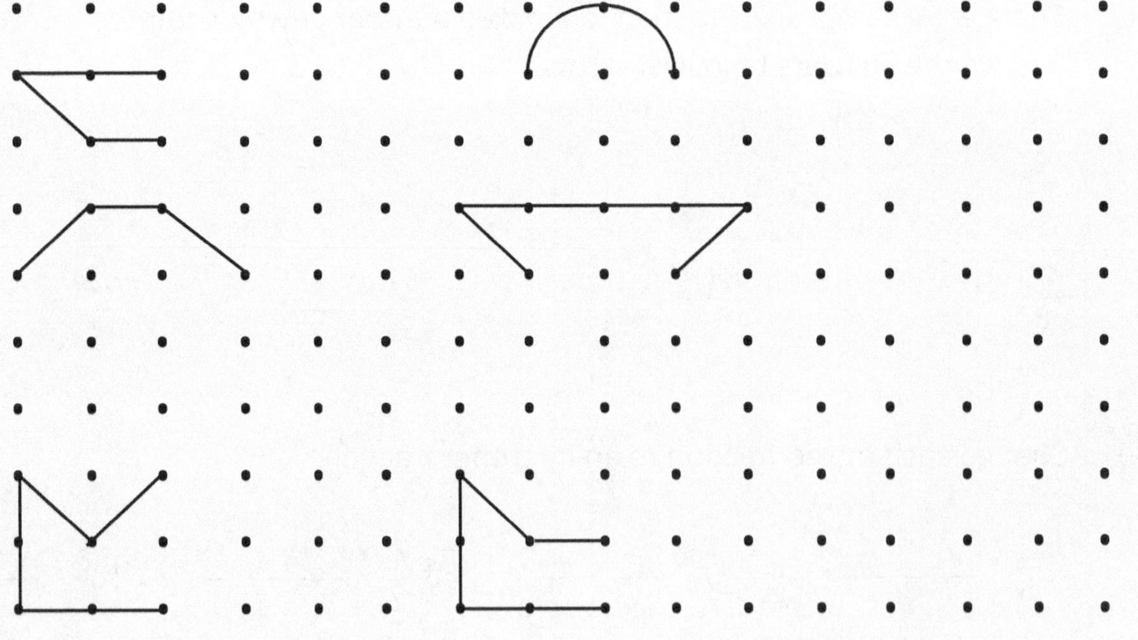

44 points total Lessons 96-105

1 Give the number of faces, edges, and vertices. 6 pts. total for this exercise.

Triangular Prism			Rectangular Pyramid		
Faces___	Edges___	Vertices ___	Faces___	Edges___	Vertices ___

2 Match the figure with the definition. 5 pts. total for this exercise.

1. All points are the same distance from the center.
2. Two parallel polygon bases. All other faces are rectangles.
3. A base that is not a polygon. Curved sides.
4. Two parallel bases that are not polygons. Curved sides.
5. One polygon base. All faces are triangles that meet at a point.

Cone

Prism 

Sphere 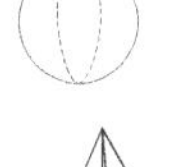

Pyramid 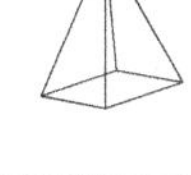

Cylinder

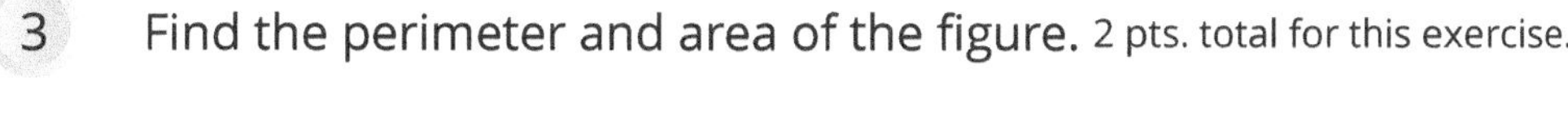

3 Find the perimeter and area of the figure. 2 pts. total for this exercise.

8 meters

20 meters

The perimeter is __________.

The area is ______________.

4 Find the volume of the figure. 1 pt. for this exercise.

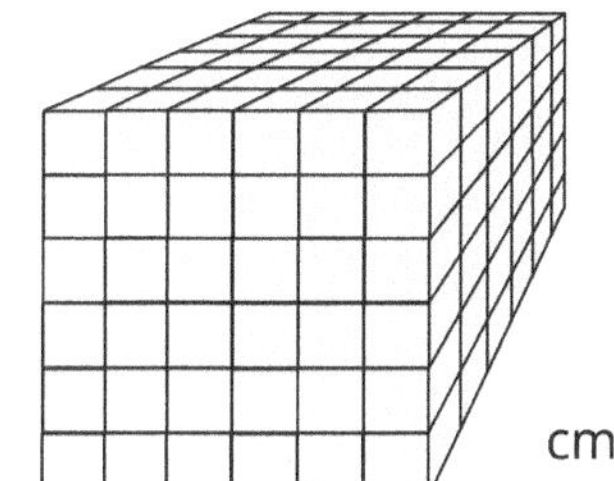

The volume of the figure is ______________.

5 Complete the fraction. 4 pts. total for this exercise.

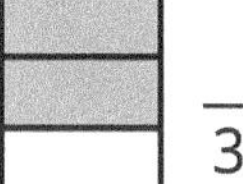 $\frac{\quad}{3}$

$\frac{\quad}{6}$

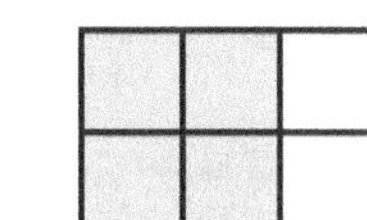 $\frac{\quad}{8}$

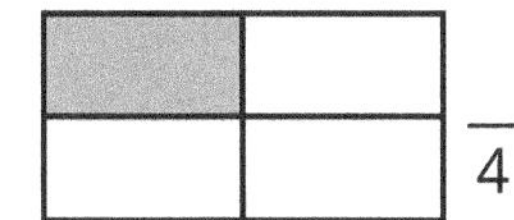 $\frac{\quad}{4}$

6 Label the numerator and denominator of the fraction. 2 pts. total for this exercise.

$\frac{6}{7}$ ____________________

____

7 Match the fractions with word names. 5 pts. total for this exercise.

one-third	$\frac{0}{5}$
zero-fifths	$\frac{4}{5}$
seven-eighths	$\frac{7}{8}$
six-eighteenths	$\frac{1}{3}$
four-fifths	$\frac{6}{18}$

8 What fraction of each set is red? 3 pts. total for this exercise.

__________ __________ __________

9 Give the missing numerator. 5 pts. total for this exercise.

$\frac{4}{5} = \frac{\quad}{25}$ $\frac{5}{8} = \frac{\quad}{32}$ $\frac{1}{7} = \frac{\quad}{14}$ $\frac{3}{9} = \frac{\quad}{81}$ $\frac{2}{12} = \frac{\quad}{36}$

10 Find the common factors and greatest common factors for each pair of numbers.6 pts.

8:	13:	12:
16:	15:	16:
common factors:	common factors:	common factors:
greatest common factor:	greatest common factor:	greatest common factor:

11 Write each fraction in lowest terms. 5 pts. total for this exercise.

$\frac{5}{20} =$ $\frac{3}{12} =$ $\frac{4}{20} =$ $\frac{6}{36} =$ $\frac{14}{49} =$

Subtraction with Like Fractions

Thomas had $\frac{6}{10}$ of a cake left after his birthday dinner.

If he and a friend ate $\frac{2}{10}$ of it, how much would be left?

$$\frac{6}{10} - \frac{2}{10} = \frac{4}{10} = \frac{2}{5}$$

↑ (We change $\frac{4}{10}$ to lowest terms.)

When you subtract fractions with like denominators, subtract the numerators and keep the denominators the same.

1 Find the difference. Make sure the answer is in lowest terms.

$\frac{8}{10} - \frac{3}{10} =$ $\frac{7}{8} - \frac{2}{8} =$ $\frac{12}{13} - \frac{10}{13} =$ $\frac{6}{8} - \frac{2}{8} =$

$\frac{9}{11} - \frac{7}{11} =$ $\frac{5}{12} - \frac{3}{12} =$ $\frac{11}{12} - \frac{5}{12} =$ $\frac{18}{20} - \frac{8}{20} =$

$\frac{14}{15} - \frac{4}{15} =$ $\frac{6}{6} - \frac{3}{6} =$ $\frac{3}{4} - \frac{1}{4} =$ $\frac{8}{9} - \frac{5}{9} =$

2 Find the sum. Make sure the answer is in lowest terms.

$\frac{5}{7} + \frac{2}{7} =$ $\frac{1}{9} + \frac{1}{9} =$ $\frac{1}{2} + \frac{1}{2} =$ $\frac{4}{6} + \frac{1}{6} =$

$\frac{9}{15} + \frac{1}{15} =$ $\frac{1}{5} + \frac{1}{5} =$ $\frac{1}{12} + \frac{1}{12} =$ $\frac{1}{8} + \frac{2}{8} =$

$\frac{6}{9} + \frac{2}{9} =$ $\frac{7}{12} + \frac{1}{12} =$ $\frac{4}{10} + \frac{4}{10} =$ $\frac{6}{8} + \frac{1}{8} =$

3 Solve. (Be sure to use the A.M. or P.M. symbol when appropriate.)

1. It is 1:10 P.M. and Amanda has to leave for a dentist appointment at 3:00 P.M. Does she have time to watch a movie that lasts 120 minutes? Explain.

2. Tina's soccer game began at 4:15 P.M. If it lasted 80 minutes, what time was it over?

3. Alexander boarded a bus in Atlanta, Georgia at 10:07 A.M. If it takes 13 hours to get to Columbus, Ohio by bus, what time will it be when he arrives?

4. Cecilia must practice piano for 240 minutes a week. How many hours must she practice?

5. Steve went to work at 8:00 P.M. If he worked 8 hours, what time did he get off work?

4 Follow a path of true equations. There are two possible paths. Can you find them both?

End↓ (above the third column)

$2\frac{1}{8} = \frac{17}{8}$	$\frac{4}{3} = 1\frac{1}{3}$	$2\frac{1}{4} = \frac{9}{4}$	$4\frac{1}{8} = \frac{12}{8}$
$1\frac{1}{9} = \frac{10}{9}$	$\frac{5}{2} = 3\frac{1}{2}$	$1\frac{1}{2} = \frac{3}{2}$	$5\frac{1}{9} = \frac{50}{9}$
$4\frac{3}{4} = \frac{19}{4}$	$\frac{12}{9} = \frac{5}{9}$	$\frac{13}{5} = 2\frac{3}{5}$	$8\frac{1}{3} = \frac{30}{3}$
$\frac{7}{4} = 1\frac{3}{4}$	$\frac{16}{3} = 4\frac{1}{2}$	$\frac{14}{3} = 4\frac{2}{3}$	$\frac{6}{4} = 1\frac{1}{4}$
$2\frac{7}{8} = \frac{23}{8}$	$\frac{7}{4} = 2\frac{1}{8}$	$6\frac{1}{3} = \frac{19}{3}$	$2\frac{1}{5} = \frac{11}{5}$
$\frac{5}{4} = 1\frac{1}{4}$	$1\frac{1}{9} = \frac{12}{9}$	$\frac{7}{6} = 1\frac{2}{6}$	$\frac{7}{2} = 3\frac{1}{2}$
$\frac{3}{2} = 1\frac{1}{2}$	$\frac{5}{2} = 2\frac{1}{2}$	$\frac{15}{8} = 1\frac{7}{8}$	$\frac{8}{3} = 2\frac{2}{3}$
$\frac{7}{6} = 1\frac{1}{6}$	$1\frac{1}{2} = \frac{5}{4}$	$2\frac{1}{2} = \frac{8}{2}$	$1\frac{2}{3} = \frac{9}{3}$

Begin↑ (below the first column)

5 Find the sum.

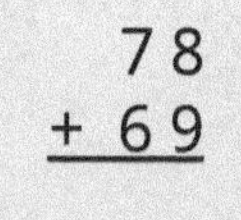

$$\begin{array}{r} 39 \\ +\ 89 \\ \hline \end{array} \qquad \begin{array}{r} 78 \\ +\ 69 \\ \hline \end{array} \qquad \begin{array}{r} 37 \\ +\ 87 \\ \hline \end{array}$$

$$\begin{array}{r} 99 \\ +\ 23 \\ \hline \end{array} \qquad \begin{array}{r} 51 \\ +\ 69 \\ \hline \end{array}$$

6 Find the product.

$$\begin{array}{r} 152 \\ \times\ \ 21 \\ \hline \end{array} \qquad \begin{array}{r} 902 \\ \times\ \ 87 \\ \hline \end{array} \qquad \begin{array}{r} 682 \\ \times\ \ 14 \\ \hline \end{array}$$

$$\begin{array}{r} 103 \\ \times\ \ 43 \\ \hline \end{array} \qquad \begin{array}{r} 714 \\ \times\ \ 76 \\ \hline \end{array}$$

7 Draw a congruent and similar figure to the one shown.

Addition and Subtraction of Like Fractions

Candy needed $\frac{1}{8}$ of a yard of ribbon for one Christmas ornament, and $\frac{3}{8}$ of a yard for another. How much ribbon did Candy need in all?

The problem asks for how much ribbon she needs IN ALL, so we add the fractions.

$$\frac{1}{8} + \frac{3}{8} = \frac{4}{8} = \frac{1}{2}$$

↑ (We change $\frac{4}{8}$ to lowest terms.)

Mary had $\frac{6}{8}$ of a yard of lace. She used $\frac{5}{8}$ of a yard to decorate an ornament. How much was left?

The problem asks for how much ribbon IS LEFT, so we subtract.

$$\frac{6}{8} - \frac{5}{8} = \frac{1}{8}$$

1 Add or subtract the fractions as indicated. Make sure the answer is in lowest terms.

$\frac{1}{8} + \frac{2}{8} =$ $\frac{2}{5} + \frac{3}{5} =$ $\frac{7}{12} + \frac{2}{12} =$

$\frac{8}{9} - \frac{3}{9} =$ $\frac{6}{10} - \frac{1}{10} =$ $\frac{14}{15} - \frac{4}{15} =$

$\frac{4}{9} + \frac{5}{9} =$ $\frac{4}{7} + \frac{2}{7} =$ $\frac{2}{10} + \frac{3}{10} =$

$\frac{11}{12} - \frac{10}{12} =$ $\frac{5}{8} - \frac{1}{8} =$ $\frac{10}{11} - \frac{8}{11} =$

      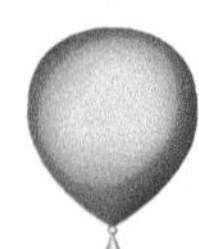

2 Find each sum. Write the answer in lowest terms. Locate the answer in the table and shade in that block. Read the hidden message.

T	B	O	E	N	N	O	I	T	Y
$\frac{15}{16}$	$\frac{7}{12}$	$\frac{1}{4}$	$\frac{9}{20}$	$\frac{5}{7}$	$\frac{1}{6}$	$\frac{6}{7}$	$\frac{1}{3}$	$\frac{1}{2}$	$\frac{5}{8}$
A	**G**	**F**	**O**	**R**	**N**	**A**	**I**	**Z**	**D**
$\frac{3}{8}$	$2\frac{9}{13}$	$\frac{3}{16}$	$\frac{3}{14}$	$\frac{3}{4}$	$\frac{4}{5}$	$\frac{5}{9}$	$\frac{2}{3}$	$\frac{7}{8}$	$\frac{10}{11}$

$\frac{1}{12} + \frac{6}{12} =$ $\frac{1}{8} + \frac{2}{8} =$ $\frac{1}{16} + \frac{2}{16} =$ $\frac{4}{9} + \frac{1}{9} =$

$\frac{6}{20} + \frac{3}{20} =$ $\frac{14}{21} + \frac{1}{21} =$ $\frac{1}{4} + \frac{2}{4} =$ $\frac{1}{7} + \frac{5}{7} =$

$\frac{2}{12} + \frac{6}{12} =$ $\frac{1}{10} + \frac{4}{10} =$ $\frac{6}{11} + \frac{4}{11} =$

Place the shaded letters on the lines below. Start with the first one in the table and go left to right.

___ ___   ___ ___ ___   ___ ___ ___ ___ ___ ___

3 Find the difference. Write the answers in lowest terms.

$\frac{8}{10} - \frac{1}{10} =$ $\frac{7}{18} - \frac{2}{18} =$ $\frac{10}{13} - \frac{1}{13} =$ $\frac{3}{4} - \frac{2}{4} =$

$\frac{9}{9} - \frac{7}{9} =$ $\frac{11}{12} - \frac{2}{12} =$ $\frac{10}{15} - \frac{5}{15} =$ $\frac{8}{20} - \frac{6}{20} =$

4 Solve. (Use the A.M. or P.M. symbol when appropriate.)

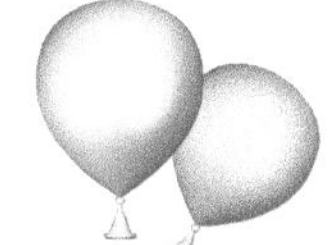

1. Sarah started walking to her friend's house at 3:15 P.M. It took her 17 minutes to get there. What time did she arrive?

2. Paul finished his paper route at 7:00 A.M. If it took him 86 minutes to complete, what time did he start?

3. Amelia started on her math homework at 3:30 P.M. She finished working at 4:18 P.M. How long did she work?

4. If Susan started work at 9:00 A.M. and worked 6 hours, what time did she finish?

5 Find the product. (These problems have been changed and may not match the answers in the key.)

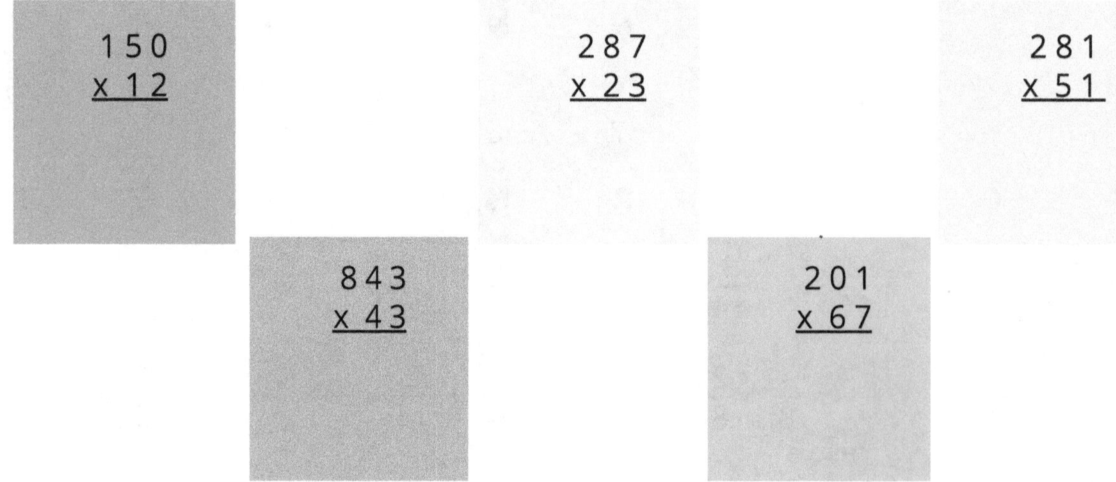

6 Find the quotient. Write the remainder over the divisor as a fraction. Reduce the fraction remainder if possible.

$82\overline{)639}$ $37\overline{)891}$ $45\overline{)967}$ $48\overline{)712}$ $27\overline{)381}$

7 Draw a shape using the grid as a guide. Draw a figure that is similar to the original shape and a figure that is congruent to the original shape.

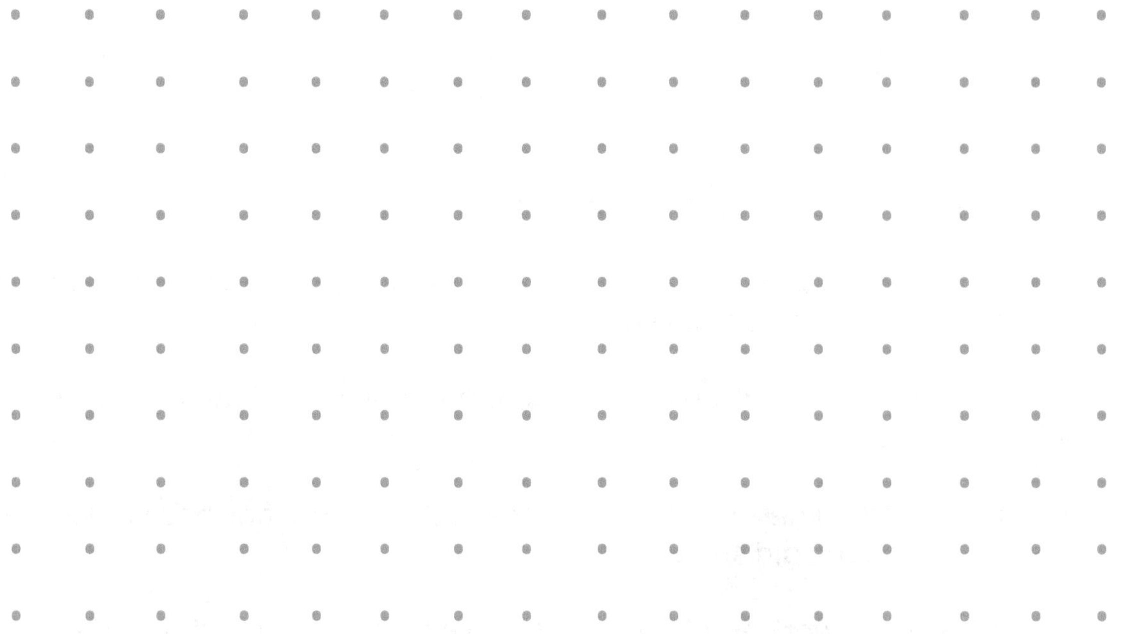

Addition of Unlike Fractions

Paul said he could eat $\frac{1}{3}$ of a pizza, and Alex said he could eat $\frac{3}{6}$ of a pizza. How much pizza can they both eat together?

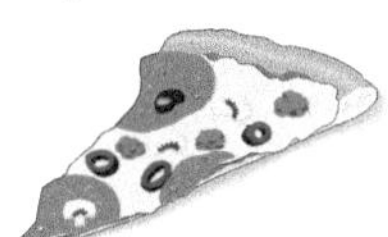

$\frac{1}{3}$ and $\frac{3}{6}$ have different denominators. To add fractions, they need to have the same denominator. Use fraction bars or fraction strips to help. We can see that $\frac{1}{3}$ equals $\frac{2}{6}$.

 $\frac{1}{3}$

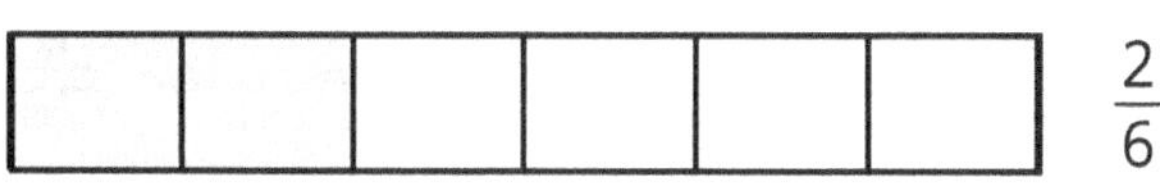 $\frac{2}{6}$

Now that we have two fractions with common denominators, they are easy to add.

$$\frac{2}{6} + \frac{3}{6} = \frac{5}{6}$$

1 Use fraction bars or strips to help you find common denominators before you add the fractions.

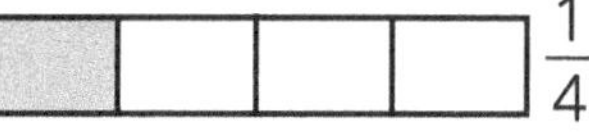 $\frac{1}{4}$

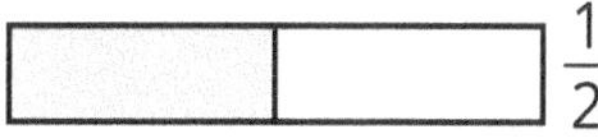 $\frac{1}{2}$

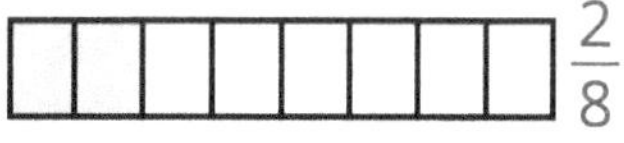 $\frac{2}{8}$

$\frac{3}{6}$

$\frac{1}{4} = \frac{2}{8}$

$\frac{1}{2} = \frac{3}{6}$

$\frac{1}{4} + \frac{3}{8} =$

$\frac{1}{2} + \frac{3}{6} =$

$\frac{2}{8} + \frac{3}{8} =$ ______

$\frac{3}{6} + \frac{3}{6} =$ ______

$\frac{2}{10} + \frac{1}{2} =$ $\frac{3}{4} + \frac{1}{8} =$ $\frac{1}{5} + \frac{3}{10} =$

$\frac{1}{6} + \frac{2}{3} =$ $\qquad$ $\frac{1}{6} + \frac{5}{12} =$ $\qquad$ $\frac{3}{4} + \frac{1}{12} =$

2 Find the difference. Make sure the answer is in lowest terms.

$\frac{8}{12} - \frac{4}{12} =$ $\qquad$ $\frac{7}{9} - \frac{1}{9} =$ $\qquad$ $\frac{6}{7} - \frac{1}{7} =$ $\qquad$ $\frac{6}{8} - \frac{1}{8} =$

$\frac{9}{10} - \frac{8}{10} =$ $\qquad$ $\frac{5}{6} - \frac{1}{6} =$ $\qquad$ $\frac{3}{12} - \frac{1}{12} =$ $\qquad$ $\frac{8}{20} - \frac{5}{20} =$

3 Find the sum. Make sure the answer is in lowest terms.

$\frac{5}{12} + \frac{2}{12} =$ $\qquad$ $\frac{1}{8} + \frac{1}{8} =$ $\qquad$ $\frac{3}{6} + \frac{3}{6} =$ $\qquad$ $\frac{4}{8} + \frac{1}{8} =$

$\frac{3}{5} + \frac{1}{5} =$ $\qquad$ $\frac{1}{10} + \frac{1}{10} =$ $\qquad$ $\frac{4}{12} + \frac{2}{12} =$ $\qquad$ $\frac{1}{15} + \frac{2}{15} =$

4 Find the sum.

$\begin{array}{r} 135 \\ 387 \\ 702 \\ +\ 500 \\ \hline \end{array}$ $\qquad$ $\begin{array}{r} 298 \\ 800 \\ 712 \\ +\ 354 \\ \hline \end{array}$ $\qquad$ $\begin{array}{r} 901 \\ 278 \\ 231 \\ +\ 750 \\ \hline \end{array}$ $\qquad$ $\begin{array}{r} 274 \\ 245 \\ 361 \\ +\ 110 \\ \hline \end{array}$ $\qquad$ $\begin{array}{r} 761 \\ 902 \\ 147 \\ +\ 322 \\ \hline \end{array}$

5 Find the difference.

$$\begin{array}{r} 78 \\ -\ 38 \\ \hline \end{array} \qquad \begin{array}{r} 90 \\ -\ 39 \\ \hline \end{array} \qquad \begin{array}{r} 32 \\ -\ 15 \\ \hline \end{array}$$

$$\begin{array}{r} 64 \\ -\ 57 \\ \hline \end{array} \qquad \begin{array}{r} 82 \\ -\ 79 \\ \hline \end{array}$$

6 Circle each hidden division problem. There are four in each square. Work from left to right and top to bottom.

83	2	7	3
9	9	1	50
9 r 2	8	7	7
5	1	0	7 r 1

3	37	5	7 r 2
6	6	1	9
1	6 r 1	2	0
14	3	4 r 2	7

7 Write the name of each figure using symbols.

1. • K

2. X ———— Y

3. M ←——→ N

4. A ————→ B

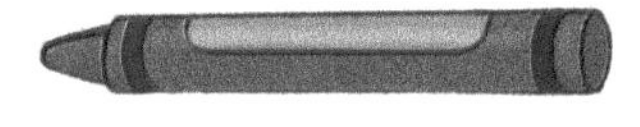  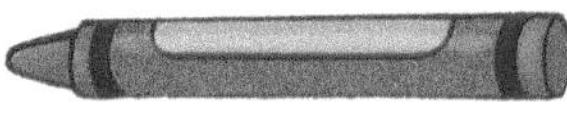 

Subtraction of Unlike Fractions

Paula had $\frac{3}{4}$ yard of material. She used $\frac{1}{2}$ yard of it to make a dress for her doll. How much material will be left over?

$\frac{3}{4}$ and $\frac{1}{2}$ have different denominators. To subtract fractions, they need to have the same denominator. Use the fraction bars or fraction strips to help. We see that $\frac{1}{2}$ equals $\frac{2}{4}$.

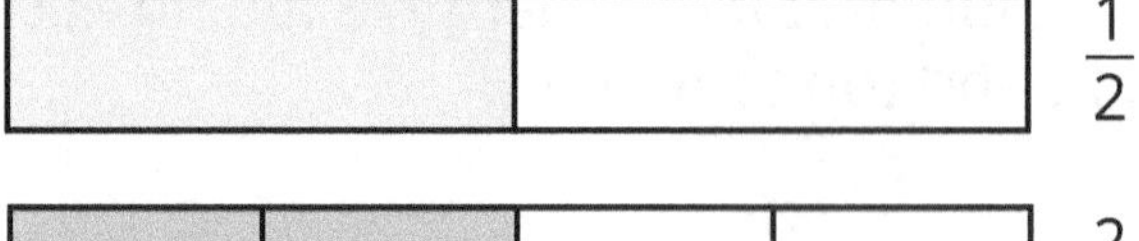

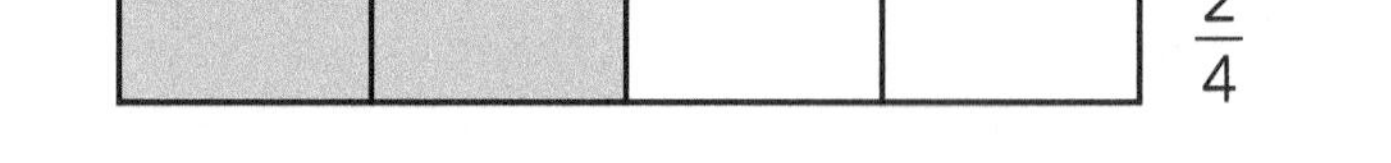

Now that we have two fractions with common denominators, they are easy to subtract.

$$\frac{3}{4} - \frac{2}{4} = \frac{1}{4} \text{ yard}$$

1 Use fraction bars or strips to help you find the common denominators before you subtract the fractions.

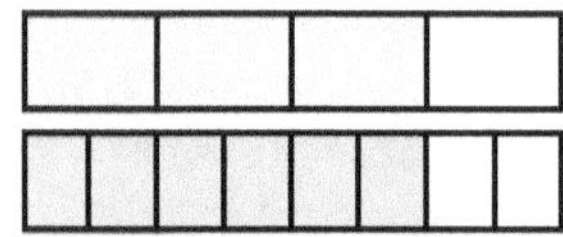

$\frac{3}{4} = \frac{6}{8}$

$\frac{7}{8} - \frac{3}{4} =$

$\frac{7}{8} - \frac{6}{8} =$

$\frac{1}{2} = \frac{3}{6}$

$\frac{5}{6} - \frac{1}{2} =$

$\frac{5}{6} - \frac{3}{6} =$

$\frac{7}{10} - \frac{1}{2} =$ $\qquad \frac{9}{10} - \frac{4}{5} =$ $\qquad \frac{1}{2} - \frac{1}{4} =$

$\frac{4}{10} - \frac{1}{5} =$ $\qquad \frac{5}{6} - \frac{2}{3} =$ $\qquad \frac{3}{4} - \frac{2}{12} =$

2 Use fraction bars or strips to help you find common denominators before you add the fractions.

$\frac{3}{8} + \frac{2}{4} =$ $\frac{2}{6} + \frac{3}{12} =$ $\frac{1}{2} + \frac{1}{6} =$

$\frac{3}{10} + \frac{1}{5} =$ $\frac{2}{6} + \frac{1}{3} =$ $\frac{4}{10} + \frac{1}{2} =$

3 Write the sum or difference in the box. Write the answer in lowest terms. Place the appropriate letter above each fraction at the bottom of the page to spell out the answer to the riddle: ***What do you call a baby goat that is sleeping?***

Problem	Letter	Problem	Letter	Problem	Letter
$\frac{2}{12} + \frac{3}{12} =$	**P**	$\frac{4}{9} + \frac{4}{9} =$	**P**	$\frac{1}{7} + \frac{5}{7} =$	**A**
$\frac{3}{15} + \frac{2}{15} =$	**A**	$\frac{4}{12} - \frac{2}{12} =$	**I**	$\frac{12}{15} - \frac{2}{15} =$	**I**
$\frac{12}{13} - \frac{10}{13} =$	**N**	$\frac{4}{10} + \frac{6}{10} =$	**K**	$\frac{3}{4} - \frac{2}{4} =$	**N**
$\frac{18}{20} - \frac{6}{20} =$	**G**	$\frac{7}{8} - \frac{3}{8} =$	**D**	$\frac{1}{5} + \frac{3}{5} =$	**!**

____ ____ ____ ____ ____ ____ ____ ____ ____ ____ ____ ____

$\frac{1}{3}$ 1 $\frac{1}{6}$ $\frac{1}{2}$ $\frac{2}{13}$ $\frac{6}{7}$ $\frac{8}{9}$ $\frac{5}{12}$ $\frac{2}{3}$ $\frac{1}{4}$ $\frac{3}{5}$ $\frac{4}{5}$

4 Round each number to the nearest 10.

1,346 ______	16,891 ______	57 ______	189 ______
6,999 ______	23,102 ______	98 ______	267 ______
2,389 ______	67,999 ______	27 ______	679 ______

5 Find the difference.

$$\begin{array}{r} 3009 \\ -\ 2341 \\ \hline \end{array} \quad \begin{array}{r} 7900 \\ -\ 6145 \\ \hline \end{array} \quad \begin{array}{r} 6030 \\ -\ 5721 \\ \hline \end{array} \quad \begin{array}{r} 1000 \\ -\ 813 \\ \hline \end{array} \quad \begin{array}{r} 8010 \\ -\ 6781 \\ \hline \end{array}$$

6 Solve the equations and check.

$6 \times n = 48$ ______ Check:

$n \times 8 = 64$ ______ Check:

$4 \times n = 32$ ______ Check:

7 Draw and label the following as indicated.

1. Point B
2. Line Segment AB
3. Line PQ
4. Ray XY

Addition and Subtraction of Unlike Fractions

Andrew is cutting plywood to make a bench. $\frac{1}{2}$ of the wood will make the seat, and $\frac{1}{4}$ of the wood will make the legs.
How much of the wood will be used in all?

The problem asks for how much wood will be used IN ALL, so we add the fractions.

$$\frac{1}{2} + \frac{1}{4} =$$

Use fraction bars or fraction strips to help. We see that $\frac{1}{2}$ equals $\frac{2}{4}$.

$\frac{1}{2}$

$\frac{2}{4}$

Now that we have two fractions with common denominators, they are easy to add.

$\frac{2}{4} + \frac{1}{4} = \frac{3}{4}$ of the wood will be used in all.

Andrew had $\frac{7}{8}$ of a piece of wood and needs $\frac{3}{4}$ of it to make a wooden swing.

How much wood will he have left?

The problem asks for how much wood WILL BE LEFT, so we subtract.

$$\frac{7}{8} - \frac{3}{4} =$$

Use fraction bars or fraction strips to help. We see that $\frac{3}{4}$ equals $\frac{6}{8}$.

$\frac{3}{4}$

$\frac{6}{8}$

Now that we have two fractions with common denominators, they are easy to subtract.

$\frac{7}{8} - \frac{6}{8} = \frac{1}{8}$ of the wood will be left.

1 Solve. Use fraction bars or fraction strips to help.

1. Samantha had $\frac{5}{6}$ of a yard of fabric. She used $\frac{2}{3}$ yard. How much was left?

2. Samantha spent $\frac{1}{2}$ of an hour laying out the pattern. She spent $\frac{1}{4}$ of an hour cutting the fabric. How much time did she spend in all?

3. Samantha spent $\frac{1}{10}$ of an hour reading the instructions and $\frac{1}{2}$ hour sewing. How much time did she spend in all?

4. It took Samantha $\frac{5}{6}$ of an hour to put the sleeves into the doll's dress.

It tookher $\frac{1}{3}$ hour to sew the zipper and seams. How much longer did it take her to sew in the sleeves than to sew the zipper and seams?

2 Find the sum or difference. Make sure each fraction is in lowest terms.
Shade the answers that equal 1/2 to read the answer to the riddle:
What do hogs use to write? Read the answer from left to right.

$\frac{1}{4} + \frac{2}{8} =$ **P**	$\frac{7}{12} - \frac{6}{12} =$ **A**	$\frac{2}{3} + \frac{1}{6} =$ **T**	$\frac{9}{10} - \frac{4}{10} =$ **I**	$\frac{1}{12} + \frac{6}{12} =$ **P**
$\frac{2}{5} + \frac{1}{10} =$ **G**	$\frac{12}{14} - \frac{2}{14} =$ **R**	$\frac{7}{9} - \frac{1}{3} =$ **O**	$\frac{3}{4} - \frac{1}{2} =$ **L**	$\frac{6}{8} - \frac{1}{4} =$ **P**
$\frac{8}{9} + \frac{1}{9} =$ **K**	$\frac{1}{20} + \frac{9}{20} =$ **E**	$\frac{1}{3} + \frac{2}{6} =$ **R**	$\frac{1}{4} + \frac{1}{4} =$ **N**	$\frac{8}{12} - \frac{2}{12} =$ **S**

_____ _____ _____ _____ _____ _____ _____

3 Find the quotients. Write the remainder over the divisor as a fraction. Reduce the fraction remainder if possible.

$5\overline{)26}$ $6\overline{)14}$ $3\overline{)25}$ $8\overline{)42}$ $9\overline{)85}$ $7\overline{)50}$

Round each number to the nearest 10. Place the rounded numbers in order from least to greatest in the table below. Read the missing words in the passage: **"He that dwelleth in the _________ _______ of the most high shall abide under the shadow of the Almighty."** (Psalm 91:1) The first one has been done for you.

413 _________ **R** 798 _________ **E** 1,279 _________ **T**

81 _________ **C** 15 _________ **E** 13,693 _________ **L**

9,081,302 _________ **C** 809,999 _________ **A** 9 _________ **S**

6,955 _________ **P** 45,023,876 _________ **E**

Number	Letter
10	S

5 Can you find all 15 of the prime numbers below? If you need help, refer to lesson 45.

1	2	3	4	5	6	7	8	9	10
11	12	13	14	15	16	17	18	19	20
21	22	23	24	25	26	27	28	29	30
31	32	33	34	35	36	37	38	39	40
41	42	43	44	45	46	47	48	49	50

Find the terms in the answer box and place them under the appropriate picture.

parallel lines	intersecting lines	ray
perpendicular lines	line	point

• V

__________ __________ __________

__________ __________ __________

Addition of Mixed Numbers

Paul and Leanne were making potato salad for their church dinner. Paul brought $1\frac{2}{12}$ containers of eggs.

Leanne brought $2\frac{4}{12}$ containers of eggs.

How many containers of eggs did they have in all?

STEP ONE Add the fractions.	STEP TWO Add the whole numbers.	STEP THREE Reduce to lowest terms.
$1\frac{2}{12}$	$1\frac{2}{12}$	$1\frac{2}{12}$
$+2\frac{4}{12}$	$+2\frac{4}{12}$	$+2\frac{4}{12}$
$\frac{6}{12}$	$3\frac{6}{12}$	$3\frac{6}{12} = 3\frac{1}{2}$

There will be $3\frac{1}{2}$ containers of eggs.

1 Find the sum. Reduce the answer to lowest terms.

$1\frac{1}{8} + 1\frac{1}{8}$ $\qquad$ $6\frac{2}{6} + 4\frac{1}{6}$ $\qquad$ $9\frac{2}{12} + 3\frac{4}{12}$ $\qquad$ $4\frac{2}{8} + 3\frac{4}{8}$ $\qquad$ $7\frac{3}{10} + 1\frac{1}{10}$

$3\frac{3}{7} + 1\frac{2}{7}$ $\qquad$ $4\frac{3}{9} + 2\frac{5}{9}$ $\qquad$ $5\frac{6}{12} + 3\frac{3}{12}$ $\qquad$ $3\frac{2}{8} + 1\frac{2}{8}$ $\qquad$ $6\frac{1}{4} + 1\frac{2}{4}$

2 Solve. Reduce the answer to lowest terms.

Paul sold $1\frac{3}{4}$ cases of soda at the picnic on Friday. He sold $3\frac{1}{8}$ cases on Saturday. How many cases did he sell Friday and Saturday?

Stephen was reading a fantastic adventure story that he could hardly put down.

After studies on Tuesday, he read for $1\frac{1}{4}$ hours. On Wednesday morning, he read for $\frac{1}{2}$ hour. How much did he read in all?

3 Combine the fractions in adjacent cells to equal one. Use each cell only once. You may not use cells like this: You may use cells like this:

$\frac{5}{8}$	$\frac{1}{2}$	$\frac{1}{4}$
$\frac{2}{8}$	$\frac{1}{4}$	$\frac{1}{6}$
$\frac{1}{8}$	$\frac{2}{3}$	$\frac{1}{6}$

$\frac{2}{8}$	$\frac{1}{4}$	$\frac{7}{10}$
$\frac{2}{4}$	$\frac{1}{3}$	$\frac{1}{5}$
$\frac{1}{3}$	$\frac{2}{6}$	$\frac{1}{10}$

4 Find the sum or difference. Reduce the answer to lowest terms.

$\frac{2}{10} + \frac{5}{10} =$ $\frac{2}{8} + \frac{5}{8} =$ $\frac{6}{10} + \frac{4}{10} =$ $\frac{2}{9} + \frac{6}{9} =$

$\frac{18}{20} - \frac{10}{20} =$ $\frac{15}{18} - \frac{3}{18} =$ $\frac{10}{12} - \frac{4}{12} =$ $\frac{10}{15} - \frac{5}{15} =$

5 Test each number to see if it is divisible by 2, 5, 10, or 3. Circle the correct responses.

40 is divisible by:	2	5	10	3
81 is divisible by:	2	5	10	3
205 is divisible by:	2	5	10	3
603 is divisible by:	2	5	10	3
2,126 is divisible by:	2	5	10	3

6 Beside each sentence, write A.M. or P.M.

1. Kathleen got up to go to school at 7:00 ________ .
2. The barking dog awoke Mildred in the middle of the night at 2:00 _______ .
3. The carnival was Saturday afternoon at 3:00 ______ .
4. Lunch was served at 12:05 _____ .
5. Tommy's parents got him out of bed before dawn to start their road trip to the Grand Canyon. They left the house at 4:30 _____ .
6. I was born at 12:15, just after midnight ______ .

7 Draw the lines described.

Intersecting Lines	Parallel Lines	Perpendicular Lines

Subtraction of Mixed Numbers

Robin ordered $3\frac{5}{8}$ pounds of chocolate to make all of her holiday candy.

The Chewy Delights use $1\frac{3}{8}$ pounds of the chocolate. How much will be left?

STEP ONE **Subtract the fractions.**	**STEP TWO** **Subtract the whole numbers.**	**STEP THREE** **Reduce to lowest terms.**
$3\frac{5}{8}$	$3\frac{5}{8}$	$3\frac{5}{8}$
$-1\frac{3}{8}$	$-1\frac{3}{8}$	$-1\frac{3}{8}$
$\frac{2}{8}$	$2\frac{2}{8}$	$2\frac{2}{8} = 2\frac{1}{4}$

$2\frac{1}{4}$ pounds will be left.

1 Find the difference. Reduce the answer to lowest terms.

$1\frac{5}{8} - 1\frac{1}{8}$

$6\frac{4}{6} - 1\frac{1}{6}$

$5\frac{10}{12} - 4\frac{4}{12}$

$4\frac{7}{8} - 3\frac{5}{8}$

$7\frac{7}{10} - 1\frac{2}{10}$

$3\frac{3}{7} - 1\frac{2}{7}$

$14\frac{8}{9} - 2\frac{5}{9}$

$7\frac{6}{12} - 3\frac{3}{12}$

$9\frac{7}{8} - 1\frac{6}{8}$

$2\frac{3}{4} - 1\frac{2}{4}$

$3\frac{7}{7} - 2\frac{6}{7}$

$17\frac{2}{3} - 6\frac{1}{3}$

$8\frac{10}{10} - 7\frac{4}{10}$

2 Find the sum. Reduce the answer to lowest terms.

$9\frac{3}{6}$	$2\frac{1}{9}$	$5\frac{1}{4}$	$8\frac{2}{8}$	$3\frac{3}{7}$
$+1\frac{2}{6}$	$+2\frac{1}{9}$	$+1\frac{1}{4}$	$+1\frac{3}{8}$	$+3\frac{2}{7}$

3 Use the picture to answer the questions about the United States. Remember there are 50 states in the United States. Reduce the answers to lowest terms.

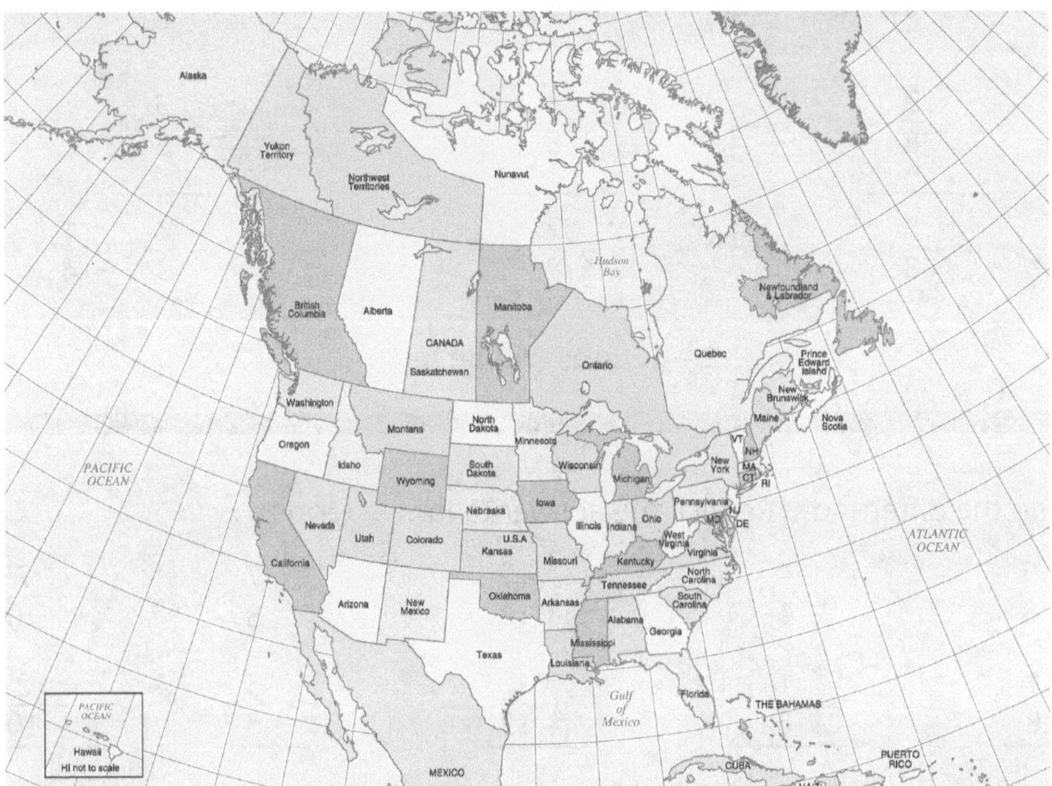

1. What fraction of the states border the Gulf of Mexico? ________
2. What fraction of the states border the Pacific Ocean? ________
3. What fraction of the states have two-word names? ________
4. $\frac{2}{50}$ or $\frac{1}{25}$ of the states border no other American state. Name them.

____

5. What fraction of the states are completely surrounded by the Pacific Ocean?

____

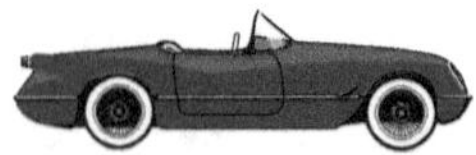

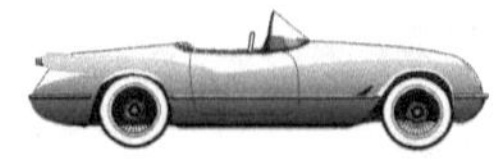

4 Find the sum or difference. Use fraction bars or strips to help find equivalent fractions. Reduce the answer to lowest terms.

$\frac{1}{2} + \frac{1}{4} =$ ______ $\frac{3}{5} + \frac{1}{10} =$ ______ $\frac{1}{6} + \frac{2}{3} =$ ______

$\frac{6}{9} - \frac{1}{3} =$ ______ $\frac{1}{2} - \frac{1}{3} =$ ______ $\frac{3}{4} - \frac{1}{2} =$ ______

5 Draw and label the angles as described.

Right Angle Label ∠ ABC	Acute Angle Label ∠ XYZ	Obtuse Angle Label ∠ CDE

6 Solve the equations and check.

$6 + n = 4 \times 5$ $n + 8 = 9 \times 2$ $4 + n = 2 \times 5$

Check: Check: Check:

$4 \times n = 15 + 1$ $8 \times n = 20 + 4$ $7 \times n = 29 + 20$

Check: Check: Check:

7 Find the average.

17, 19, 24 34, 32, 33 68, 64, 60

Addition of Mixed Numbers: Renaming Sums

Review changing improper fractions to mixed numbers. For more practice, refer to Lesson 108.

$\frac{17}{5} = 3\frac{2}{5}$ $\frac{10}{9} = 1\frac{1}{9}$ $\frac{18}{6} = 3$ $\frac{26}{5} = 5\frac{1}{5}$ $\frac{39}{4} = 9\frac{3}{4}$

Andrew and Carl are making bread for the neighborhood soup kitchen. They are buying flour. For one recipe they need 10 and 3/4 cups of flour. For another recipe they need 5 and 2/4 cups. How much flour do they need in all?

STEP ONE **ADD the fractions.**	**STEP TWO** **ADD the whole numbers.**	**STEP THREE** **Rename**
$10\frac{3}{4}$	$10\frac{3}{4}$	$10\frac{3}{4}$
$+5\frac{2}{4}$	$+5\frac{2}{4}$	$+5\frac{2}{4}$
$\frac{5}{4}$	$15\frac{5}{4}$	$15\frac{5}{4} = 16\frac{1}{4}$

Andrew and Carl will need $16\frac{1}{4}$ cups of flour.

1 Find the sum. Reduce to lowest terms.

$1\frac{7}{8} + 2\frac{7}{8}$ $4\frac{7}{10} + 3\frac{5}{10}$ $3\frac{5}{6} + 5\frac{4}{6}$ $2\frac{8}{10} + 7\frac{2}{10}$

$5\frac{4}{5} + 4\frac{3}{5}$ $10\frac{2}{3} + 12\frac{2}{3}$ $9\frac{5}{7} + 8\frac{6}{7}$ $11\frac{1}{2} + 13$

2 Complete the pyramid by filling in the boxes. The number in each box is the sum of the numbers in the two boxes below. The first row has been done for you. Reduce to lowest terms.

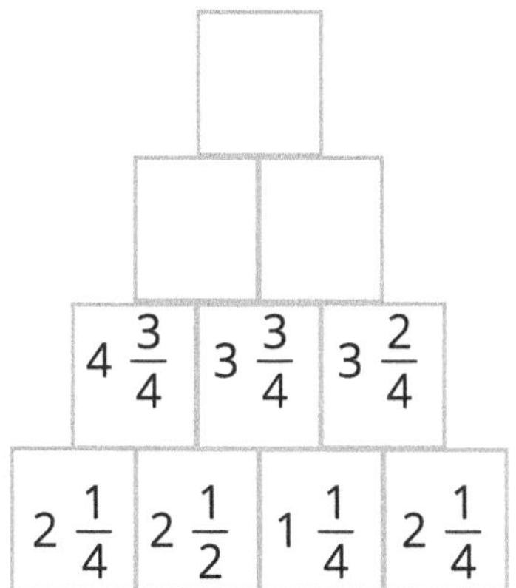

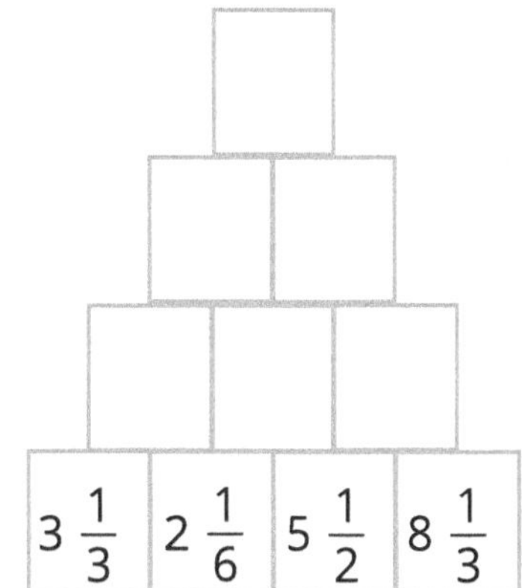

3 Find the difference. Reduce to lowest terms.

$7\frac{7}{8} - 1\frac{3}{8}$ $\qquad$ $16\frac{4}{9} - 11\frac{1}{9}$ $\qquad$ $5\frac{11}{12} - 1\frac{8}{12}$ $\qquad$ $4\frac{3}{4} - \frac{2}{4}$ $\qquad$ $4\frac{7}{16} - 3\frac{2}{16}$

4 Solve the equations.

$n - 4 = 17 - 8$ $n - 4 = 9$ $+4 \quad +4$ $n = 9 + 4$ $n = 13$ Check: $13 - 4 = 17 - 8$ $9 = 9$	$n - 6 = 40 - 11$ Check:	$n - 3 = 18 - 2$ Check:	$n - 9 = 29 - 19$ Check:

5 Count the change. Use the fewest coins and bills possible. Write the total amount due.

Price	Paid	Change Due
$1.36	$2.00	4 pennies, 1 dime, 2 quarters
$3.75	$5.00	
$9.13	$10.00	
$25.00	$30.00	
$11.56	$20.00	
$89.76	$100.00	
$57.00	$100.00	

6 Given the date, state the century.

583 AD _______ century

798 AD _______ century

1647 AD _______ century

7 AD _______ century

1999 AD _______ century

1147 AD _______ century

1811 AD _______ century

2010 AD _______ century

7 Define the angle as acute, obtuse, or right.

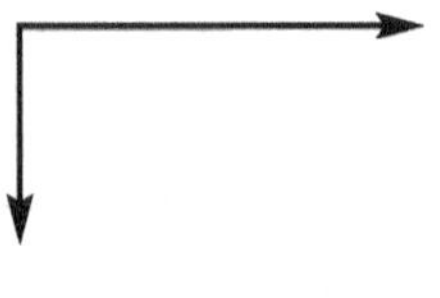

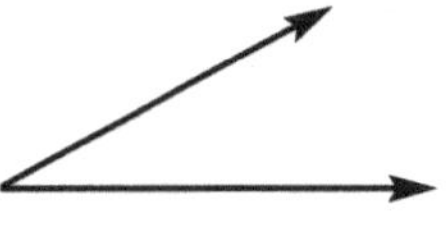

__________ __________ __________

Logical Reasoning

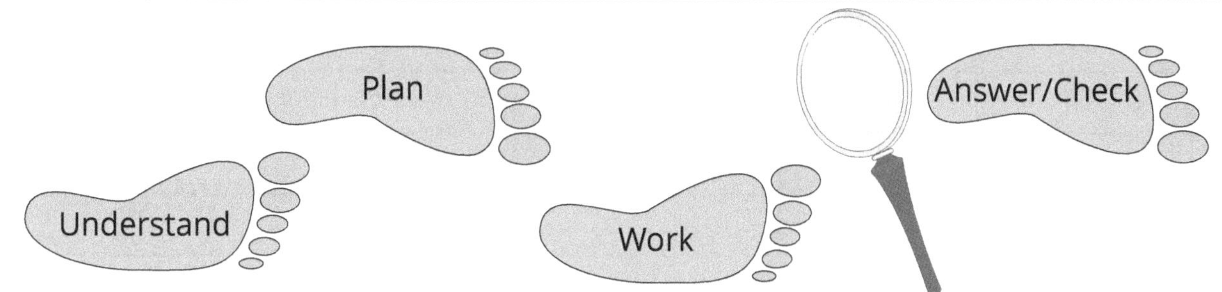

There are 12 children in Mrs. Anthony's class. They are pictured below. How many children have brown hair or brown eyes?

UNDERSTAND: A child with brown hair or brown eyes could be one of the following: a child with brown hair and blue eyes, a child with brown hair and brown eyes, or a child with brown eyes and blonde hair. A child with blonde hair and blue eyes WOULD NOT fit the description.

PLAN: Count the students described above. 3 + 3 + 3

WORK: 3 + 3 + 3 = 9

ANSWER / CHECK: Reread the problem. Is the answer 9 reasonable? Yes.

1 Use the pictures of the children above to answer the following questions.

1. How many children have blonde hair and blue eyes? ____________
2. How many children have brown hair? ____________
3. How many children have blonde hair or blue eyes? ____________
4. How many children have brown hair and brown eyes? ____________
5. How many children have blonde hair or brown eyes? ____________

2 Count the change. Use the fewest coins and bills possible. Write the total amount due.

Price	Paid	Change Due
$0.37	$1.00	
$1.15	$1.25	
$1.63	$1.75	
$4.87	$5.00	
$3.43	$5.00	
$12.62	$20.00	
$78.90	$100.00	

3 Match.

____ 2 hours　　　　A. 2 years

____ 60 seconds　　　　B. 1 day

____ 24 hours　　　　C. 120 minutes

____ 12 months　　　　D. 1 hour

____ 60 minutes　　　　E. 1 minute

____ 24 months　　　　F. 1 year

* Just for fun... Can you determine how many months, weeks, and days old you are?

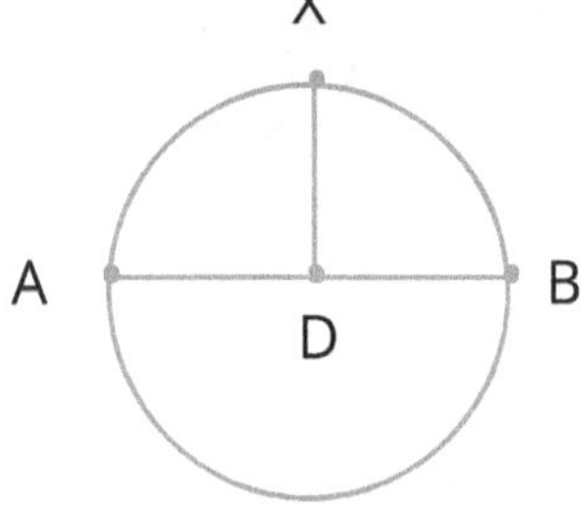

Name the circle above. ________

Name the 3 radii. ______________________

Name the diameter. __________

If the radius is 25m, what is the diameter? ______________________

5 Give the missing numerator.

$\frac{1}{2} = \frac{\_\_\_}{18}$ $\frac{4}{5} = \frac{\_\_\_}{45}$ $\frac{6}{7} = \frac{\_\_\_}{63}$ $\frac{3}{15} = \frac{\_\_\_}{30}$ $\frac{1}{8} = \frac{\_\_\_}{64}$

6 Write each fraction in lowest terms.

$\frac{10}{30}$ $\frac{5}{25}$ $\frac{2}{16}$ $\frac{6}{30}$ $\frac{12}{48}$

$\frac{30}{90}$ $\frac{12}{24}$ $\frac{18}{36}$ $\frac{80}{100}$ $\frac{9}{81}$

7 Compare with the correct sign (>, <, =).

$\frac{3}{6}$ _____ $\frac{7}{18}$ $\frac{6}{12}$ _____ $\frac{8}{12}$ $\frac{3}{12}$ _____ $\frac{1}{4}$ $\frac{8}{9}$ _____ $\frac{12}{18}$

$\frac{1}{3}$ _____ $\frac{2}{6}$ $\frac{1}{2}$ _____ $\frac{3}{4}$ $\frac{7}{8}$ _____ $\frac{2}{4}$ $\frac{3}{5}$ _____ $\frac{5}{6}$

Reading Decimals

Remember the place value chart? There are two sides to the place value chart; the whole number side and the decimal side. Until now we have mainly worked with the whole number side which is Ones, Tens, Hundreds, Thousands, and so on. We will now talk about the decimal side. Decimals and fractions are actually the same side of the place value chart. A fraction is part of a whole, and so is a decimal. Think about money; 50¢ is part of a dollar. Look at the place value chart below.

Hundreds	Tens	Ones		Tenths	Hundredths
		1	•	5	
	3	5	•	2	
1	0	5	•	4	

1 **and** $\frac{5}{10}$ One **and** five tenths 1.5

35 **and** $\frac{2}{10}$ Thirty-five **and** two tenths 35.2

105 **and** $\frac{4}{10}$ One hundred five **and** four tenths 105.4

Any time you see the word AND in math, this means a decimal is present in the problem.

Karen painted one whole side of a trailer and 4 of the 10 sections on the back side of the trailer. How can she use numbers to tell someone about the amount of the trailer she has painted?

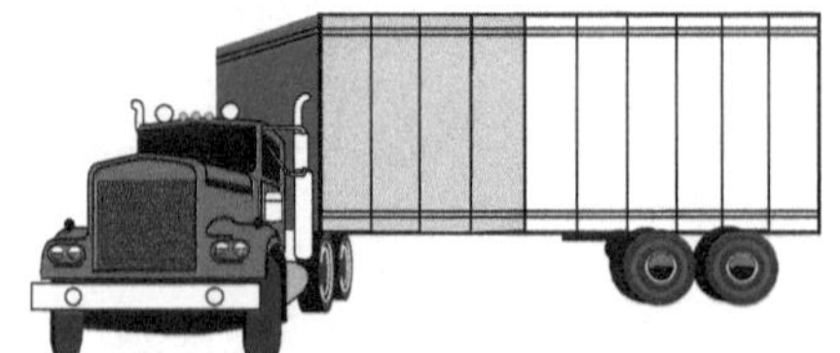

Karen has painted 1 side and 4 out of 10 panels on the other side.

Using a fraction:	**Using a decimal:**
(One whole side) → $1\frac{4}{10}$ ↓ (Number of panels painted in the next section) ↑ (Total number of panels in the section)	(One whole side) ↓ 1.4 ← (Total number of panels painted in the next section out of a total of 10.)
We read: "One and four tenths"	**We read:** "One and four tenths"

Karen can say she has painted 1.4 sides of the trailer.

Look at these other examples.

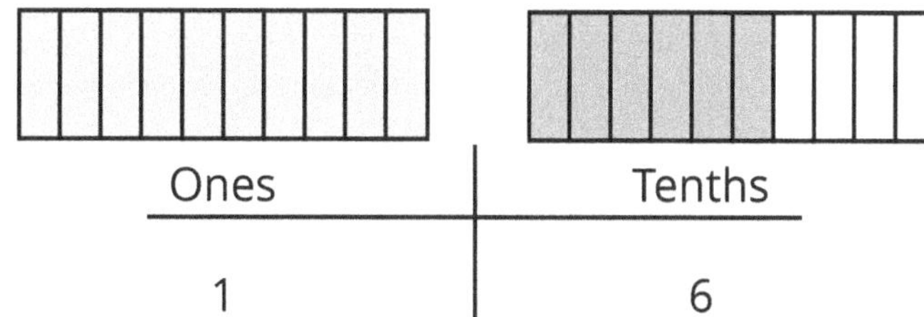

Ones	Tenths
1	6

We write: 1.6
We read: "one and six tenths"

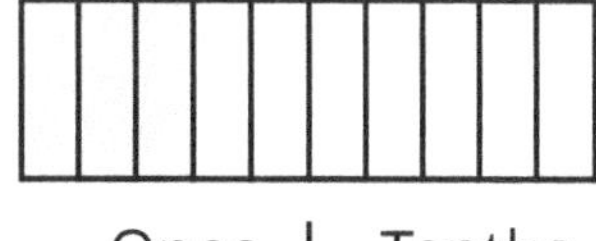

Ones	Tenths
0	3

We write: 0.3
We read: "three tenths"

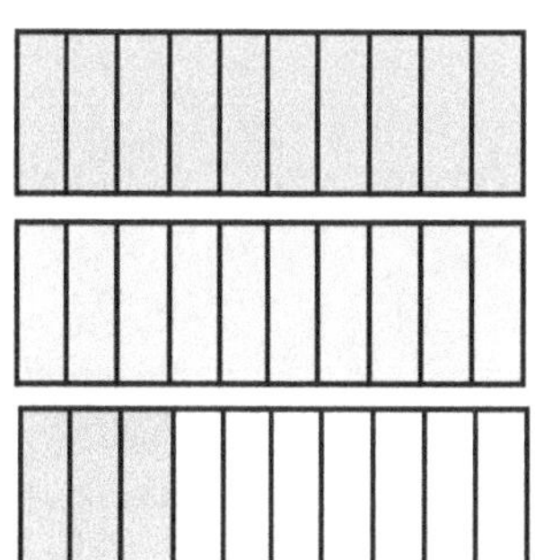

Ones	Tenths
2	3

We write: 2.3
We read: "two and three tenths"

1 Solve.

We write: ___________

We read: ________________________

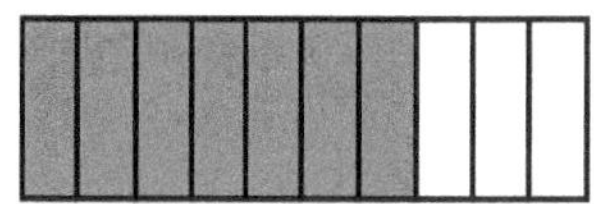

We write: ___________

We read: ________________________

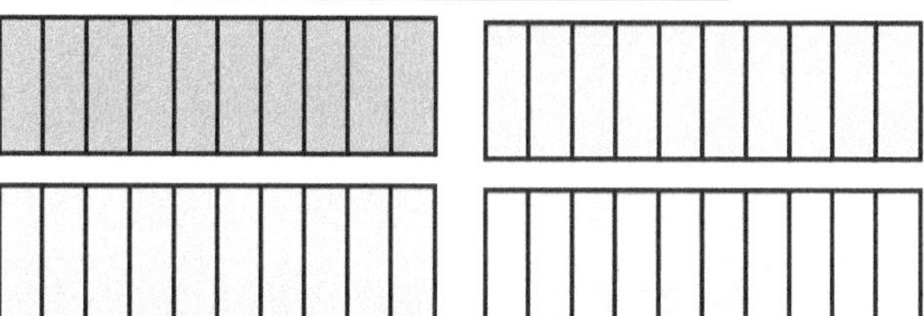

We write: ___________

We read: ________________________

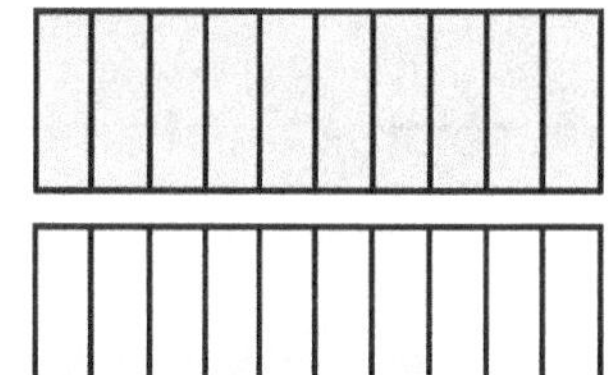

We write: ___________

We read: ________________________

2 Solve.

$2\frac{1}{4} + 1\frac{1}{4} =$ ______

$10\frac{3}{11} + 5\frac{1}{11} =$ ______

$5\frac{4}{9} - 3\frac{2}{9} =$ ______

$6\frac{5}{12} - 6\frac{4}{12} =$ ______

$12\frac{3}{17} + 10\frac{7}{17} =$ ______

$2\frac{4}{7} - 1\frac{4}{7} =$ ______

3 Divide. The remainders in the quotients spell out a message. Use the secret code to write the message.

Example:

$79\overline{)403}$ 5 r [8] → [F]

$41\overline{)84}$ r [ ] → [ ]

$36\overline{)193}$ r [ ][ ] → [ ][ ]

$33\overline{)75}$ r [ ] → [ ]

$31\overline{)687}$ r [ ] → [ ]

$50\overline{)104}$ r [ ] → [ ]

$28\overline{)91}$ r [ ] → [ ]

0	1	2	3	4	5	6	7	8	9
M	R	O	G	E	V	L	N	F	I

____

Jeremiah 31:34

4 Match.

____ 1 hour	A. 300 seconds
____ 120 seconds	B. 2 days
____ 24 hours	C. 60 minutes
____ 48 hours	D. 3 hours
____ 180 minutes	E. 2 minutes
____ 5 minutes	F. 1 day

5 Label.

In what color is the radius drawn?

____

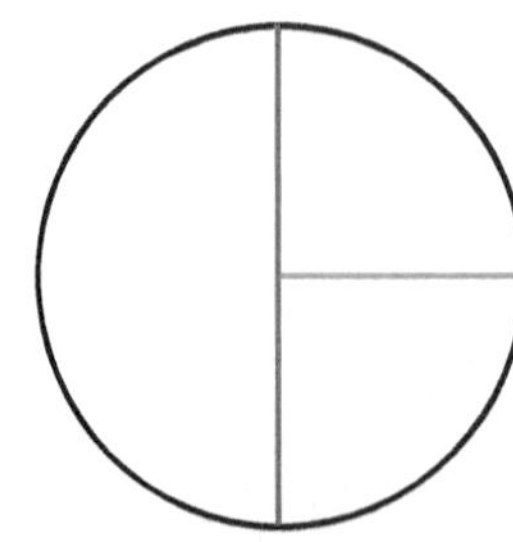

Label the radius $\overline{AB}$.

In what color is the diameter drawn?

____

Label the diameter $\overline{CD}$.

6 Match.

$\frac{1}{2}$	$\frac{8}{18}$
$\frac{1}{3}$	$\frac{4}{8}$
$\frac{1}{5}$	$\frac{3}{9}$
$\frac{3}{7}$	$\frac{3}{15}$
$\frac{4}{9}$	$\frac{6}{14}$

48 points total Lessons 106-115

1 Compare with the correct sign. (>, <, =) 8 pts. total for this exercise.

$\frac{2}{8}$ ___ $\frac{3}{8}$ $\frac{2}{3}$ ___ $\frac{1}{3}$ $\frac{2}{14}$ ___ $\frac{1}{14}$ $\frac{2}{3}$ ___ $\frac{5}{6}$

$\frac{1}{3}$ ___ $\frac{2}{6}$ $\frac{2}{5}$ ___ $\frac{2}{10}$ $\frac{2}{4}$ ___ $\frac{1}{2}$ $\frac{4}{5}$ ___ $\frac{5}{10}$

2 Change each mixed fraction to an improper fraction. 8 pts. total for this exercise.

$1\frac{2}{8}$ = ______ $2\frac{1}{7}$ = ______ $3\frac{1}{4}$ = ______ $1\frac{5}{7}$ = ______

$4\frac{2}{5}$ = ______ $2\frac{1}{9}$ = ______ $2\frac{2}{3}$ = ______ $9\frac{2}{9}$ = ______

3 Change each improper fraction to a whole number or mixed fraction. Reduce the answer to lowest terms. 8 pts. total for this exercise.

$\frac{17}{4}$ = ______ $\frac{12}{4}$ = ______ $\frac{36}{6}$ = ______ $\frac{14}{2}$ = ______

$\frac{20}{4}$ = ______ $\frac{20}{9}$ = ______ $\frac{11}{2}$ = ______ $\frac{12}{10}$ = ______

4 Use simpler numbers to write a number sentence for the problem. Then, solve the problem with the actual numbers. 2 pts. total for this exercise.

Ben had 315 Legos™. He needed to divide the Legos™ among 9 students. How many Legos™ would each student get?

Jeannine needs 27 beads to make a necklace. How many beads will she need to make 5 necklaces?

5 Find the sum. Make sure the answer is in lowest terms. 4 pts. total for this exercise.

$\frac{1}{7} + \frac{4}{7}$ = $\frac{1}{8} + \frac{5}{8}$ = $\frac{2}{10} + \frac{2}{10}$ = $\frac{1}{5} + \frac{2}{5}$ =

6 Find the difference. Make sure the answer is in lowest terms. 4 pts.

$\frac{11}{12} - \frac{3}{12} =$ $\frac{3}{4} - \frac{2}{4} =$ $\frac{6}{7} - \frac{1}{7} =$ $\frac{8}{8} - \frac{1}{8} =$

7 Add or subtract the fractions as indicated. Make sure the answer is in lowest terms. 4 pts. total for this exercise.

$\frac{1}{6} + \frac{2}{6} =$ $\frac{2}{8} + \frac{4}{8} =$ $\frac{7}{14} - \frac{3}{14} =$ $\frac{5}{6} - \frac{2}{6} =$

8 Use fraction bars or strips to help you find common denominators before you add the fractions. Make sure the answer is in lowest terms. 4 pts. total for this exercise.

$\frac{1}{4} + \frac{2}{8} =$ $\frac{2}{6} + \frac{1}{3} =$ $\frac{1}{2} + \frac{3}{6} =$ $\frac{1}{8} + \frac{2}{4} =$

9 Use fraction bars or strips to help you find common denominators before you subtract the fractions. Make sure the answer is in lowest terms. 4 pts.

$\frac{7}{8} - \frac{3}{4} =$ $\frac{5}{6} - \frac{2}{12} =$ $\frac{1}{2} - \frac{1}{6} =$ $\frac{6}{10} - \frac{1}{5} =$

10 Solve. Use fraction bars or fraction strips to help. 2 pts. total for this exercise.

Tom spent $\frac{1}{2}$ hour researching about Indians. He spent $\frac{3}{4}$ of an hour writing a report. How much more time was spent writing than researching?

Sarah and Pam were making cookies for a church bake sale. One recipe called for $\frac{1}{8}$ cup of chocolate chips, and another recipe called for $\frac{3}{4}$ cup of chocolate chips. How many cups of chocolate chips are needed in all?

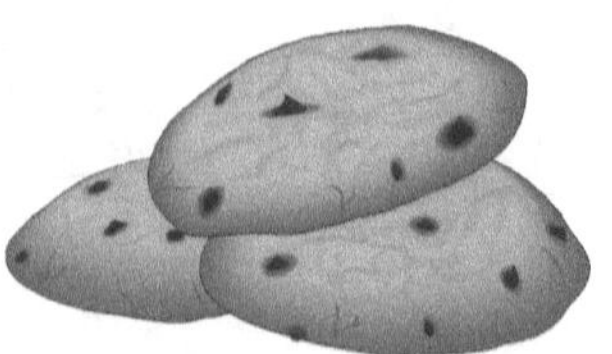

Reading and Writing Fractions as Decimals

Monica took up her old kitchen floor and began to replace it with green tile. How can she use numbers to tell someone about the amount of the floor she has covered with the tile?

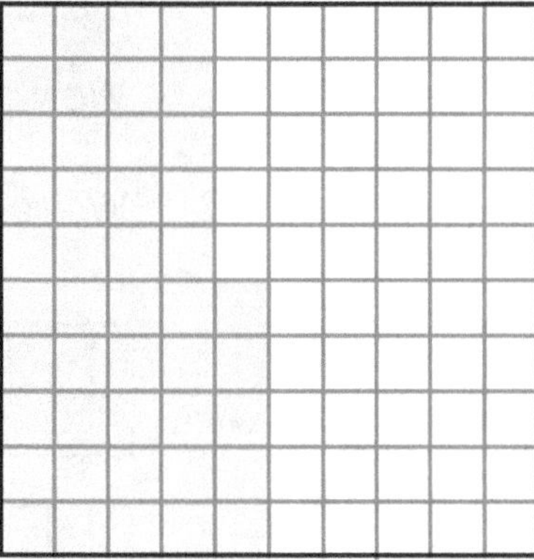

Using a fraction:
$\frac{45}{100}$ ← Number of tiles in place. / ← Total number of tiles needed.

We read: "forty-five hundredths"

Using a decimal:
0.45 ← Number of tiles in place out of a 100 total tiles.

We read: "forty-five hundredths"

Monica has tiled 0.45 of the kitchen floor.

1 Match.

a. 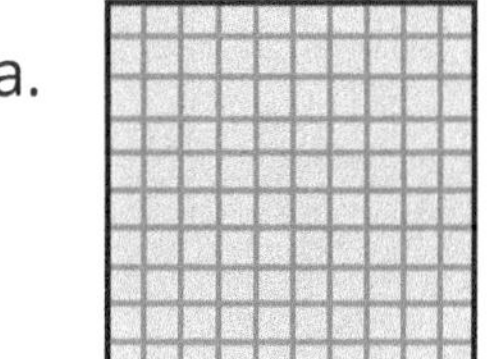 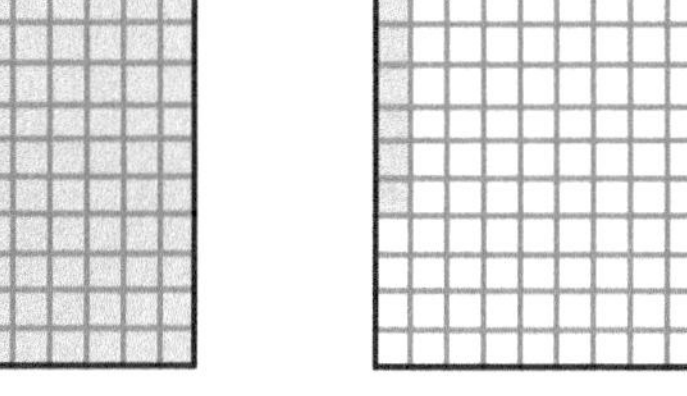

b. 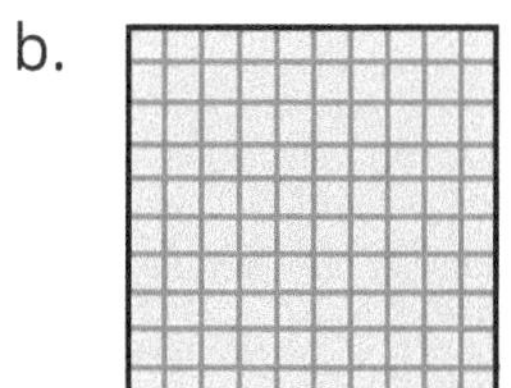 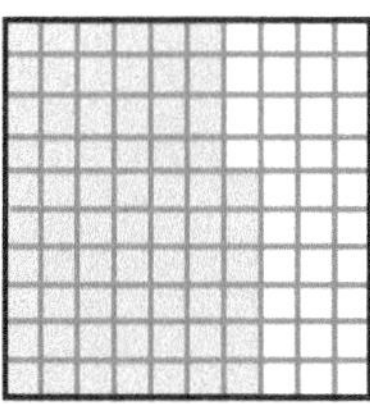

c. 

10's	1's	10ths	100ths
		7	5

10's	1's	10ths	100ths
	1	0	6

10's	1's	10ths	100ths
	1	6	6

2 Solve.

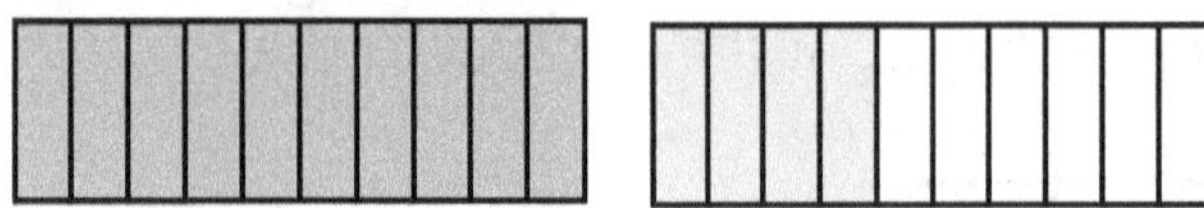

We write: ___________

We read: ________________________

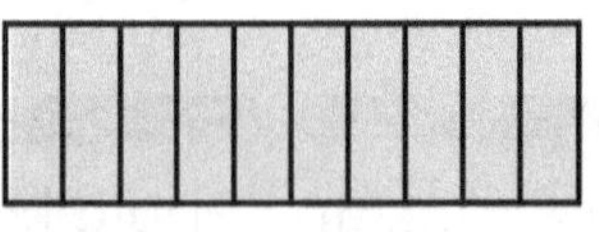
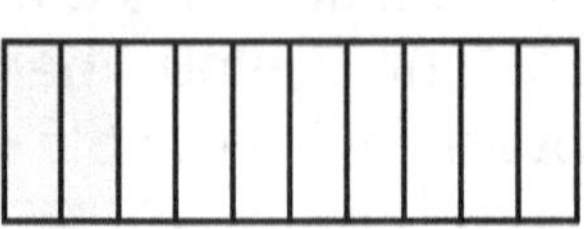

We write: ___________

We read: ________________________

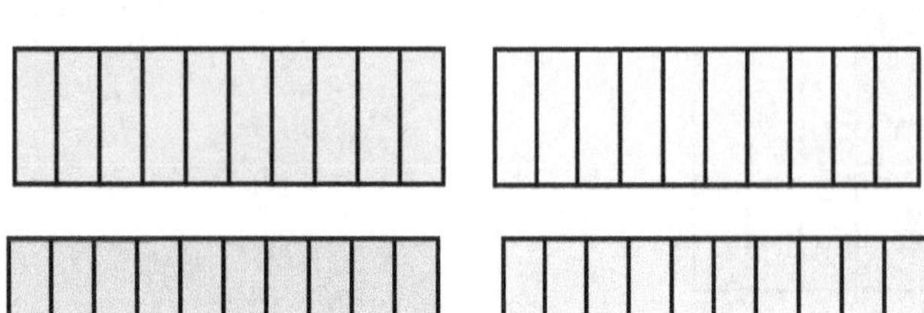
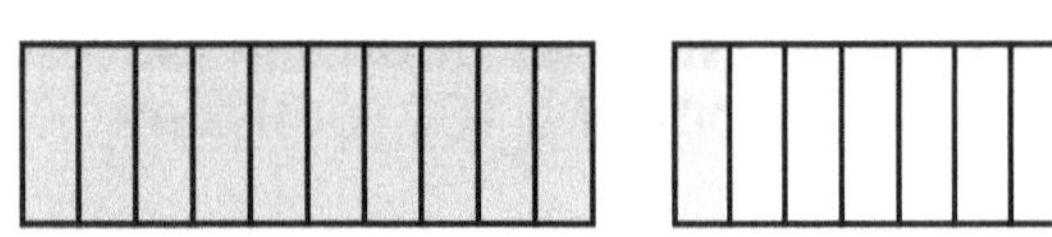

We write: ___________

We read: ________________________

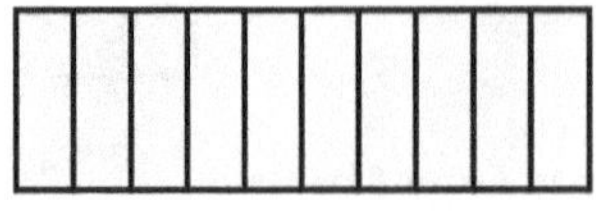
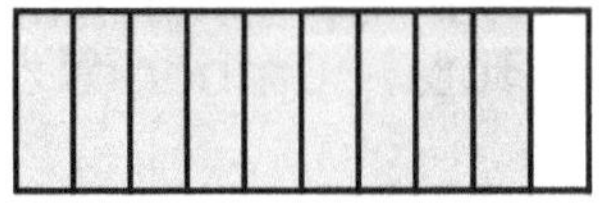

We write: ___________

We read: ________________________

3 Add or Subtract.

$$4\frac{2}{10} + 3\frac{3}{10} = \underline{\qquad}$$

$$8\frac{10}{16} - 7\frac{5}{16} = \underline{\qquad}$$

$$9\frac{5}{15} + 10\frac{6}{15} = \underline{\qquad}$$

$$22\frac{14}{20} - 11\frac{7}{20} = \underline{\qquad}$$

$$4\frac{1}{6} + 4\frac{1}{6} = \underline{\qquad}$$

$$3\frac{2}{8} + 1\frac{1}{8} = \underline{\qquad}$$

4 Find the difference.

910 – 234 =   643 – 158 =   945 – 179 =   675 – 280 =

5 Divide.

$19\overline{)135}$ $33\overline{)171}$ $22\overline{)169}$ $50\overline{)441}$

6 Solve.

1978 is in the _________ century.

1761 is in the _________ century.

1542 is in the _________ century.

2021 is in the _________ century.

7 Solve.

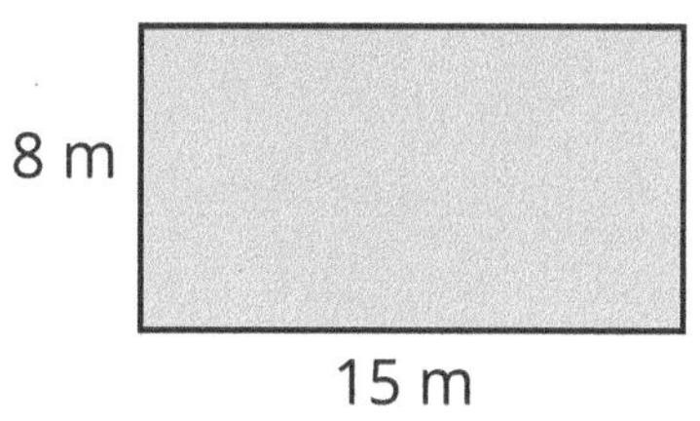

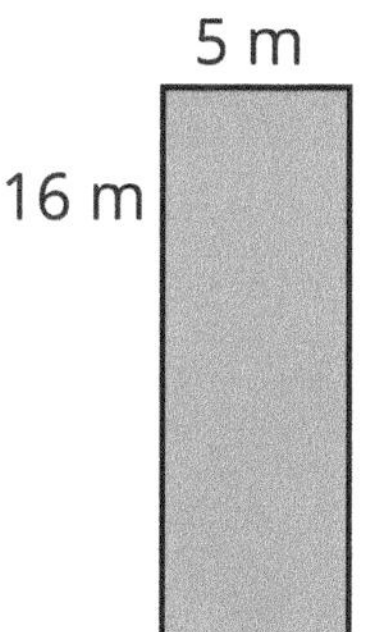

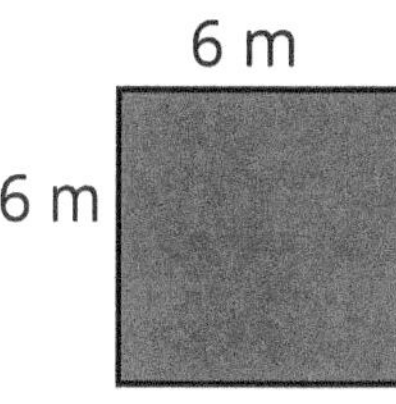

Perimeter =
Area =

Perimeter =
Area =

Perimeter =
Area =

Compare Decimals

While watching the 1996 World Series, Lisa wanted to know which of the Atlanta Braves starting pitchers had the lowest Earned Run Average (ERA).

Earned Run Average for Starting Pitchers in the 1996 World Series.

John Smoltz	2.94
Tom Glavine	2.98
Greg Maddux	2.72
Denny Neagle	5.59

Compare these averages to see which pitcher had the lowest ERA that season. We compare decimals the same way we compare other numbers. The steps below will help you compare and order decimals.

1. Compare each digit starting at the left.
2. When 2 digits are the same, continue to move to the right and find the first place where the digits are different. Compare these digits to see which is larger.
3. The number with the larger digit is the larger number.

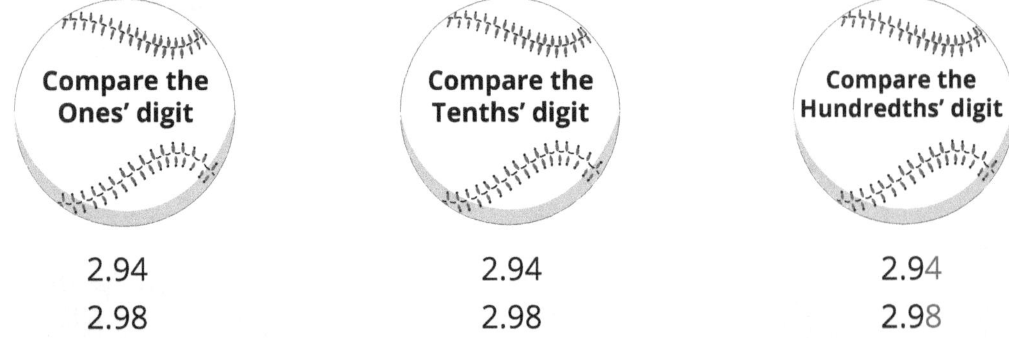

2.94	2.94	2.94
2.98	2.98	2.98

4 is smaller than 8, so 2.94 is smaller than 2.98. The lowest ERA is 2.94.

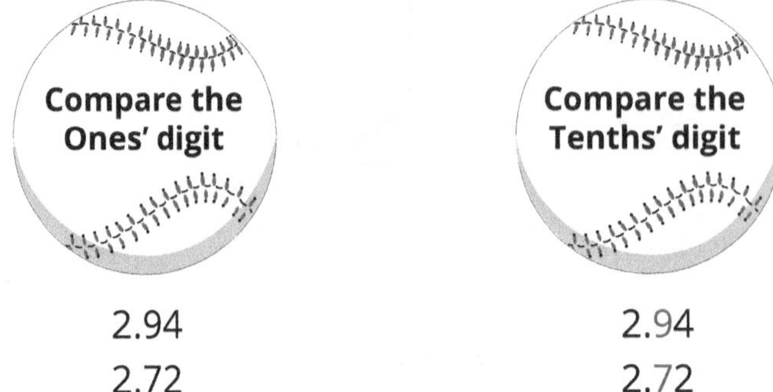

2.94	2.94
2.72	2.72

7 is lower than 9 so 2.72 is smaller than 2.94. The lowest ERA is 2.72.

Going into the 1996 World Series, Greg Maddux had the lowest ERA of the Braves starting pitchers.

1 <, >, or =.

4.6 ◯ 8.4   1.95 ◯ 1.59   9.05 ◯ 9.01   1.86 ◯ 1.68

4.69 ◯ 5.23   0.02 ◯ 0.01

2 Match.

one and forty-three hundredths	2.50
five and seven hundredths	17.15
two and fifty hundredths	1.43
seventeen and fifteen hundredths	5.07

3 Find the numbers in written form.

DATA BANK: 0.8   7.1   0.5   1.3

```
N S E V E N A N D O N E T E N T H
P K I L M C D A E T Y U A E M I O
R A G E A U I N D L B M X C Z N T
S E H G W B E K D F D F G S H J K
H I T V R V E O S I J I O A B V C
B C T T C H H I K V N U I H D P K
O N E A N D T H R E E T E N T H S
M K N X A I P F L T W K T D V N M
L G T M E L Z D M E P P G D H J E
C H H O D B X X N N Q T X M K H V
E J S P O D V L N T W F G Q R Y T
T F T E I F U N B H E Z F J Q U P
O D K J Y T H B R S D B N L S I O
```

4 Find the missing fraction.

$4\frac{1}{4}$ + 2 ____ = $6\frac{3}{4}$

$10\frac{6}{7}$ − 5 ____ = $5\frac{3}{7}$

2 ____ + $3\frac{1}{5}$ = $5\frac{3}{5}$

11 ____ − $10\frac{2}{5}$ = $1\frac{1}{5}$

5 Find the difference.

$$\begin{array}{r} 6{,}002 \\ -\ 1{,}012 \\ \hline \end{array} \qquad \begin{array}{r} 8{,}005 \\ -\ 5{,}007 \\ \hline \end{array} \qquad \begin{array}{r} 9{,}003 \\ -\ 2{,}013 \\ \hline \end{array} \qquad \begin{array}{r} 2{,}004 \\ -\ 1{,}022 \\ \hline \end{array}$$

6 Divide.

185 ÷ 5 = 170 ÷ 20 = 165 ÷ 33 = 442 ÷ 22 =

7 Solve.

_______ is in the 20th century.

_______ is in the 18th century.

_______ is in the 17th century.

_______ is in the 19th century.

DATA BANK:
1986
1854
1654
1725

8 Solve.

12 m

12 m

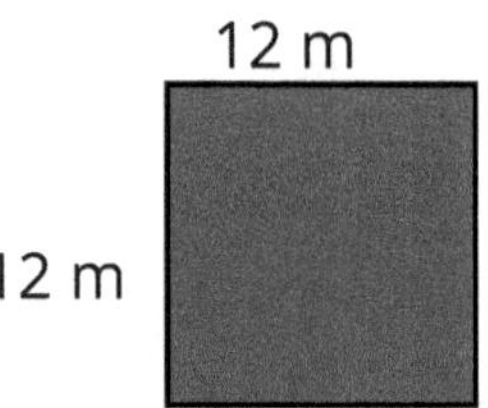

18 m

3 m

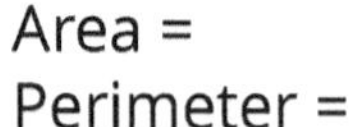

Area =
Perimeter =

Area =
Perimeter =

Order Decimals

Earned Run Average for Starting Pitchers
in the 1996 World Series.

John Smoltz	2.94
Tom Glavine	2.98
Greg Maddux	2.72
Denny Neagle	5.59

Using the chart above, place the Earned Run Averages of each pitcher in order from the smallest to the largest.

We can follow the same three steps previously used when comparing numbers to place decimals in order.

1. Compare each digit starting at the left.
2. When 2 digits are the same, continue to move to the right and find the first place where the digits are different. Compare these digits to see which is larger.
3. The number with the larger digit is the larger number.

5.59
2.72
2.94
2.98

5 is larger than any of the other digits in the ones' place, so 5.59 is the largest of these numbers.

2.72
2.94
2.98

7 is smaller than any of the other digits in the tenths' place, so 2.72 is the smallest of these numbers.

Compare the Hundredths' digit

2.94
2.98

4 is smaller than 8 so, 2.94 is smaller than 2.98.

Smallest Number →			→ **Largest Number**
2.72	**2.94**	**2.98**	**5. 59**

The Earned Run Averages for each pitcher, in order from the smallest to the largest, are 2.72, 2.94, 2.98, & 5.59.

1 Order from smallest to largest.

Batting Averages of Starting Pitchers at Start of 1996 World Series.

Glavine	.289
Maddux	.147
Neagle	.143
Smoltz	.218

Batting Averages of Braves Switch Hitters at Start of 1996 World Series.

Jones	.309
Lemke	.323
Pendleton	.204

Pitchers' Batting Averages:

____
____
____
____

Switch Hitters' Batting Averages:

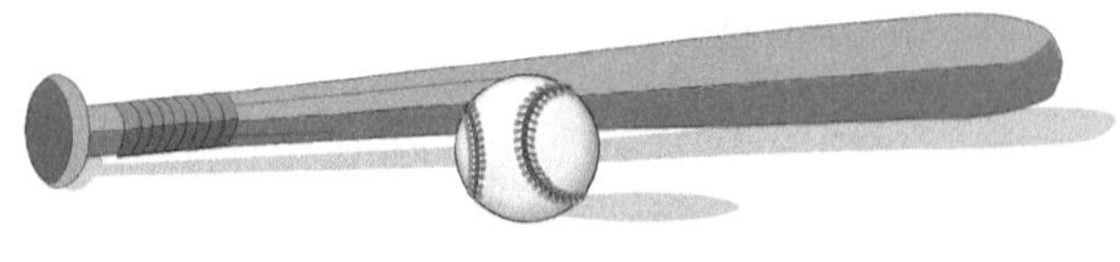

____
____
____

2 Write <, >, or =.

23.65 ___ 32.56 42.25 ___ 42.52 1.69 ___ 1.96 8.3 ___ 8.30

3 Write the written problem as a standard problem and solve.

two and three hundredths + one and two tenths =

six and five tenths + four and twelve hundredths =

seven hundredths + one tenth =

4 Write the number in the tenths' place.

23.65 _______ 45.96 _______ 432.05 _______ 983.61 _______ 14.16 _______

5 Round to the nearest ten.

89 _______ 1,565 _______ 2,481 _______ 782 _______ 463 _______

6 Solve.

$n - 48 = 21$ $n - 31 = 10$ $n - 1 = 1 + 3$ $12 + 1 = n + 5$

7 Divide.

$22\overline{)484}$ $33\overline{)1,089}$ $50\overline{)1,500}$ $45\overline{)450}$

8 Solve.

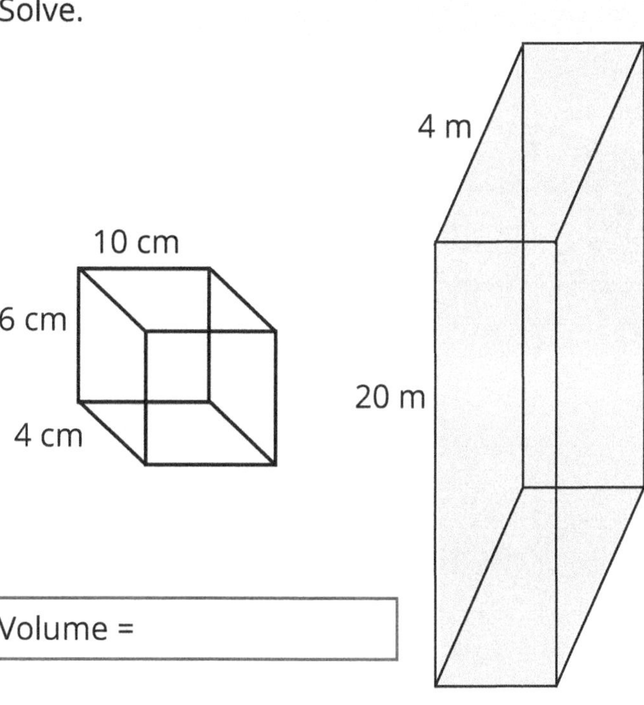

3 mm
15 mm
4 mm

Volume =

Volume =

Volume =

Round Decimals

Earned Run Average for Starting Pitchers in the 1996 World Series.

John Smoltz	2.94
Tom Glavine	2.98
Greg Maddux	2.72
Denny Naegle	5.59

What is each pitcher's Earned Run Average (ERA), rounded to the nearest whole number?

Use what you know about rounding whole numbers to help you round decimals. When looking at each number think of a number line. Is 2.94 closer to 2 or 3? It is closer to three therefore 2.94 rounds up to 3.

2.00 2.50 2.94 3.00

Below are two easy steps to follow when rounding to the nearest whole number (or dollar).

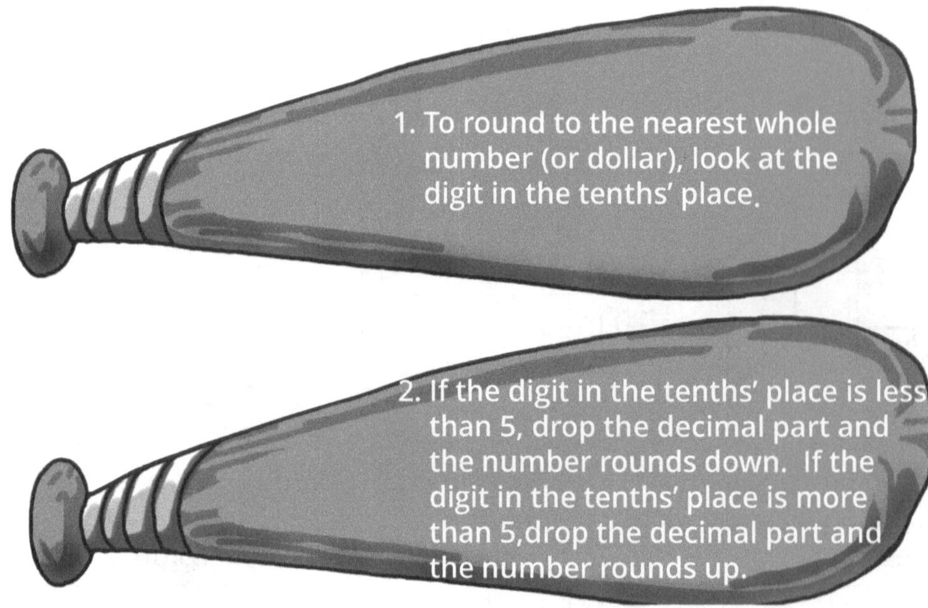

5.59 5.59 rounded to the nearest whole number is 6.

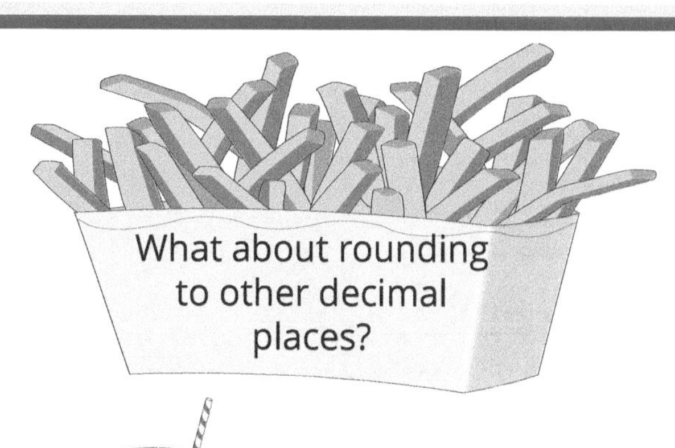

3.501 rounded to the nearest **whole number** is **4**.

4.256 rounded to the nearest **tenth** is **4.3**.

8.629 rounded to the nearest **tenth** is **8.6**.

Look at the digit to the right of the place to which you want to round.

1 Round.
Round to the nearest whole number.

4.3 ______ 7.8 ______ 12.83 ______ 9.24 ______

Round to the nearest tenth.

0.27 ______ 2.45 ______ 3.96 ______ 0.071 ______

2 Circle the smaller number in each pair. Find the hidden message.

6.61	P	G	6.32
4.36	O	R	5.23
3.18	D	S	3.20
0.88	I	M	0.99
8.03	T	S	0.83
4.66	L	B	4.85
5.44	C	I	5.11
7.31	F	G	7.14
2.34	H	W	2.43
9.50	U	T	9.05

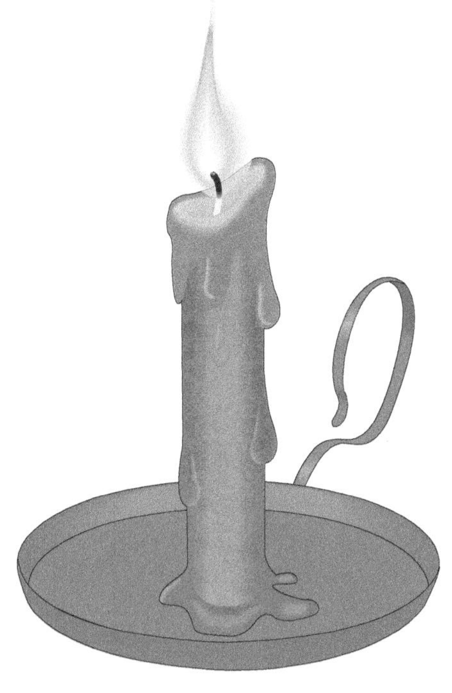

___ ___ ___ ___ ___ ___ ___ ___ ___ ___
1 John 1:5

3 Write in written form.

0.23 = ______________________________

1.34 = ______________________________

5.72 = ______________________________

6.31 = ______________________________

9.06 = ______________________________

8.11 = ______________________________

4 Round to the tens.

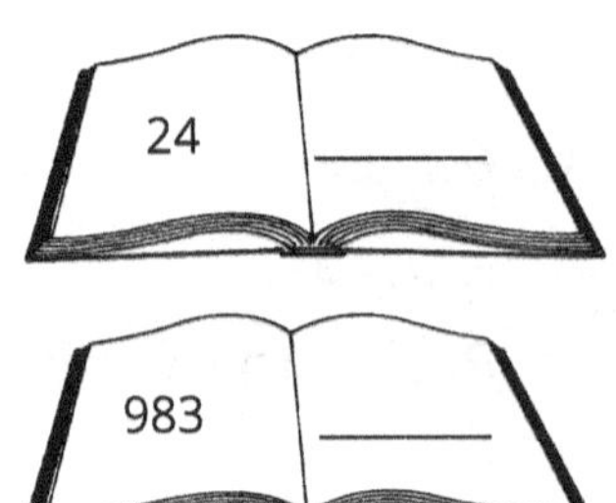

5 Solve.

$n - 1 = 13 - 10$ $8 + 9 = n + 9$ $n - 9 = 18$

$n - 6 = 14$ $n - 4 = 12 + 5$ $n - 10 = 15$

6 Divide.

$37\overline{)530}$ $46\overline{)620}$ $33\overline{)705}$ $21\overline{)382}$

7 Solve.

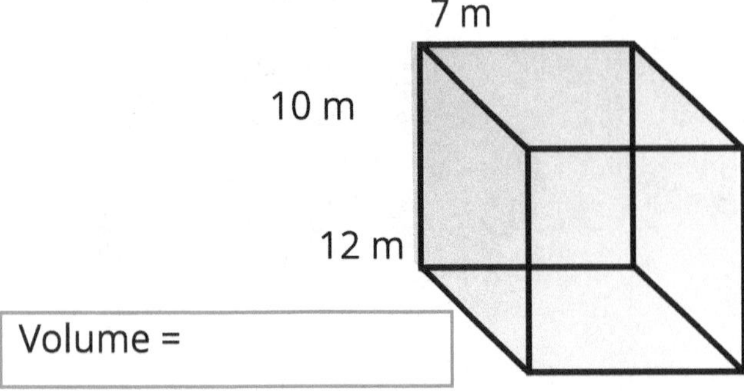

Volume =

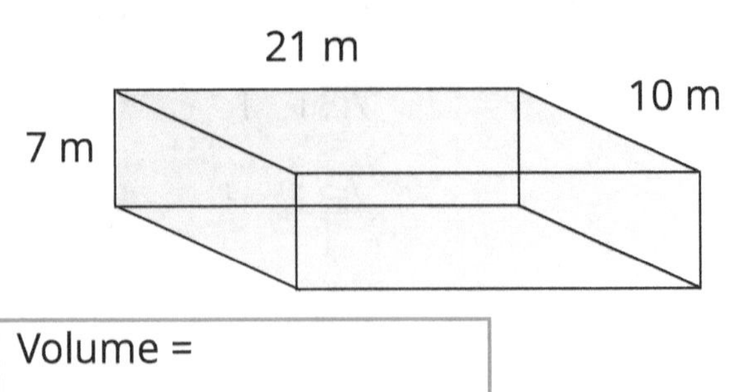

Volume =

Add Decimals

Connie is sending Erin a rock collection. Each rock has been weighed and measured for shipping purposes. The total weight of each rock is listed below. Connie needs to know the total weight of all the rocks in order to ship them. What is it?

Decimals are added and subtracted in the same way as money is added and subtracted. It is important to place the decimal points directly beneath each other. This is to keep all place value columns straight so that no errors occur.

Rock 1	2.25 g
Rock 2	5.26 g
Rock 3	3.98 g
Rock 4	6.04 g

Add together keeping decimals in line:

	Ones	Tenths	Hundredths
	2	. 2	5
	5	. 2	6
	3	. 9	8
+	6	. 0	4
1	7	. 5	3

The total weight of all the rocks is 17.53 grams.

1 Add.

```
  1.86        14.60        17.04
+ 4.45      +  9.07      +  5.00

     11.00        35.07
   +  7.25      + 18.23
```

2 Round to the nearest whole number.

1.48 ______ 7.75 ______ 23.89 ______ 1.85 ______ 15.27 ______

Round to the nearest tenth.

4.42 ______ 9.89 ______ 19.32 ______ 0.07 ______

3 Order from largest to smallest.

1.41 13.7 13.61 0.342 0.437

______ ______ ______ ______ ______

4 Round to the nearest 100.

1,388 ______ 12,187 ______ 4,921 ______

15,252 ______ 843 ______ 168 ______

5 Average.

25, 90, 65, 70, 25

88, 92, 76, 86, 33

6 Label each time zone. Write the missing times on the time zone clocks.

7 Solve.

$\frac{1}{3} + \frac{1}{3} =$ $\frac{3}{10} + \frac{1}{10} =$ $\frac{2}{5} - \frac{1}{5} =$ $\frac{7}{12} - \frac{4}{12} =$

Subtract Decimals

Kimberly needs 10.75 meters of ribbon to wrap a package. If she has 7.25 already, how much more does she need?

Decimals are subtracted and added in the same way as money is subtracted and added. It is important to place the decimal points directly beneath each other. This is to keep all place value columns straight so that no errors occur.

$$\begin{array}{r} 10.75 \\ -\ 7.25 \\ \hline 3.50 \end{array} \text{ meters}$$

1 Find the difference.

$$\begin{array}{r} 12.24 \\ -\ 5.20 \\ \hline \end{array} \qquad \begin{array}{r} 11.41 \\ -\ 10.40 \\ \hline \end{array} \qquad \begin{array}{r} 62.53 \\ -\ 11.72 \\ \hline \end{array}$$

$$\begin{array}{r} 104.80 \\ -\ 70.80 \\ \hline \end{array} \qquad \begin{array}{r} 7.85 \\ -\ 5.25 \\ \hline \end{array} \qquad \begin{array}{r} 41.26 \\ -\ 20.14 \\ \hline \end{array}$$

2 Add.

$$\begin{array}{r} 1.68 \\ +\ 2.38 \\ \hline \end{array} \qquad \begin{array}{r} 42.35 \\ +\ 5.98 \\ \hline \end{array} \qquad \begin{array}{r} 0.79 \\ +\ 0.25 \\ \hline \end{array}$$

$$\begin{array}{r} 23.49 \\ +\ 20.51 \\ \hline \end{array} \qquad \begin{array}{r} 71.25 \\ +\ 6.00 \\ \hline \end{array}$$

3 Shade the spaces in each row that round to the number given on the left.

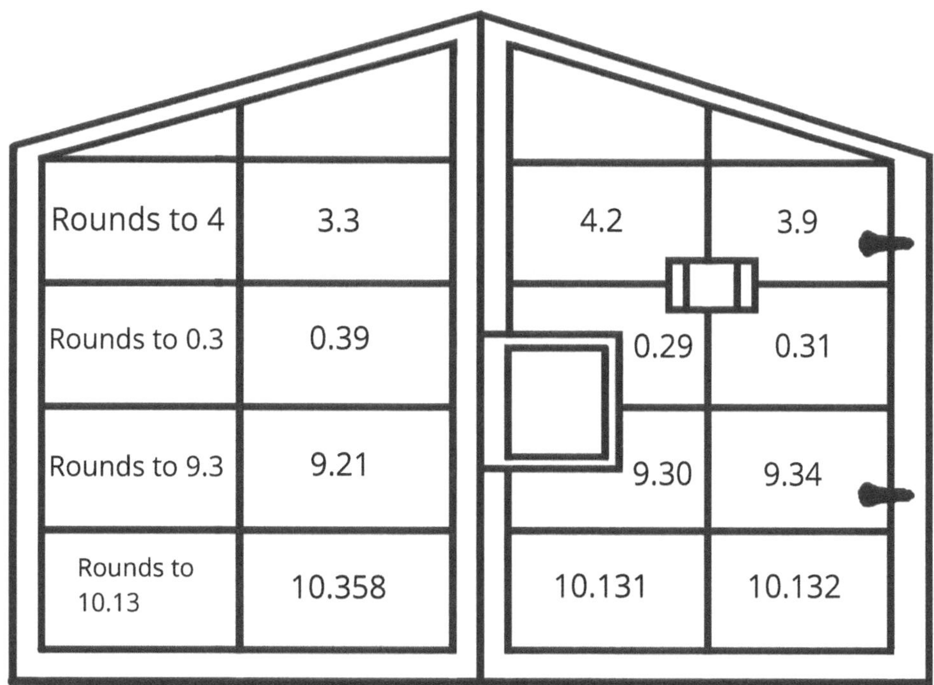

"Behold, I stand at the door, and knock: If any man hear my voice, and open the door, I will come in to him, and will sup with him, and he with me."

Revelation 3:20

4 Order from smallest to largest.

0.12 0.04 .025 0.42 0.39

_______ _______ _______ _______ _______

5 Find all numbers which round to 300 and color them yellow.
Find all numbers which round to 500 and color them green.

203	198	354	229
152	242 298	304 561	387
212	365 289	98	426
562 521	489	525	356

6 Solve.

$6 + n = 5 \times 2$ $4 + n = 5 \times 3$ $n + 7 = 3 \times 6$

7 Solve.

If it is 10:00 A.M. in Dallas, Texas, what time is it in the following cities:

New York? _________ San Francisco? _________ Anchorage? _________

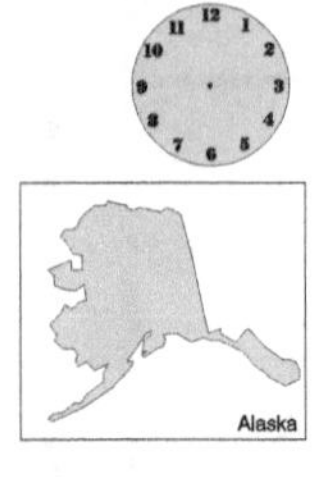

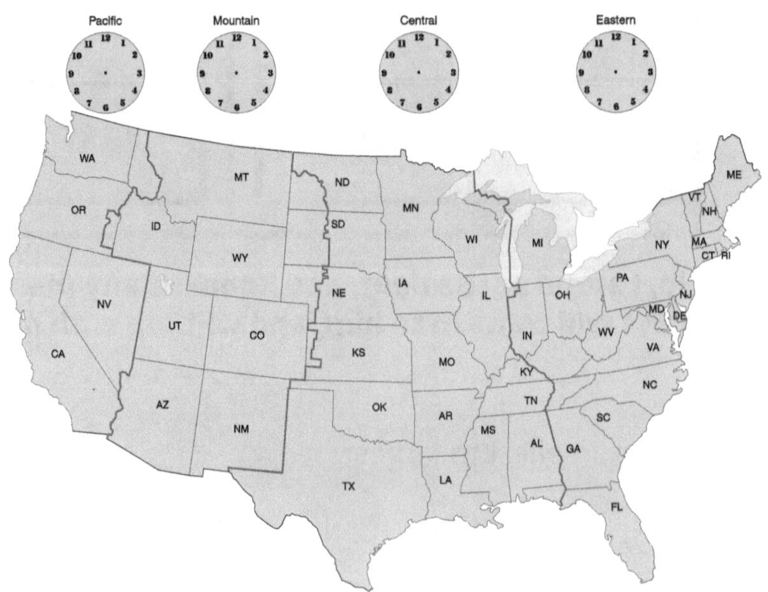

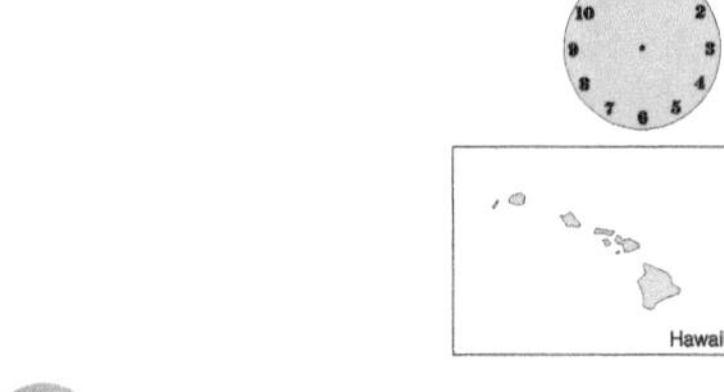

8 Solve.

$\frac{5}{15} - \frac{3}{15} =$ $\frac{35}{50} + \frac{3}{50} =$

$\frac{2}{5} + \frac{1}{5} =$ $\frac{9}{17} - \frac{6}{17} =$

Estimate Addition

Estimating is a skill used almost every day. To estimate, we round each addend to the nearest whole number, or dollar, and then add or subtract.

Actual		Rounded	
8.89		9	
+ 10.40		+ 10	
19.29	Actual answer	19	Estimated answer

Actual		Rounded	
2.56		3	
– 1.23		– 1	
1.33	Actual answer	2	Estimated answer

1 Estimate the sum or difference by rounding to the nearest whole number.

$\begin{array}{r} 8.49 \\ +\ 3.76 \\ \hline \end{array}$ $\begin{array}{r} 9.24 \\ -\ 5.70 \\ \hline \end{array}$ $\begin{array}{r} 15.49 \\ +\ 9.46 \\ \hline \end{array}$

$\begin{array}{r} 7.36 \\ -\ 1.39 \\ \hline \end{array}$ $\begin{array}{r} 66.30 \\ +\ 15.41 \\ \hline \end{array}$ $\begin{array}{r} 36.89 \\ -\ 12.06 \\ \hline \end{array}$

2 Solve.

$\begin{array}{r} 3.7 \\ +\ 1.\square \\ \hline 5.2 \end{array}$ $\begin{array}{r} 6.2 \\ -\ 2.\square \\ \hline 4.0 \end{array}$ $\begin{array}{r} 0.8\square \\ +\ 0.25 \\ \hline 1.10 \end{array}$ $\begin{array}{r} 8.\square \\ -\ 2.2 \\ \hline 6.2 \end{array}$ $\begin{array}{r} 19.3 \\ +\square.1 \\ \hline 39.4 \end{array}$

3 Write two numbers which would round to the given number.

6.1 ______ ______

9.4 ______ ______

24.0 ______ ______

5.6 ______ ______

4 Follow the numbers which round to 3,000 or 7,000 in order to find a path through the maze.

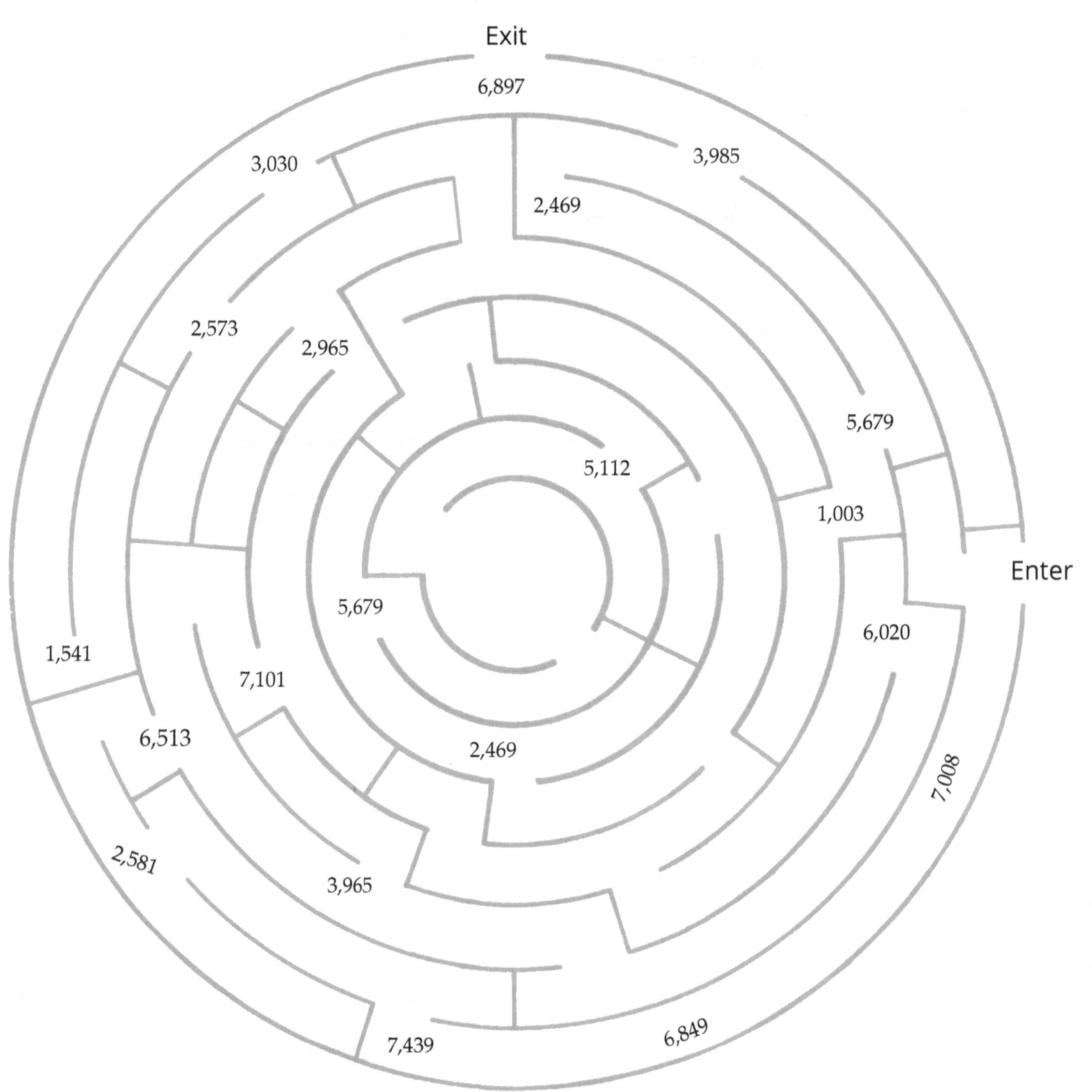

"Straight is the gate, and narrow is the way, which leadeth unto life, and few there be that find it."

Matthew 7:14

5 Solve.

$7{,}823 + 460 + n = 8{,}293$	$539 + n + 6 = 562$	$n + 692 + 48 = 747$

6 Choose the correct term from the Word Box.

Christ was born almost two _________ ago.

Lori is 30 years old. That is three ________.

Noah's son Shem died when he was 500 years, or 5 ________ old.

Word Box:
decades
centuries
millennium
years

7 Circle the numbers with a 4 in the tenths' place.

12.36 0.23 5.43 0.49 65.04 10.42

Estimate Money

Molly went to the grocery store to purchase a few items. She only had $10.00 to spend, and needed to make sure she didn't go over that amount. She decided to try and add each item as she shopped, so she would know when she had $10.00 worth of merchandise. How can she do this in her head, without a calculator, and still be accurate?

Sometimes we don't need an exact answer to an addition or subtraction problem; especially when we are adding several numbers, or dollar, amounts. An estimated answer will do in situations like these. To estimate a problem, round each number to be added or subtracted to the nearest dollar, or whole number.

Molly picked up the following items:			In her head Molly **rounded and added**:	
milk	$2.69		$3.00	milk
bread	$1.15	→	$1.00	bread
salami	$3.69	→	$4.00	salami
cheese	$1.59	→	$2.00	cheese
actual total:	$9.12	→	$10.00	estimated total

1 Add.
Sally has $4.00 to spend in the candy store. She may purchase 3 different bags of candy. Round each amount to the nearest dollar and then circle the 3 items she may purchase and still stay under $4.00.

Chocolate bars	$2.69 per bag	______
Hard Candy	$1.75 per bag	______
Lollipop	$0.75 per bag	______
Bubble Gum	$2.55 per bag	______
Licorice	$1.25 per bag	______
Chocolate covered cherries	$3.00 per bag	______

2 Some of the problems are incorrect. Circle the correct problems.

$$\begin{array}{r} 13.7 \\ +\ 34.8 \\ \hline 45.8 \end{array} \qquad \begin{array}{r} 7.81 \\ -\ 5.61 \\ \hline 2.20 \end{array} \qquad \begin{array}{r} 9.57 \\ +\ 0.48 \\ \hline 10.05 \end{array} \qquad \begin{array}{r} 0.76 \\ -\ 0.21 \\ \hline 0.97 \end{array} \qquad \begin{array}{r} 7.86 \\ +\ 0.18 \\ \hline 8.04 \end{array}$$

3 Round to the nearest 1,000.

15,689	54,460	3,561	1,289	123,945	978
______	______	______	______	______	______

4 Write the correct word.

5 + 4 = 9, 4 + 5 = 9 is an example of the ______________ property of addition.

8 – 0 = 8 is an example of the ___________ property.

In the equation 25 ÷ 5 = 5 the red number is the ___________.

In the number 145,258,489,309 the 2 is in the ___________________ place.

5 Write A.M. or P.M.

Brett ate lunch at 12:45 _______.

Cindy called the doctor when his office opened at 8:30 _______.

Chad went to bed at 10:00 _______.

Kathryn ate breakfast at 7:30 _______.

6 Use the following numbers to write a number with a 2 in the tenths' place.

8 2 0 3 4

____

7 Keith and Megan are practicing their rounding skills at the grocery store while their mother is shopping. Help them through the maze by finding prices that round to an odd dollar amount.

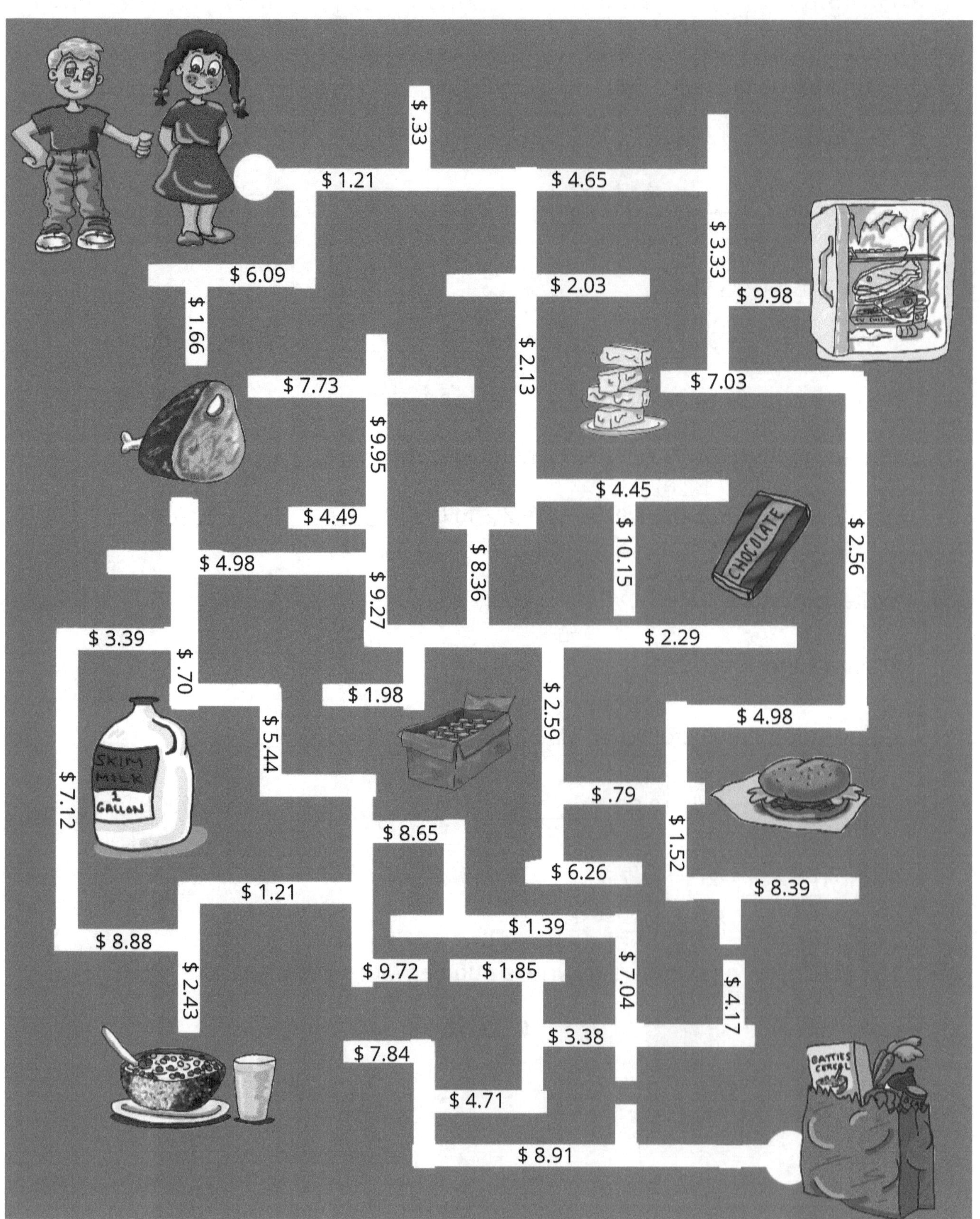

Problem Solving

Katie needs to hang a wallpaper border in a rectangular room. One wall is 16 feet long and another wall is 24 feet long. How much wallpaper border will she need?

Draw pictures to help you solve problems. Katie knows that the room is a rectangle:

Katie also knows that one wall is 16 ft and another wall is 24 feet:

16 ft

24 ft

We know that a rectangle's opposing sides are of equal length, so there are 2 sides that are 24 ft and two sides that are 16 ft.

24 + 24 + 16 + 16 = 80 ft (or) (24 x 2) + (16 x 2) = 80 ft

Katie will need at least 80 feet of border.

1 Draw a picture and solve.

The Pentagon in Washington, DC is a building built with 5 equal sides. If one side of the building is 320 feet long, what is the perimeter of the building?

Sabrina needs to have a picture framed. The picture is a rectangle with a width of 24 inches. The length is twice as long as the width. Calculate the perimeter of the picture so Sabrina will know how much picture frame moulding to buy.

Kevin is purchasing a piece of land and needs to fence the entire property. The land is in a triangular shape. Side one is 450 feet long. Side two is half that long. The third side is 15 feet longer than the second side. What is the perimeter of the lot?

2 Match.

$10.00 – 5.35	4 - one dollar bills, 2 - quarters
$25.00 – 20.50	4 - one dollar bills, 1 - quarter
$5.00 – .75	4 - one dollar bills, 2 - quarters, 1 - nickel, 1 - dime

3 Correct the incorrect problems.

Carla went to bed at 10:30 A.M.

Susie ate breakfast at 8:00 A.M.

Sarah ate lunch at 12:45 A.M.

Mary & Becky got out of school at 3:00 A.M.

4 Write the correct answer on the blank from the word bank.

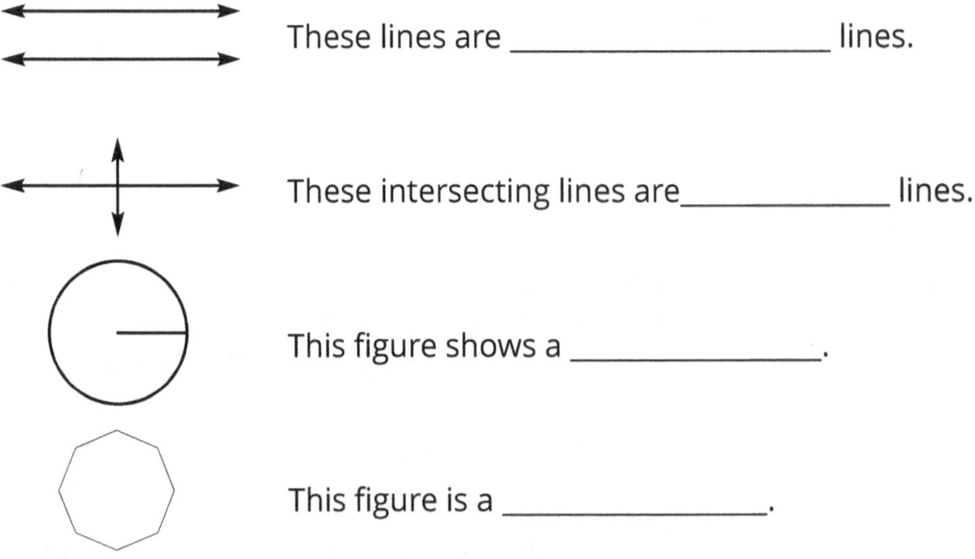

These lines are ____________________ lines.

These intersecting lines are_____________ lines.

This figure shows a _______________.

This figure is a ________________.

Word Bank: (not all will be used)

hexagon octagon radius diameter parallel perpendicular intersecting

5 Write an equivalent fraction.

$\frac{1}{2} =$ $\frac{1}{3} =$

$\frac{1}{5} =$ $\frac{3}{5} =$

6 Reduce.

$\frac{10}{20} =$ $\frac{50}{100} =$

$\frac{2}{4} =$ $\frac{3}{6} =$

$\frac{12}{16} =$ $\frac{9}{21} =$

7 Order from smallest to largest.

$\frac{1}{2}$ $\frac{1}{3}$ $\frac{1}{6}$ $\frac{1}{4}$

______ ______ ______ ______

8 Add or subtract.

$\frac{1}{8} + \frac{3}{4} =$ $\frac{1}{3} + \frac{1}{2} =$ $\frac{1}{3} - \frac{1}{6} =$ $\frac{7}{8} - \frac{2}{4} =$

Measure to the $\frac{1}{4}$ inch

Rita used a drill bit to make a hole. How long was the drill bit?

Several units of length are used in the customary system of measurement. The inch (in) is one of these units which is used to measure short lengths.

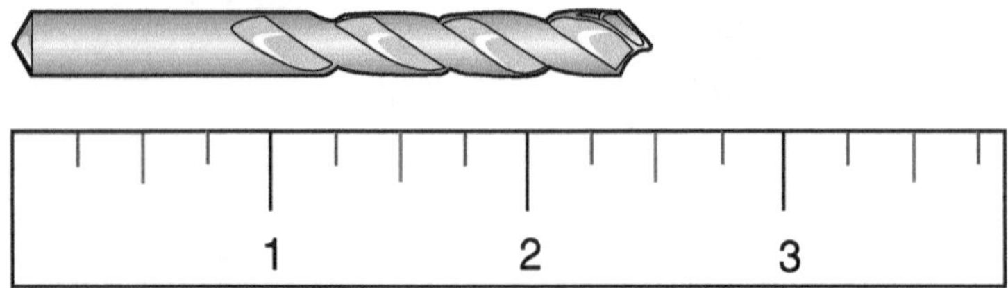

When looking at the ruler above, the numbered lines indicate how many inches long the drill bit is. The red lines indicate a measurement spacing of $\frac{1}{2}$ of an inch. The blue lines indicate a measurement spacing of $\frac{1}{4}$ of an inch.

When we place the drill bit next to the ruler, we can see that the drill bit which Rita used was $2\frac{1}{2}$ inches long.

Look at the following example.

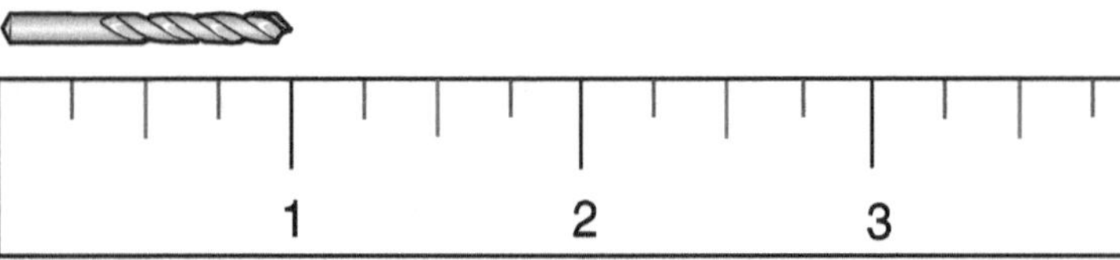

The drill bit shown is 1 inch long.

Answer.

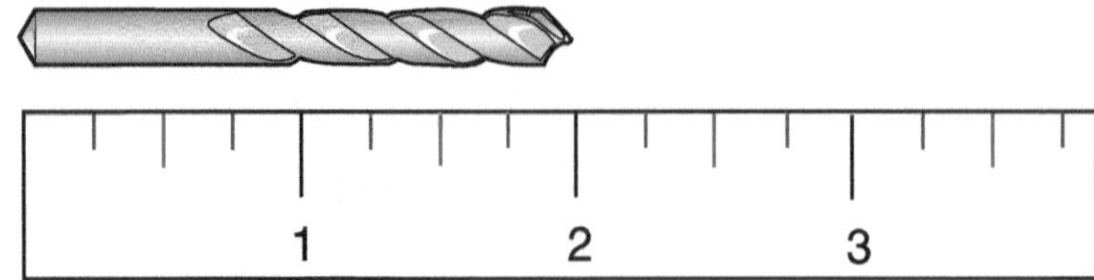

__________ inches long.

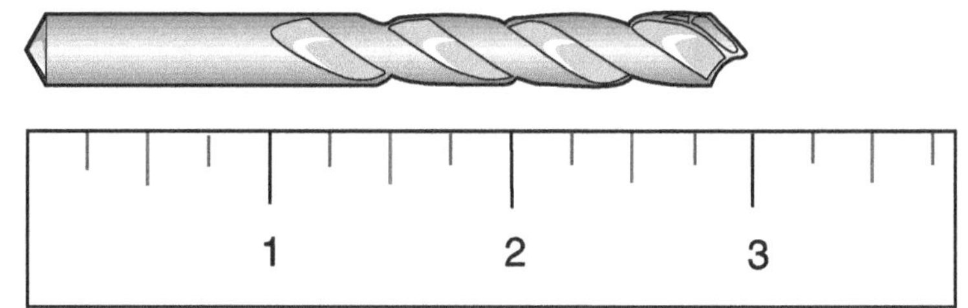

___________ inches long.

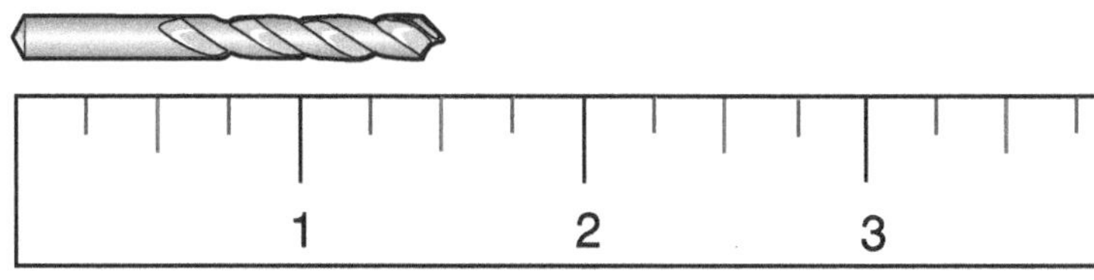

___________ inches long.

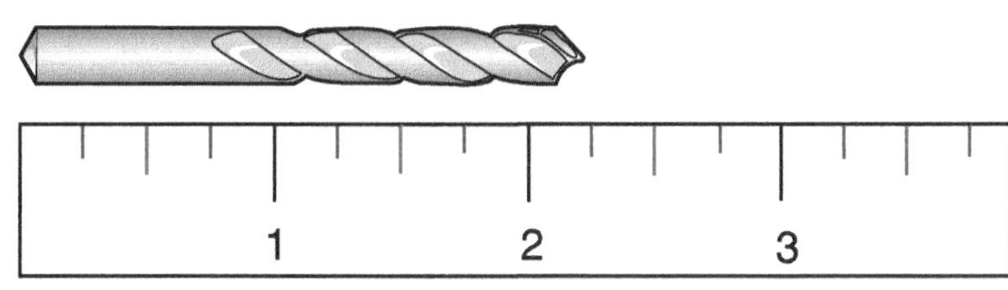

___________ inches long

2 Solve. Find the answers and connect the dots by following the order in which the problems are written.

42.05 - 0.85	34.91 - 6.29	25.41 - 9.50	71.30 - 12.60	52.31 - 7.90
38.9 - 9.25	29.65 - 5.8	31.65 - 3.03	12.86 - 10.47	

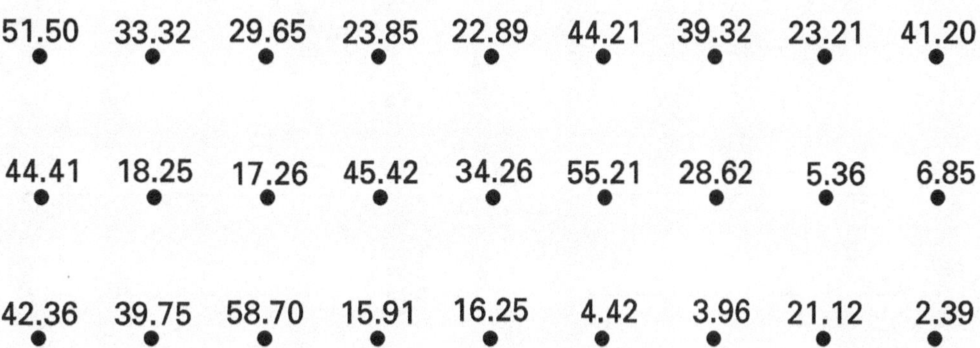

3 Estimate by rounding to the nearest dollar.

```
  $6.00        $7.25        $4.35
+  2.98      -  3.56      +  4.50

      $6.97        $2.05
    -  1.87      +  5.67
```

4 Find the difference.

```
  554     874     687     542     803     605
- 260   - 763   - 198   - 439   - 596   - 164
```

5 Divide.

$28\overline{)148}$ $37\overline{)228}$ $53\overline{)426}$ $82\overline{)419}$

6 Write the change due.

Total Purchase	Amount Given	Change Due
$86.20	$100.00	
$140.25	$150.00	
$24.49	$25.00	
$2.97	$5.00	

7 Write two equivalent fractions.

$\frac{1}{4}$ = ______________ $\frac{1}{3}$ = ______________

$\frac{1}{2}$ = ______________ $\frac{1}{5}$ = ______________

Test 13

50 points total Lessons 116-125

1 Find the sum. Reduce the answer to lowest terms. 5 pts. total for this exercise.

$4\frac{4}{8} + 3\frac{2}{8}$ $\qquad$ $3\frac{4}{7} + 4\frac{1}{7}$ $\qquad$ $8\frac{3}{15} + 8\frac{4}{15}$ $\qquad$ $1\frac{2}{9} + 3\frac{4}{9}$ $\qquad$ $17\frac{3}{10} + 2\frac{2}{10}$

2 Find the difference. Reduce the answer to lowest terms. 5 pts. total for this exercise.

$3\frac{4}{7} - 3\frac{1}{7}$ $\qquad$ $5\frac{4}{8} - 1\frac{1}{8}$ $\qquad$ $8\frac{10}{10} - 3\frac{4}{10}$ $\qquad$ $5\frac{5}{8} - 3\frac{5}{8}$ $\qquad$ $17\frac{5}{6} - 9\frac{4}{6}$

3 Find the sum. Reduce to lowest terms. 4 pts. total for this exercise.

$3\frac{6}{8} + 5\frac{6}{8} =$ $\qquad$ $2\frac{7}{12} + 1\frac{5}{12} =$ $\qquad$ $6\frac{5}{7} + 8\frac{4}{7} =$ $\qquad$ $12\frac{9}{10} + 7\frac{9}{10} =$

4 Use the pictures of the dogs to answer the following questions. 5 pts. total for this exercise.

1. How many dogs have red collars?
2. How many black dogs have red collars?
3. How many black dogs have red collars or blue collars?
4. How many dogs have brown hair and blue collars?
5. How many dogs have black hair or blue collars?

5 4 pts. total for this exercise.

We write: _________ We write: _________

We read: ________________ We read: ________________

6 Match. 4 pts. total for this exercise.

0.45	ninety hundredths
1.45	forty-five hundredths
0.09	nine hundredths
0.90	one and forty-five hundredths

7 < , > , or =. 8 pts. total for this exercise.

4.7 ◯ 4.4 1.07 ◯ 1.70 9.67 ◯ 9.78 0.06 ◯ 0.84

0.760 ◯ 0.740 5.070 ◯ 5.700 .607 ◯ .067 0.306 ◯ 0.340

8 Round to the nearest whole number. 5 pts. total for this exercise.

3.3 _____ 7.5 _____ 11.80 _____ 123.14 _____ 105.09 _____

9 Round to the nearest tenth. 5 pts. total for this exercise.

0.24 _____ 0.99 _____ 1.91 _____ 0.07 _____ 8.67 _____

10 Add. 5 pts. total for this exercise.

$$\begin{array}{r} 4.90 \\ +\ 8.09 \\ \hline \end{array} \quad \begin{array}{r} 34.55 \\ +\ 1.09 \\ \hline \end{array} \quad \begin{array}{r} 55.21 \\ +\ 4.50 \\ \hline \end{array} \quad \begin{array}{r} 77.00 \\ +\ 9.88 \\ \hline \end{array} \quad \begin{array}{r} 69.09 \\ +\ 68.93 \\ \hline \end{array}$$

Linear Measurement Conversions

The Lord instructed Noah to build an ark 450 ft long, 75 ft wide, and 45 ft high. Once you understand customary units of measurement, you will be able to understand the gigantic proportions of this boat.

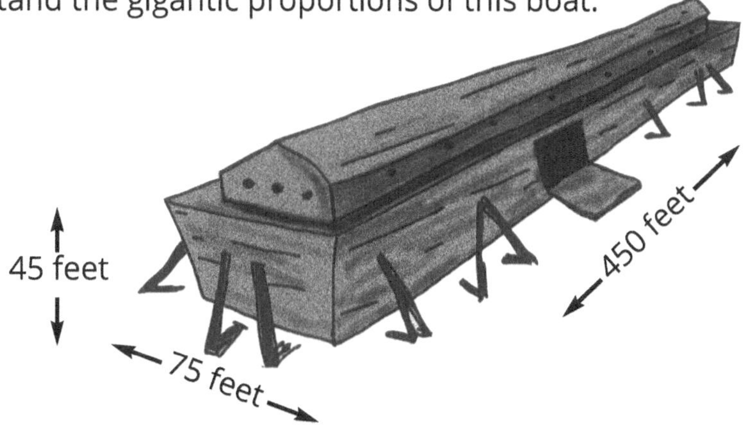

Other customary units of measure, besides inches, are feet (ft), yards (yd), and miles (mi).

12 in = 1 foot (ft)
3 ft = 1 yard (yd)
5,280 ft = 1,760 yards (yd) = 1 mile (mi)

Would a car be 8 inches long or 8 feet long?

> A pen is about 8 inches long. A car would be much longer than this; therefore the car would be 8 feet long.

Would you measure the size of a playground in inches, feet, or yards?

> Playgrounds are large areas. It would make more sense to measure this area in yards and feet rather than inches.

Would you measure the distance between two towns in inches, feet, yards, or miles?

> The distance between towns is usually a long way. For this reason, we would measure this distance in miles.

A baseball bat is about 1 yard long. How many feet would that be? (3)

The room is 9 feet long. How many yards is this? (3)

1 Look at the following items. Would each one be measured in feet, yards, or miles?

The small room was 7 ____________ long. (feet, yards, or miles)
The ceiling was 8 ____________ tall. (feet, yards, or miles)
The house was 10 ____________ from town. (feet, yards, or miles)
The football field was 120 ____________ long. (feet, yards, or miles)

2 Complete.

6 yd = _____ ft

2 yd = _____ ft

24 ft = _____ yd

2 miles = _____ yd

220 yd = _____ ft

3 Complete.

3 ft = _____ in 6 ft = _____ in 2 ft = _____ in 10 ft = _____ in

4 Use the chart to find the price of each item. Round the price to the nearest dollar. Round prices that are less than a dollar to the nearest half or whole dollar. Then find the estimated cost of the items in the grocery bag.

Cheese	$2.89 per lb	Apples	$0.49 per lb
Bread	$1.59	Cereal	$3.98
Milk	$2.49 per gal	Squash	$0.40 per lb
Eggs	$1.25 doz.	Soup	$0.95

Which grocery bag was the most expensive? _____________________

5 Solve.

```
  4.17      3.54     12.09      9.85     13.68
- 1.86    + 1.74   -  4.35    + 4.50   -  8.75
```

6 Solve.

```
  306      200     5,000     8,001
- 128    - 155   - 3,201   - 6,220
```

7 Divide.

12)60   11)99   21)63   15)60

8 Complete.

1243 is in the __________ century.

1546 is in the __________ century.

1971 is in the __________ century.

1889 is in the __________ century.

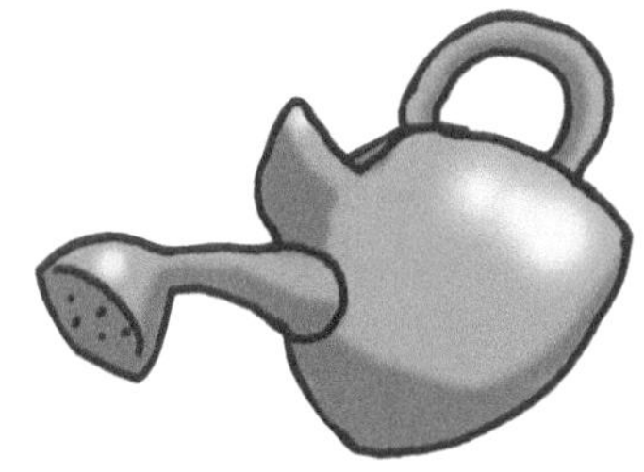

9 Complete the Fraction flower by writing in fractions which reduce (rename to lowest terms) to the fraction in the middle of the flower.

Weight Conversions

Customary Units of Measurement

Length	**Weight**
inch (in)	ounce (oz)
foot (ft)	pound (lb)
yard (yd)	ton (T)
mile (mi)	

Mr. Jones runs an old general store in a small mountain town. He sells coffee, flour, sugar, and other cooking items by weight. It is important for him to understand customary units of weight like ounces, pounds, and tons. Look at the examples below:

Butter 4 sticks	Hot Chocolate	16 ounces = 1 pound 2000 pounds = 1 ton
1 pound	1 ounce	1 ton

Would a watermelon weigh 2 ounces, 2 pounds, or 2 tons?

Since one ounce is about the weight of a package of hot chocolate, and one ton is about the weight of a pick-up truck, the watermelon would weigh 2 pounds.

If a customer asked Mr. Jones for $\frac{1}{2}$ a pound of hamburger meat, how many ounces is this?

16 ounces equals 1 lb, so 8 ounces equals $\frac{1}{2}$ a lb.

1 Write the correct unit of measure.

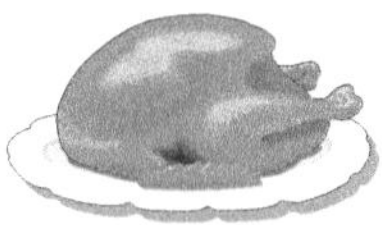

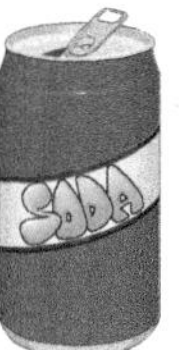

The bus weighs 2 _____. The turkey weighs 10 _____. The can weighs 12 _____.

The onion rings weigh 8 _____. The bag of flour weighs 5 _____.

2 Solve.

Write foot, yard, or mile.	Convert.
The city bus measures 33 ______ long.	3 yd = _____ feet
The Amazon River is 3,912 _______ long.	_____ ft = 1 mile
The football field is 100 _______ long.	24 feet = _____ yd

3 Choose the correct answer.

The spikes which were used to crucify Jesus were about 11 __________ long.

The cross on which Jesus was crucified was approximately 10 __________ tall.

4 Use a ruler to measure the following.

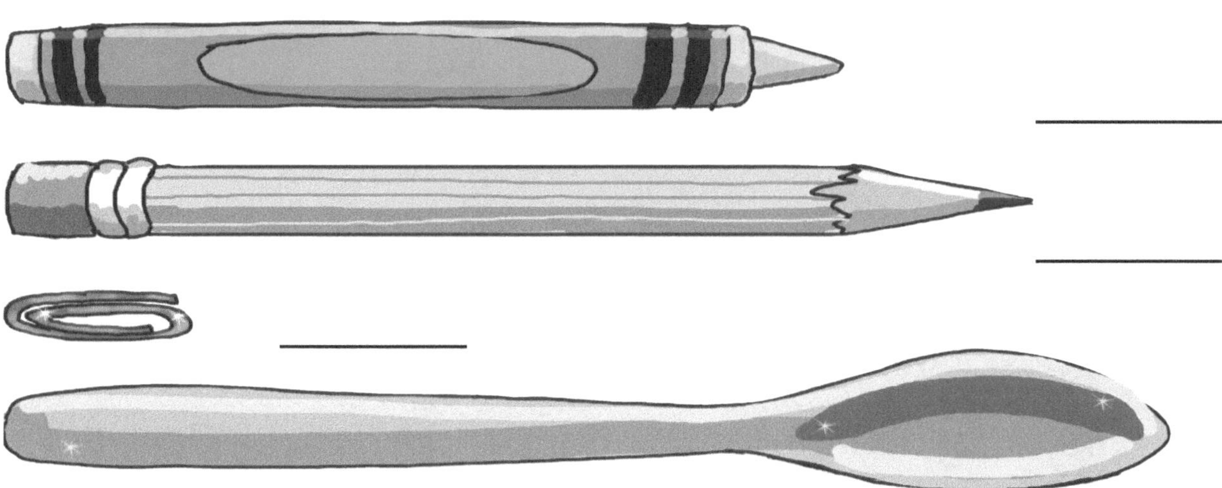

5 Estimate by rounding to the nearest hundred or thousand.

\$553.00	\$780.00	\$5,541.00	\$6,088.00
+ 260.00	- 520.00	+ 3,429.00	- 3,198.00

6 Solve.

$n - 1 = 8 \div 8$ $\quad$ $n - 0 = 50 + 0$ $\quad$ $n \times 8 = 4 \times 10$ $\quad$ $n \times 1 = 26 - 1$

7 Divide.

33)705 $\quad$ 50)550 $\quad$ 22)382 $\quad$ 31)696

8 Write a year for each century.

18th century __________

19th century __________

15th century __________

17th century __________

9 Reduce to lowest terms.

$\frac{50}{100}$ = __________ $\quad$ $\frac{4}{12}$ = __________

$\frac{9}{27}$ = __________ $\quad$ $\frac{5}{25}$ = __________

Liquid Measure

Kathy needed to water her ferns and give them some plant food. The directions on the container of plant food instructed her to mix two scoops of food with one gallon of water. If Kathy only has quart size containers how much will equal one gallon?

=

4 quarts equal 1 gallon. Kathy will need to mix 4 quart size containers with two scoops of food to equal a gallon container.

Look at these:

8 quarts = ____ gallon(s)

=

8 pints = ____ gallon(s)

=

1 Solve.

3 gal = ____ qt

4 pt = ____ qt

4 c = ____ qt

$\frac{1}{2}$ pt = ____ c

2 Match.

small can of soup	150 lb
a package of 2 ping pong balls	$1\frac{1}{2}$ T
refrigerator	$9\frac{1}{2}$ lb
mini-van	20 lb
a small dog	11 oz
Christmas ham	2 oz

3 Write >, <, or =.

$1\frac{1}{2}$ mi ◯ 5,360 ft   6,000 ft ◯ 2 mi   15 yd ◯ 235 ft

4 Measure each line segment in the shape below.

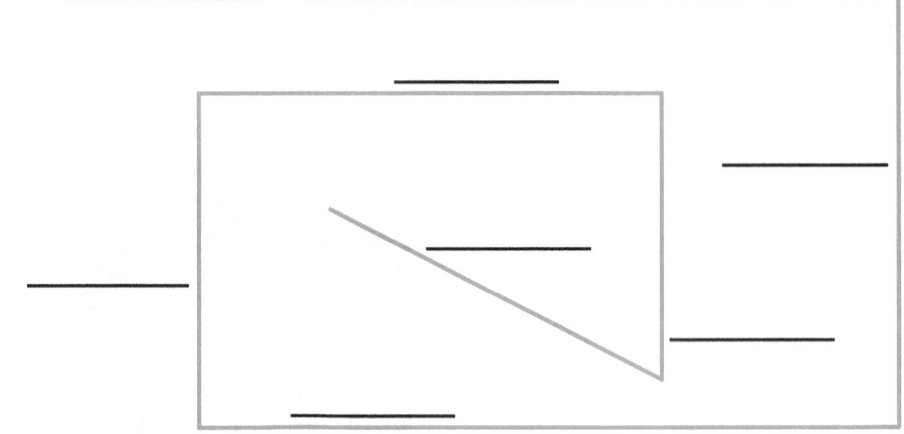

5 Solve.

$n - 5 = 10$ $n - 10 = 4$ $n - 9 = 15$ $n - 7 = 30$

6 Divide.

$2\overline{)98}$ $5\overline{)75}$ $7\overline{)91}$ $3\overline{)90}$

7 Solve.

$\frac{3}{8} + \frac{1}{4} =$ $\frac{2}{7} - \frac{1}{14} =$ $\frac{5}{9} + \frac{1}{3} =$ $\frac{8}{10} - \frac{1}{2} =$

Temperature

What is the temperature?

___________ ___________ ___________

We usually hear temperature measured in Fahrenheit degrees.
Look at the thermometer below to get an idea of the best temperature estimate for each item drawn. Write your estimates on the blanks.

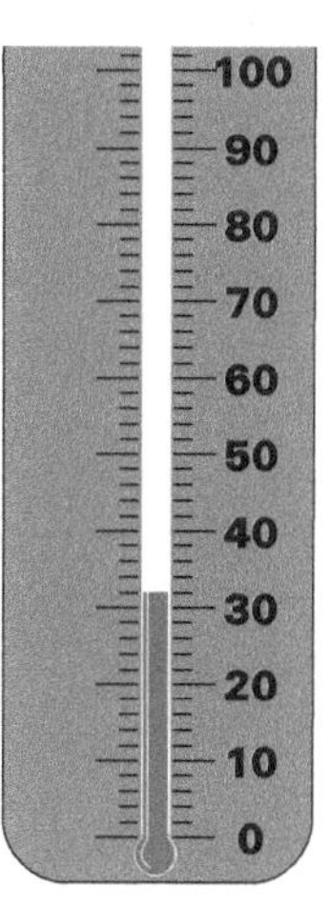

Normal Body Temperature is 98.6°

Comfortable Room Temperature is 70°

Water Freezes at 32°

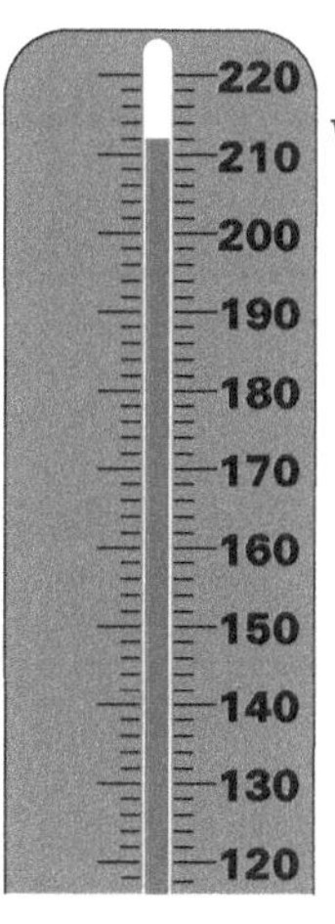

Water Boils at 212°

1 Give each temperature in degrees Fahrenheit.

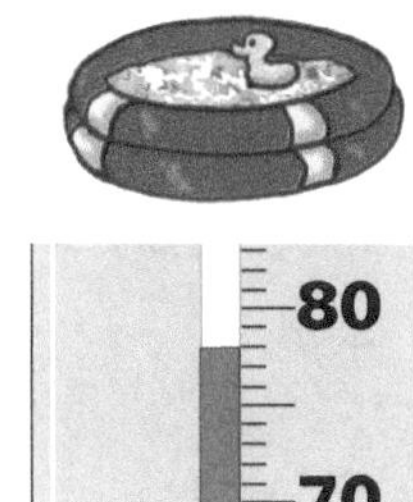

___________ ___________ ___________

2 Complete the crossword puzzle.

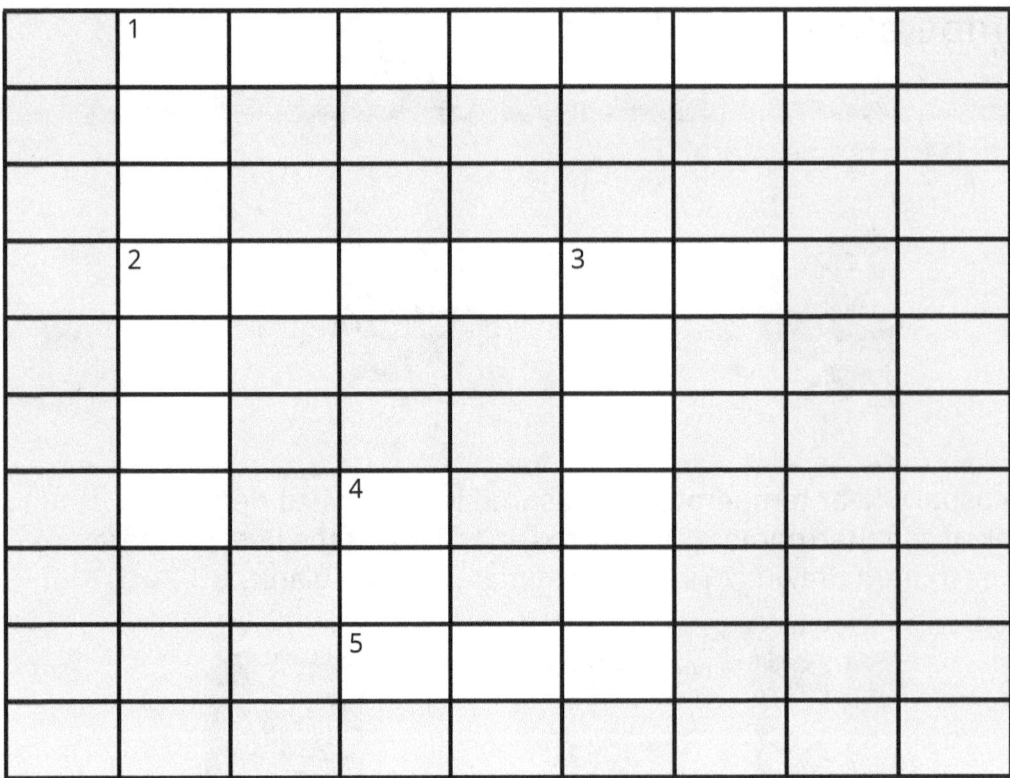

ACROSS	DOWN
1. 1 gal = ___ c	1. 2 gal = ___ pt
2. 5 qt = ___ c	3. 6 pt = ___ c
5. $\frac{1}{2}$ pt = ___ c	4. $\frac{1}{2}$ gal = ___ qt

3 Draw a circle around the best estimate.

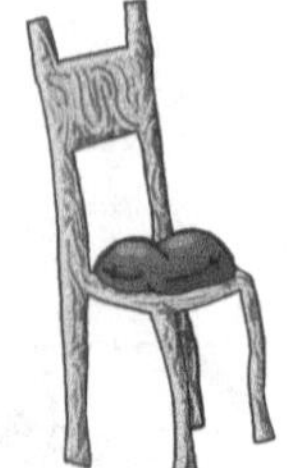		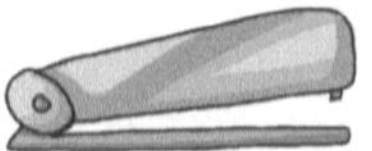	
A kitchen chair	Soda can	A hand-held stapler	A small car
3 oz	4 lb	8 oz	55 lb
3 lb	12 oz	4 T	100 oz
3 T	10 T	9 lb	1 T

4 Solve.

25 yd = ____ ft   3 mi = ____ ft   144 in = ____ yd   9 yd = ____ in

5 Add.

84	63	25	47	98	20
+ 15	+ 21	+ 13	+ 52	+ 31	+ 14

6 Average.

34, 22, 3, 25   22, 28, 24, 27, 19   34, 21, 32, 37, 73, 13

7 Solve.

$4\frac{2}{5} + 6\frac{1}{5} =$ $9\frac{7}{12} - 5\frac{3}{12} =$ $11\frac{7}{32} + 21\frac{4}{32} =$

Temperature

Charles watched the nightly news to get the weather report for the next day. When the weatherman reported the temperature, he gave a measurement in degrees Celsius. This confused Charles. He had always heard the temperature reported in Fahrenheit degrees. What is the difference?

Celsius is a Metric unit of measurement for temperature while Fahrenheit is a customary unit of measurement for temperature.

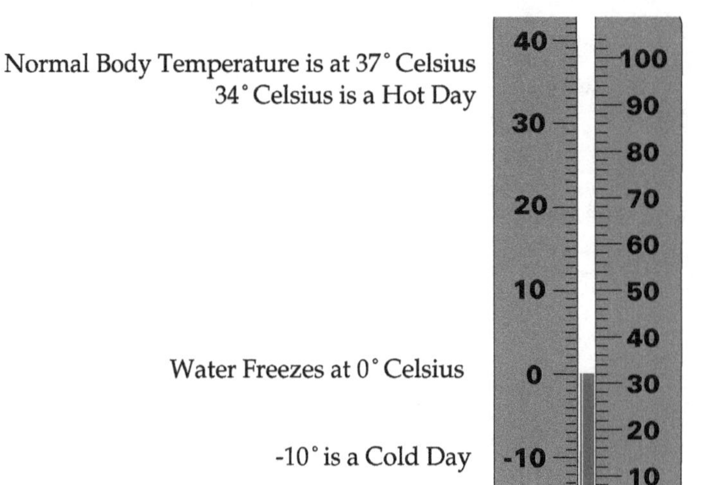

1 Write each temperature shown.

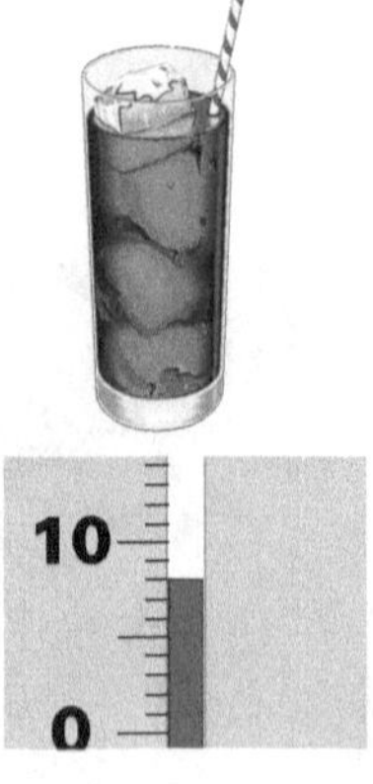

________ C ________ C ________ F

2 Answer in Fahrenheit degrees.

The normal body temperature is _____ F.

A warm day would be a temperature of _____ F.

A cold day would be a temperature of _____ F.

A freezer would have a temperature of _____ F.

3 Complete.

Y	A	R	D	G	I	N	C	H	F
R	D	A	J	F	E	Q	C	M	O
N	W	C	U	P	A	U	X	U	O
O	P	C	R	I	O	A	N	S	T
U	M	U	C	N	T	R	K	A	R
N	H	Y	L	T	L	T	O	N	E
C	P	O	U	N	D	K	L	V	M
E	N	P	V	I	D	D	Y	P	I
B	F	G	A	L	L	O	N	T	L
H	S	H	W	O	Q	F	T	Q	E

WORD BANK:

gallon quart pint cup ounce

pound ton yard foot mile inch

 Find the incorrect problems and correct them.

$$\begin{array}{r} 747 \\ +\ 556 \\ \hline 1,303 \end{array} \qquad \begin{array}{r} 724 \\ +\ 174 \\ \hline 898 \end{array} \qquad \begin{array}{r} 733 \\ +\ 125 \\ \hline 858 \end{array}$$

$$\begin{array}{r} 362 \\ +\ 113 \\ \hline 535 \end{array} \qquad \begin{array}{r} 487 \\ +\ 317 \\ \hline 704 \end{array} \qquad \begin{array}{r} 561 \\ +\ 184 \\ \hline 377 \end{array}$$

5 Write in standard form.

five tenths -

six and one tenth -

fourteen and eight tenths -

three tenths -

6 Solve.

$3 + n = 25$ $4 + n = 54$ $1 + n = 5 + 4$ $6 - 3 = n + 1$

7 Order from largest to smallest.

$\frac{7}{8}$ $\frac{0}{5}$ $\frac{1}{3}$ $\frac{1}{2}$

______ ______ ______ ______

Metric Measurements

Lisa went to the doctor for a checkup. The doctor said Lisa was 1.38 meters tall and weighed 20 kilograms. Lisa wasn't sure how much either one of these measurements were because they were in the Metric System. The Metric system is a system of weights and measures which is based on a unit of 10. The basic unit of length is called a meter (m), the basic unit of weight is called a gram, and the basic unit of capacity is called a liter. We will discuss these over the next 4 lessons.

One of the Metric system's smallest unit of length is a centimeter. Each centimeter is divided into 10 units the same exact size. This smallest unit of length is a millimeter.

10 mm = 1 centimeter
100 mm = 1 decimeter
1,000 mm = 1 meter

Caroline measured the size of her desk top. It was 24 centimeters and 4 millimeters long. She can write this information three different ways:

in both centimeter and millimeter units	24 cm / 4 mm
in only centimeter units	24.4 cm
in only millimeter units	244 mm

1 Write the three different ways each measurement may be written.

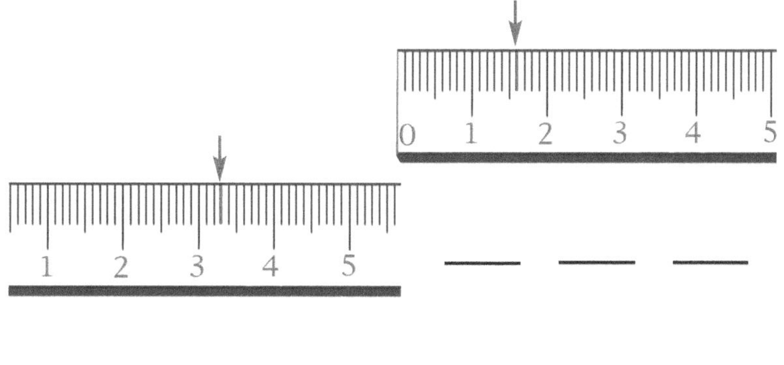

___ ___ ___

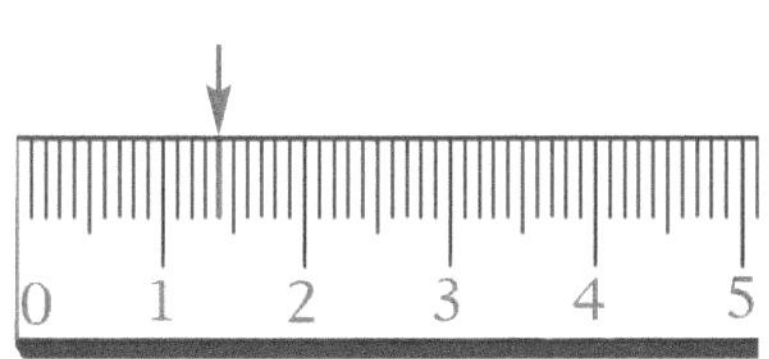

___ ___ ___

___ ___ ___

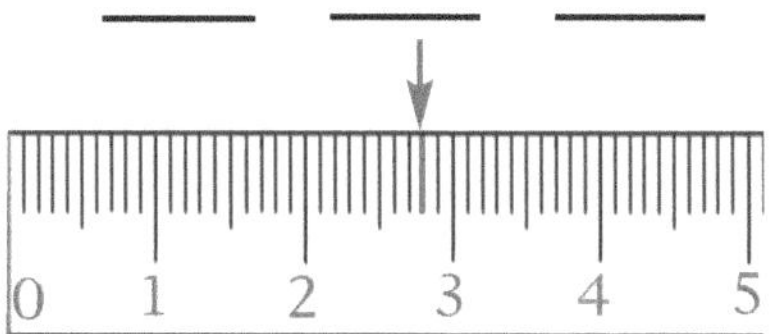

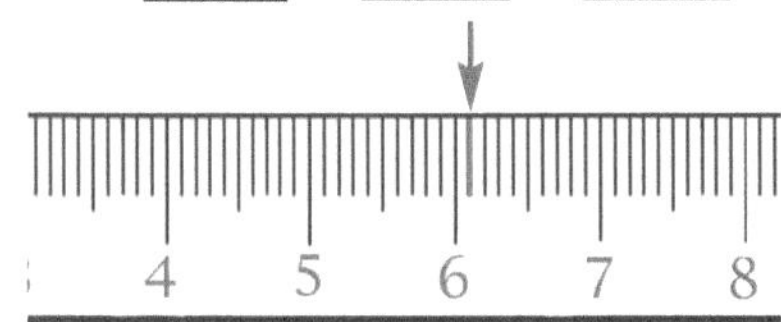

___ ___ ___

___ ___ ___

② Add.

265	119	337	409	527
921	86	252	73	762
+ 50	+ 129	+ 100	+ 661	+ 177

③ Look at each picture and tell if each temperature is Fahrenheit or Celsius.

-12° _____

170° _____

102° _____

0° _____

④ Complete.

2 gal = ______ qt

4 gal = ______ pt

4 c = ______ qt

8 pt = ______ qt

$\frac{1}{2}$ qt = ______ c

5 Color the boxes with a 5 or a 7 in the tenths' place.

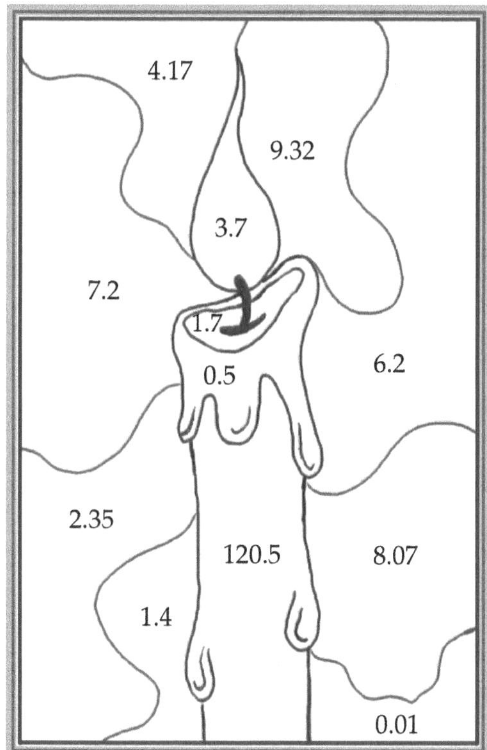

6 Write <, >, or =.

86.20 ____ 19.35 129.95 ____ 129.59

56.5 ____ 65.3 14.6 ____ 14.60

7 Match.

Right angle

Obtuse angle

Acute angle

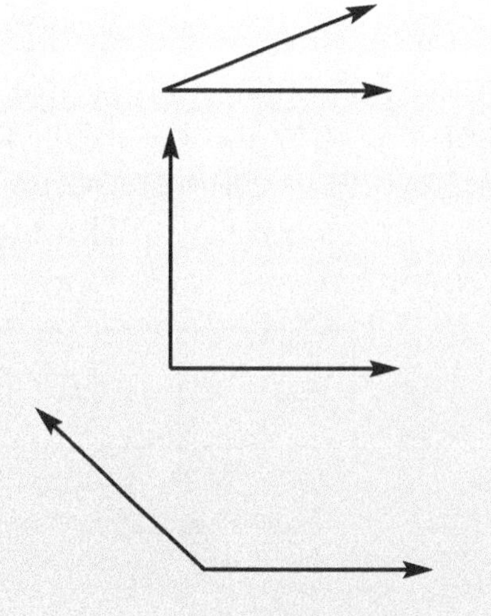

Metrics

Remember: The Metric system is a system of weights and measures which is based on a unit of 10. The basic unit of length is called a meter (m), the basic unit of weight is called a gram (g), and the basic unit of capacity is called a liter (l). All three of these units use the same prefixes to indicate a specific amount of length, weight, or liquid. Look at the conversion chart below. The prefixes are in order from the largest to the smallest going from left to right.

Kilo	Hecto	Deka	Basic Unit (Meter, Liter or Gram)	deci	centi	milli

(Kilo is the largest measurement prefix and milli is the smallest prefix measurement.)

Meter		Liter		Gram	
1000 meters	= 1 Kilometer	1000 liter	= 1 Kiloliter	1000 grams	= 1 Kilogram
100 meters	= 1 Hectometer	100 liter	= 1 Hectoliter	100 grams	= 1 Hectogram
10 meters	= 1 Dekameter	10 liter	= 1 Dekaliter	10 grams	= 1 Dekagram
Meter	= Basic Unit	Liter	= Basic Unit	Gram	= Basic Unit
0.1 meter	= 1 decimeter	0.1 liter	= 1 deciliter	0.1 gram	= 1 decigram
0.01 meter	= 1 centimeter	0.01 liter	= 1 centiliter	0.01 gram	= 1 centigram
0.001 meter	= 1 millimeter	0.001 liter	= 1 milliliter	0.001 gram	= 1 milligram

If we were measuring length, the chart below would show 12 millimeters. Because the metric system is based on units of 10, we can convert from one measurement to another measurement. (Ex: millimeter to centimeter) by simply moving a decimal because our decimal system is also based on 10. We show 12 millimeters on the conversion chart by writing the last digit of the measurement in the millimeter box. Remember from your decimal studies that if a decimal is not given in a number, we know that it is a whole number and that the decimal goes at the end. For this reason, the decimal and the number "2" are placed in the millimeter box to indicate that the original measurement was in millimeters. We are converting to centimeters so simply move the decimal one space to the left into the centimeter box. 12 millimeters = 1.2 centimeters. Check this on a ruler to see if it is correct.

					1.	2.
Kilo	Hecto	Deka	Basic Unit (Meter, Liter or Gram)	deci	centi	milli

Try another conversion: If we measured a table to be 1230 centimeters long, how many Dekameters is this?

Write the number in the conversion chart by placing the last digit "0" in the centimeter box and adding a decimal to the end since we know this is a whole number. Now simply move the decimal to the desired conversion measurement, Dekameters. 1230 centimeters = 1.230 Dekameters.

		1.	2	3	0.	
Kilo	Hecto	Deka	Basic Unit (Meter, Liter or Gram)	deci	centi	milli

Rachel Hill's mother marks her height on a special growth chart in her room. She has been marking Rachel's height since Rachel was a little girl. Today, Mrs. Hill marked Rachel's height as 139 centimeters.

How many meters is this? Use the chart below. 139 cm = 1.39 m

			1.	3	9.	
Kilo	Hecto	Deka	Basic Unit (Meter, Liter or Gram)	deci	centi	milli

Brett is 9.3 centimeters tall. How many millimeters is this?
9.3 cm = 93 mm

					9.	3.
Kilo	Hecto	Deka	Basic Unit (Meter, Liter or Gram)	deci	centi	milli

Nicolle is 1 meter **and** 10 centimeters tall. How tall is she when written only in centimeters?
Hint: Remember the word "and" means decimal when reading numbers.
1.10 m = 110 cm

			1.	1	0.	
Kilo	Hecto	Deka	Basic Unit (Meter, Liter or Gram)	deci	centi	milli

Chet is 1.80 meters tall.
How tall is he when written in centimeters?
You move the decimal to convert this number from meters to centimeters. Hint: When writing in numbers which already have a decimal in them, the decimal goes in the box that the measurement in originally given. For example: you have been given 1.80 m, so the "1" and the decimal are to be placed in the Basic Unit (Meter) box. 1.80 m = 180 cm

			1.	8	0.	
Kilo	Hecto	Deka	Basic Unit (Meter, Liter or Gram)	deci	centi	milli

1 Complete.

Kilo	Hecto	Deka	Basic Unit (Meter, Liter or Gram)	deci	centi	milli

145 mm = _____ cm

1,329 mm = _____ m

1.89 m = _____ mm

12.65 m = _____ cm

1.04 Km = _____ dm

3.40 dm = _____ mm

2 Write cm or mm.

The pencil was 8 ________ long.

The paper clip measured 25 ________.

The desktop was 27 ________ wide.

It rained 4 ________ last night.

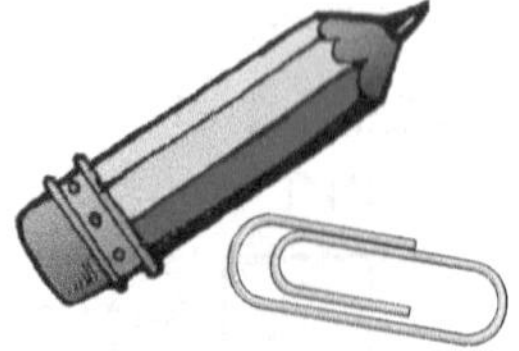

3 Complete.

Circle the best temperature estimate.

15° C 20° F 105° F

#1

0° F 0° C 20° C

#2

100° C 172° F 212° C

#3

Measuring Capacity

The Metric term **Liter** refers to the liquid unit of measurement called capacity. When going to the store to purchase a bottled soft drink, most are measured in 2 liter bottles. When dispensing medicine a doctor will sometimes prescribe a certain number of milliliters of medicine to be taken. A normal soda can holds approximately 120 ml of liquid. We can still use the Metric conversion chart from Lesson 137 to convert various liter measurements. 3,400 ml = 3.4 liters

Kilo	Hecto	Deka	Basic Unit (Meter, Liter or Gram)	deci	centi	milli

Approximately 8 liters   Approximately 700 liters   Approximately 2,500 ml

1 Complete using the conversion chart.

Kilo	Hecto	Deka	Basic Unit (Meter, Liter or Gram)	deci	centi	milli

1,000 ml = _________ L   587 L = _________ ml

1 ml = _________ L   291 ml = _________ L

33 ml = _________ L

2 Complete by writing *cm, m*, or *Km*.

A very tall telephone pole would be about 100 _______ tall.

A fighter jet is about 54 _______ long.

A knife is about 21 _______ long.

Mt. Kilimanjaro is 5,895 _______ tall.

The Nile is about 6,695 _______ long.

A pencil is 11 _______ long.

3 Match.

0°C

40°C

120°C

1°C

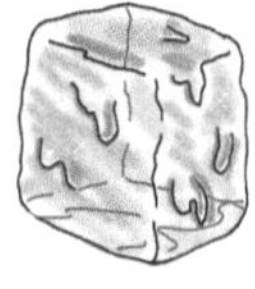

84°C

4 Solve.

$(3 + 6) + n = 15$ $n + (9 + 3) = 17$ $15 = (2 + 6) + n$

5 Draw a line which is parallel to line AB.

Draw a line which is perpendicular to line AB.

Draw a diameter in the circle below and label it segment CD.

6 Order from largest to smallest.

$\frac{1}{4}$ $\frac{9}{9}$ $\frac{1}{16}$ $\frac{3}{4}$

____ ____ ____ ____

Metric Weight

The Metric unit for measuring weight is the gram. A Kilogram is the largest measurement of weight we will discuss. We can still use our Metric conversion chart to convert weight measurements, if necessary.

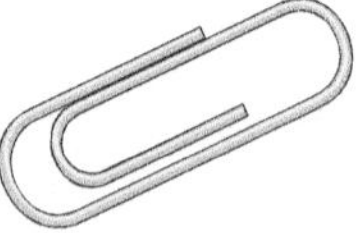

about 1 gram

about 1 gram

about 1 kilogram (Kg)

about 1 kilogram (Kg)

If a small dog weighs about 8 Kg how many grams is this?

8.	0	0	0.			
Kilo	Hecto	Deka	Basic Unit (Meter, Liter or Gram)	deci	centi	milli

8 Kg = 8,000 grams

If a small kitten weighs 125 grams how many Kilograms is this?

0.	1	2	5.			
Kilo	Hecto	Deka	Basic Unit (Meter, Liter or Gram)	deci	centi	milli

125 g = 0.125 Kg

1 Complete.

Kilo	Hecto	Deka	Basic Unit (Meter, Liter or Gram)	deci	centi	milli

Convert each weight to Kilograms (Kg) Convert each weight to grams (g)

3 g ____ 25 g ____ 710 g ____ 4 Kg ____ 56 Kg ____ 529 Kg ____

2 Choose liters or milliliters to measure each item.

The amount of water in a large bucket. ____________

The amount of tea in a glass. ____________

The amount of medicine in a dropper. ____________

The amount of jelly in a jar. ____________

The amount of gas in a drum. ____________

3 Choose kilometer, meter, centimeter, or millimeter for each measurement.

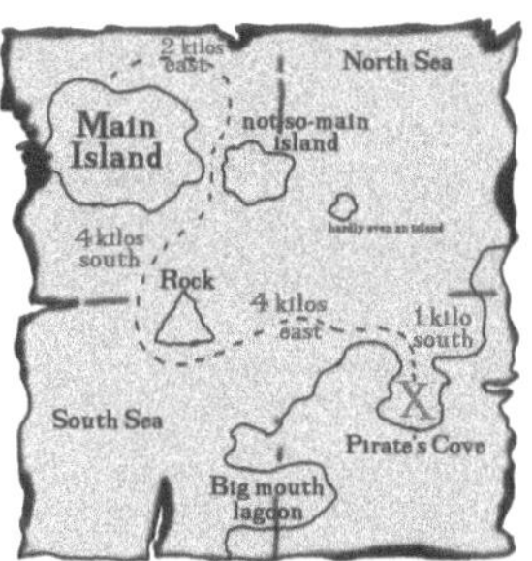

____________ ____________

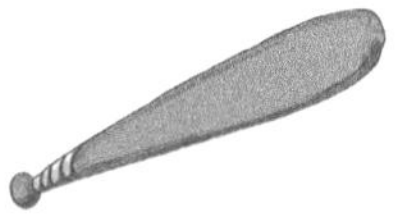

____________ ____________

(length)

(height)

_______________ _______________

4 Multiply.

```
  356      217      158      304
x  56    x  16    x  24    x  35
```

5 Write <, >, or =.

0.367 _____ 0.376   54.63 ____ 45.63   1.306 ____ 1.036

6 Add.

```
 22.85     59.27     41.55     37.59
+ 5.04    + 7.14   + 58.40    + 6.57
```

Graphs

Graphs are used to help answer questions. They show data, or information, in a visual form and many times is the best way to show information that contains numbers. Bar graphs, line graphs, pictographs, circle graphs, and coordinate graphs are the types of graphs we will discuss in the following lessons.

The Loganville First Baptist Preschool had a Fall Festival. There were several booths at the festival which made money. This information is shown in the bar graph below.

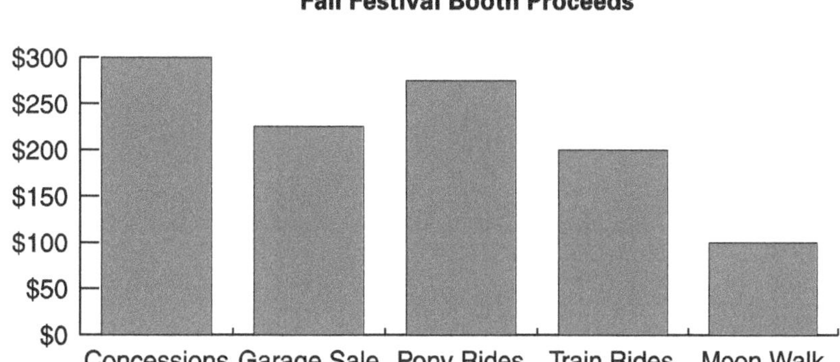

Bar graphs are used to compare related numerical information.
These graphs may be either vertical or horizontal.
This same information is presented in a horizontal bar graph below.

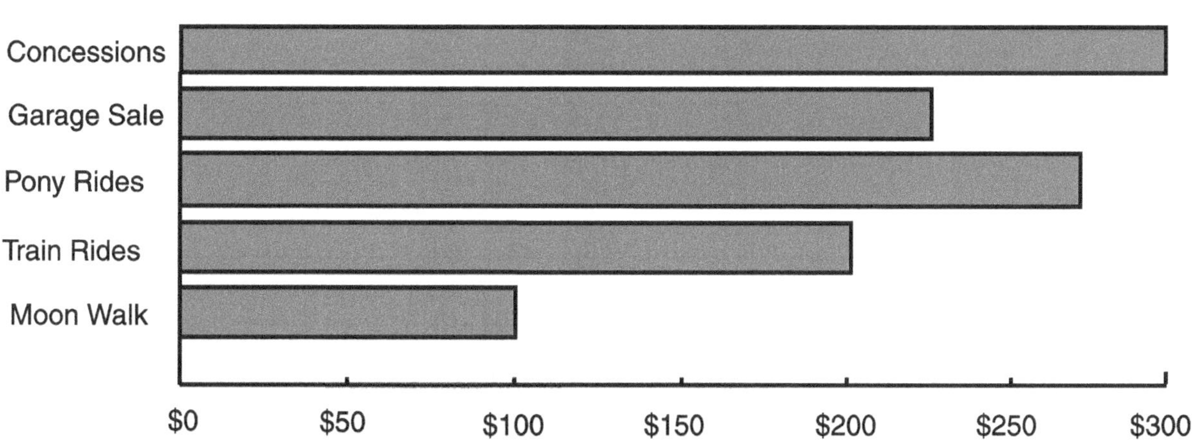

Notice the bar that is halfway between the $250.00 and the $300.00 mark. Halfway between the two numbers is $275.00. The pony rides made $275.00. How much did the garage sale and the concessions stand make together?

Concessions	$300.00
Garage Sale	+ $225.00
	$ 525.00 total sales for the concessions and the garage sale booths

1 Use the bar graphs on the previous page to answer the following questions.

How much money did the moon walk make? ______________

How much money did the festival make on train rides? ______________

Which booth made the most money? ______________

The least money? ______________

How much money did all the booths make when combined? ______________

2 Write gram or Kilogram.

Heath weighs 45 ______________.

The paper clip weighs 1 ______________.

The cup weighs 5 ______________.

The puppy dog weighs 11 ______________.

3 Complete.

Kilo	Hecto	Deka	Basic Unit (Meter, Liter or Gram)	deci	centi	milli

2,000 ml = _____ L　　　623 L = _____ ml

3 ml = _____ L　　　20 L = _____ ml

4 Circle the larger measurement in each row across to reveal a message.

P	105 cm	0.51 cm	M
E	4.2 mm	4.2 cm	R
N	20 dm	20 Km	A
O	370 cm	38 dm	Y
E	31.5 Km	31.5 Dm	N
R	1,760 mm	17.6 cm	A

"Pray without ceasing. In everything give thanks: for this is the will of God in Christ Jesus..."

1 Thessalonians 5:17-18

5 Find the difference.

$$\begin{array}{r} 521 \\ -\ 345 \\ \hline \end{array} \quad \begin{array}{r} 692 \\ -\ 108 \\ \hline \end{array} \quad \begin{array}{r} 349 \\ -\ 251 \\ \hline \end{array} \quad \begin{array}{r} 637 \\ -\ 360 \\ \hline \end{array} \quad \begin{array}{r} 507 \\ -\ 358 \\ \hline \end{array} \quad \begin{array}{r} 835 \\ -\ 223 \\ \hline \end{array}$$

6 Solve.

$n - 6 = 15$ $n - 7 = 42$ $3 - 1 = n - 5$ $n - 2 = 19 - 18$

7 Multiply.

$$\begin{array}{r} 418 \\ \times\ 43 \\ \hline \end{array} \quad \begin{array}{r} 348 \\ \times\ 27 \\ \hline \end{array} \quad \begin{array}{r} 164 \\ \times\ 52 \\ \hline \end{array} \quad \begin{array}{r} 508 \\ \times\ 39 \\ \hline \end{array} \quad \begin{array}{r} 672 \\ \times\ 81 \\ \hline \end{array}$$

1 Find the difference. 6 pts. total for this exercise.

11.00	13.49	44.59	101.49	5.33	71.96
- 6.29	- 12.40	- 10.81	- 20.47	- 5.25	- 29.99

2 Estimate the sum or difference by rounding to the nearest whole number. 4 pts.

9.99	8.80	18.50	6.32
+ 2.82	- 5.42	+ 9.87	- 2.99

3 Add. 8 pts. total for this exercise.
Trevor has $6.00 to spend in the toy store. He may purchase 2 different items. Round each amount to the nearest dollar and then circle the 2 items he may purchase and still stay under $6.00.

Lego	$3.78	truck	$5.67	mini-cars	$1.89
paint set	$4.75	game	$4.55	pencil set	$3.49

4 Draw a picture and solve. 2 pts. total for this exercise.
The square rug in Tina's room has a perimeter of 40 ft. We know that a square has 4 equal sides. What is the measure of each side of the rug?

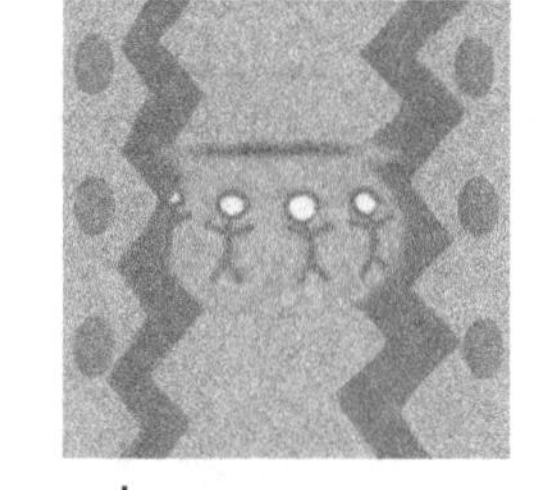

The rectangular bricks in Tony's patio each measure 10 inches in length. The perimeter of each brick is 28 inches. What is the width of each brick?

5 Measure to the nearest $\frac{1}{4}$ inch.

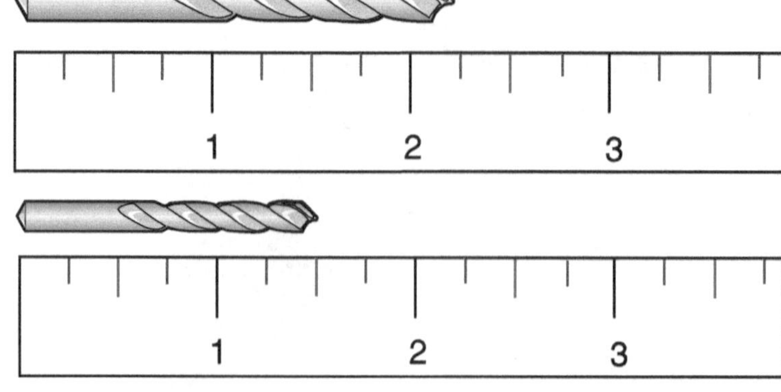

_____________ inches long

_____________ inches long

2 pts. total for above exercise.

12 inches = 1 foot (ft)	3 ft = 1 yard (yd)
1 yard = 36 inches	5,280 ft = 1,760 yards (yd) = 1 mile (mi)

6 Complete. 6 pts. total for this exercise.

2 feet = _________ inches   3 yards = _________ inches

2 yards = _________ feet   2 miles = _________ feet

36 inches = _________ yards   2 miles = _________ yards

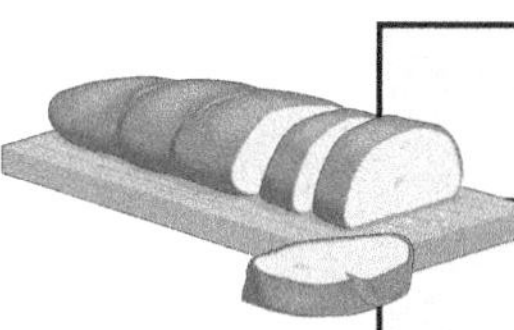

16 ounces = 1 pound	8 ounces = $\frac{1}{2}$ pound
12 ounces = $\frac{3}{4}$ pound	4 ounces = $\frac{1}{4}$ pound

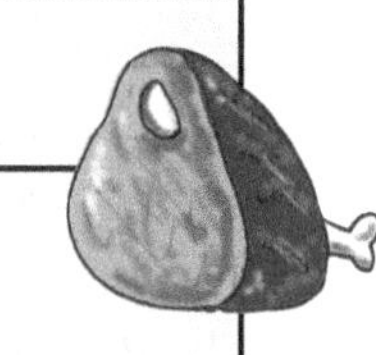

Mrs. Simms went to the deli to get food for a luncheon. She requested the items in pounds, convert these amounts to ounces. Refer to the conversion table, if necessary. 8 pts. total for this exercise.

$1\frac{1}{2}$ pounds ham = ______ ounces   2 pounds potato salad = ______ ounces

$1\frac{3}{4}$ pounds turkey = ______ ounces $2\frac{1}{2}$ pounds bean salad = ______ ounces

1 pound roast beef = ______ ounces $1\frac{1}{4}$ pounds jello = ______ ounces

3 pounds swiss cheese = ______ ounces $2\frac{3}{4}$ pounds egg salad = ______ ounces

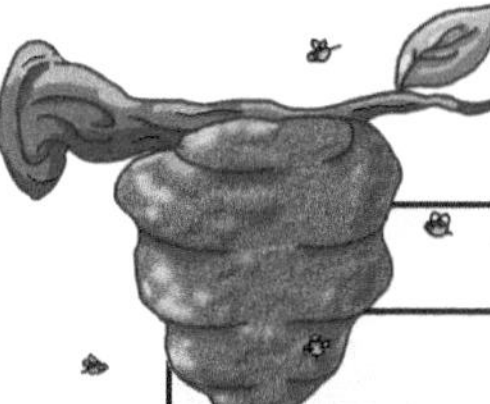

1 cup = 8 ounces	2 pints = 1 quart
2 cups = 1 pint	4 quarts = 1 gallon

It is time to gather honey from the hives. Jane and Peter are helping to pour honey into various containers. Help them with the conversions below. If necessary, refer to the conversion table. 10 pts. total for this exercise.

4 cups = _________ pint(s)   4 pints = _________ quart(s)

6 pints = _________ quart(s)   12 quarts = _________ gallon(s)

8 cups = _________ quart(s)   8 quarts = _________ gallon(s)

16 fluid ounces = _________ cup(s)   32 fluid ounces = _________ quart(s)

128 fluid ounces = _________ gallon(s)   64 fluid ounces = _________ quart(s)

7 Write the temperature in Fahrenheit under each thermometer. 4 pts.

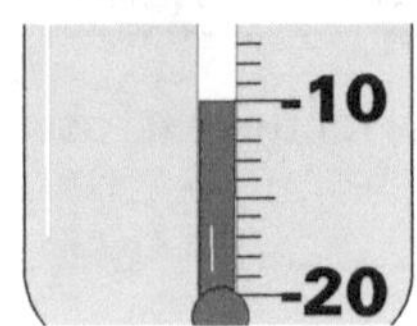

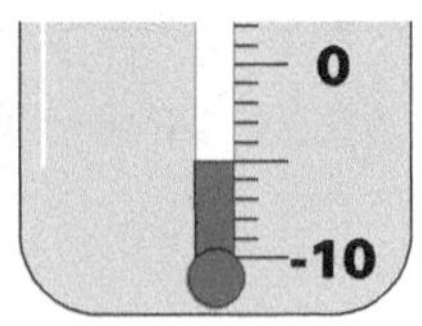

________ ________ ________ ________

8 Write the temperature in Celsius under each thermometer. 4 pts. total for this exercise.

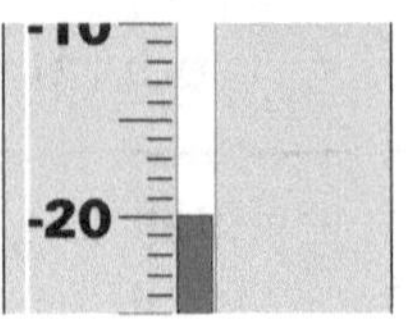

________ ________ ________ ________

9 Match the temperature to the most accurate picture. 4 pts. total for this exercise.

100°C

0°C

-20°C

22°C

Graphs

Saurian is assigned a one week science project. Each day for a week she is to keep track of the highest daily temperature. At the end of the week she is to put this information into a graph which shows the temperature changes over the course of a week. Look below.

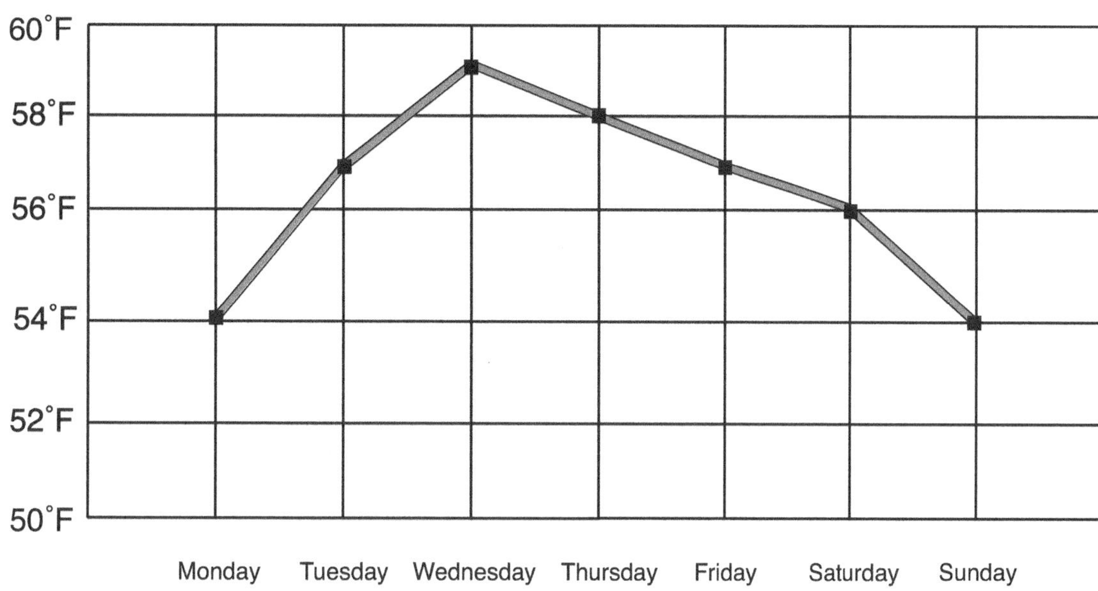

Line graphs are a good way to show changes over a period of time. Look at the line representing Monday on the graph. Follow that line up to the dot, and look across to see the temperature for that day.
The graph shows that the record daily temperature for Monday was 54° F.

What was the record temperature for Wednesday? The dot representing this temperature is half way between the 58°F line and the 60°F line. This means the temperature for Wednesday was 59°F, because 59 is between 58 and 60.

1 Use the graph above to answer the following questions.

Which day had the highest temperature for the week? ____________________

Which days had the lowest temperature for the week? ____________________

What was the temperature difference between Wed. and Sun.? ____________

2 Complete the bar graph with the following information: 5,000 trains, 8,000 table games, 4,000 dolls, & 9,000 video games.

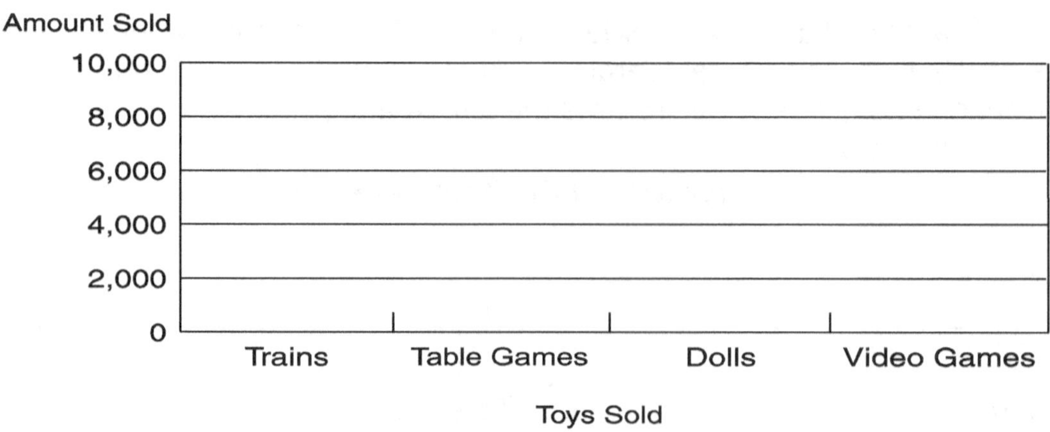

3 Use the chart to find the weight of each item. Change the total weight to kilograms. Hint: Convert all weights to grams when adding.

Item	Weight	Item	Weight
Markers	750 g	Thermos	1,400 g
Dictionary	3 Kg	Math book	1,100 g
Pencils	150 g	Spelling book	800 g
English book	1,400 g	Lunch box	2 Kg
Notebook	200 g		

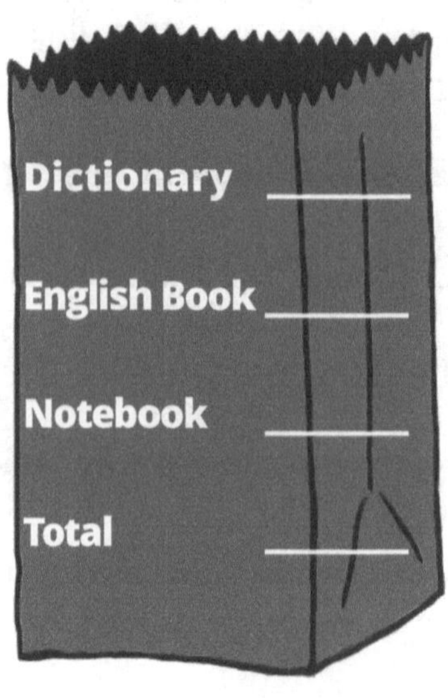

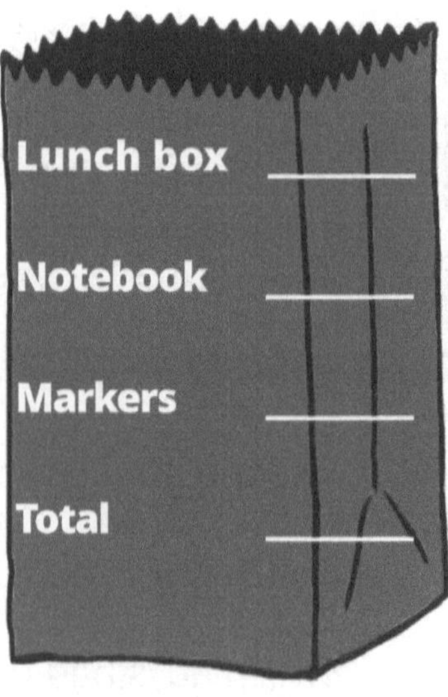

4 Complete. Connect the dots using the order of your answers.

5.4 L = __________ ml

39,321 ml = __________ L

17.49 L = __________ ml

57.02 L = __________ ml

11 L = __________ ml

9.21 L = __________ ml

125.2 ml = __________ L

46.8 ml = __________ L

61,128 ml = __________ L

32,310 ml __________ L

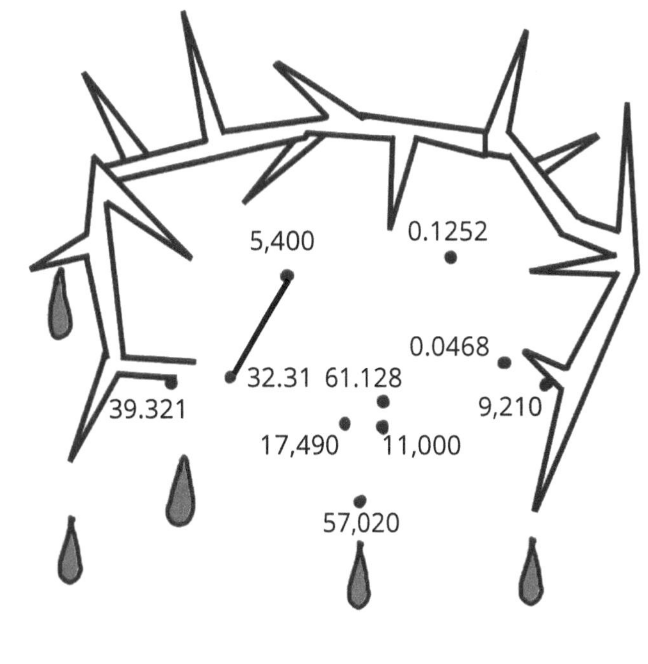

5 Find the difference.

507	601	103	503	700
− 329	− 334	− 56	− 198	− 378

6 Solve.

$13 - 6 = n - 4$ $n - 2 = 15 - 8$ $n - 5 = 12 - 4$

7 Rename in lowest terms.

$\frac{4}{20}$ = ______ $\frac{6}{8}$ = ______ $\frac{5}{10}$ = ______ $\frac{2}{14}$ = ______

Graphs

Mrs. Fowler's class conducted a census of the 4th grade students in their school. They used pictographs to show their data.

Number of Fourth Grade Students

Mrs. Fowler	🯅🯅🯅🯅🯅🯅🯅🯅🯅🯅
Mrs. Piper	🯅🯅🯅🯅🯅🯅🯅🯅🯅🯅🯅🯅
Mrs. Rodriguez	🯅🯅🯅🯅🯅🯅🯅🯅🯅🯅🯅 ½
Mrs. Zimmerman	🯅🯅🯅🯅🯅🯅🯅🯅🯅🯅🯅

🯅 = 2 students

How many students are in Mrs. Piper's class? Since there are 12 stickmen and the key tells us that 1 stickman represents 2 students, 12 x 2 = 24. There are 24 students in Mrs. Piper's class.

How many students are in Mrs. Rodriguez's class? There are 11 and 1/2 stickmen shown by Mrs. Rodriguez's name. 11 x 2 = 22. Since 1 stickman = 2 students, a 1/2 stickman = 1 student. 22 + 1 = 23. There are 23 students in Mrs. Rodriguez's class.

Which class has the fewest students? Mrs. Fowler's with 20 students.

1 Complete.
Katherine runs a hot-dog stand at the local amusement park. Her business profits for a month are shown below.

Business Profits for July

Week 1	$ $ $ $ $ $
Week 2	$ $ $ ½$
Week 3	$ $ $ $
Week 4	$ $ $ $ ½$

Each $ = $100.00

How much money did Katherine make during Week1?

How much money did she make during Week 4?

How much more money did Katherine make during Week 1 than she did during Week 2?

During which week did she make the least amount of money?

During which week did she make $400.00?

2 Complete the line graph by showing Kim's test scores:
Kim's scores: 75; 80; 90; 95; 100

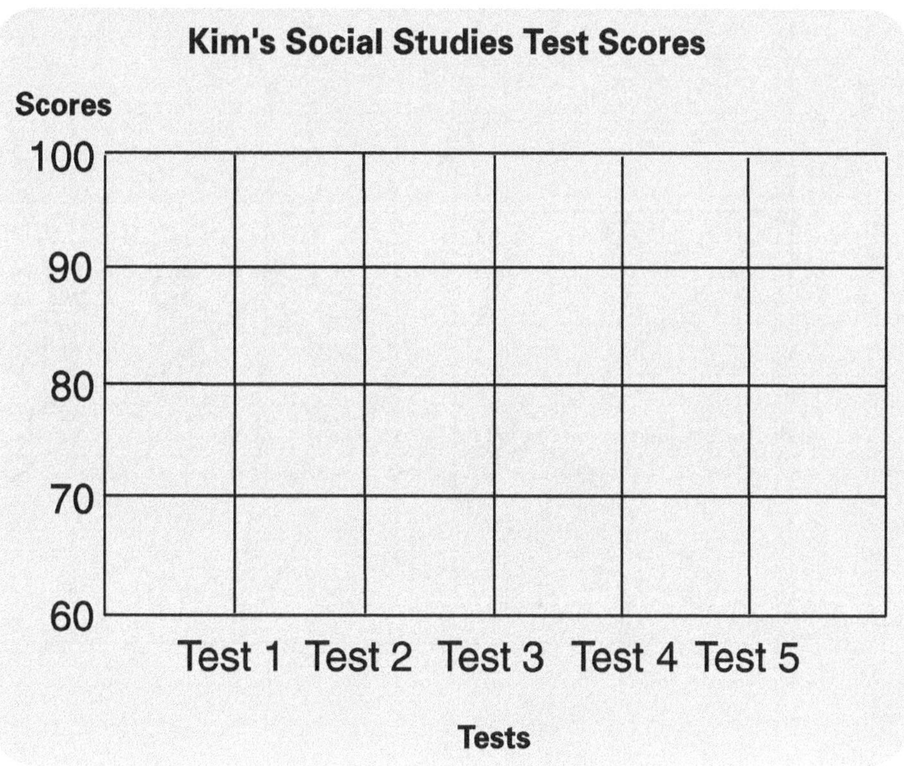

3 Make a horizontal bar graph from the following information.
Title: Favorite Subjects
Subjects: Math, Science, Social Studies, Language Arts
Number of student responses: Math - 5, Science - 7, Social Studies - 5, Language Arts - 8

4 Complete.

Kilo	Hecto	Deka	Basic Unit (Meter, Liter or Gram)	deci	centi	milli

5 Kg = ________ g

21,000 mg = ________ g

1,243 mg = ________ g

43,000 mg = ________ Kg

5 Color the composite numbers red. Color the prime numbers gold.

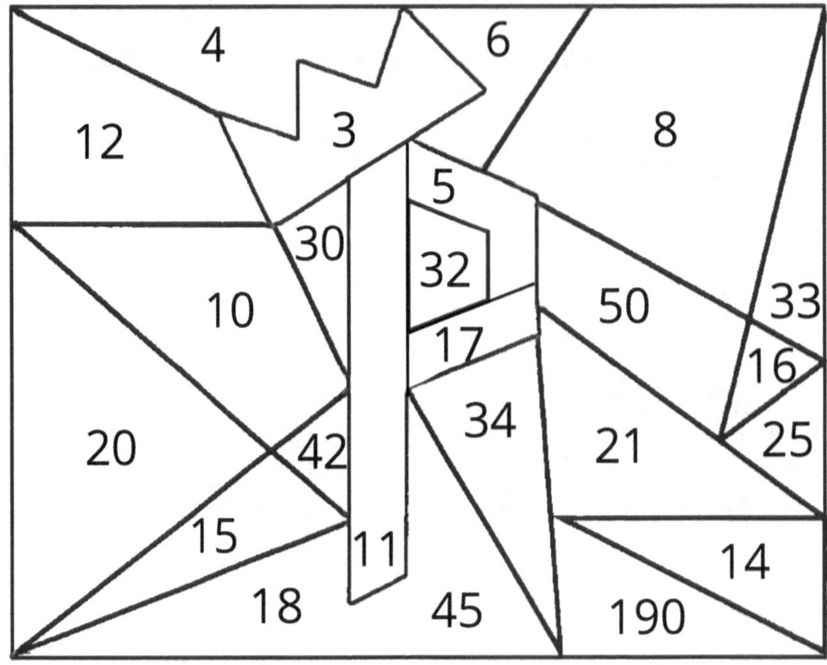

6 Solve.

6 x 5 = (2 x 6) + n

4 x n = 3 x 12

(2 x 4) x n = 4 x 6

7 Circle the fractions which have been reduced to lowest terms.

$\frac{8}{12} = \frac{2}{3}$

$\frac{20}{40} = \frac{2}{4}$

$\frac{7}{14} = \frac{1}{2}$

$\frac{12}{24} = \frac{4}{6}$

Graphs

Laura's parents made a monthly budget to show where their money is spent each month. A circle graph shows how much of their monthly salary is spent each month on items such as rent, clothing, groceries, tithing, and other household necessities. Circle graphs show how one item, or part, compares to the whole amount being discussed. A circle graph is also called a pie chart and the sections of the graph are called pie pieces. Look at the graph below.

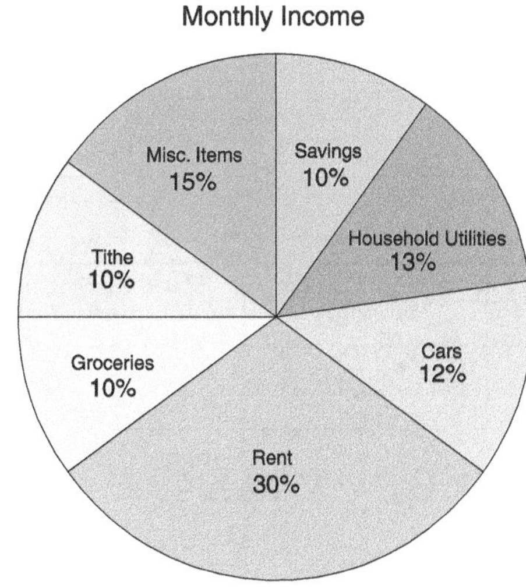

The sum of the pie pieces should always total 100. We have shown percents (%) on this pie chart, so the numbers should total 100%.
15% + 10% + 13% + 12% + 30% + 10% + 10% = 100%

Where is most of the budget spent? Look at the graph and see which pie slice is the largest. Rent is the largest because that is where most of the monthly income is spent.

How much of the income is tithed? 10%

Do Laura's parents spend more money on groceries or cars? Cars, 12%

1 Complete.
Selita works at a book store. Last week 100 magazines were sold.

Notice that the sum of the numbers on each pie should equal 100.

Use the graphs to answer the questions.

Which magazine sold the least? ____________________

Which three magazines sold the most?
How many of each were sold?

__________=______ , __________=______ , __________=______

What is the total number of Home Improvement and Cooking magazines sold? ______________________

How many more News magazines were sold than Sports magazines? ______________________

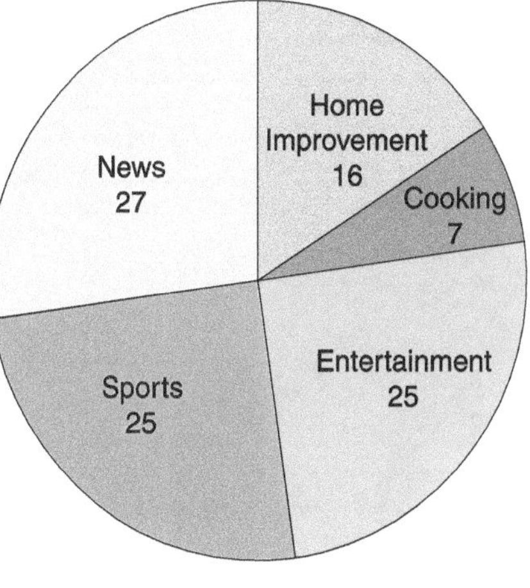

2. Make a line graph with the following information.
Information: Church offerings from the past 4 weeks

Week 1: $4,500
Week 2: $9,000
Week 3: $6,000
Week 4: $7,800

Title:______________________________

3. Draw a pictograph with the following information:
Most popular ice cream flavors sold in one week
Flavors: Chocolate - 60, Strawberry / Banana - 75, Vanilla - 30, Cookies & Cream - 45

 = 5 ice cream cones sold.

Favorite Ice Cream Flavors

Chocolate	
Strawberry/ Banana	
Vanilla	
Cookies & Cream	

 = 5 cones

4 Make a bar graph with the following information:
Sunday School Attendance: Week 1-40, Week 2-72, Week 3-49, Week 4-60.

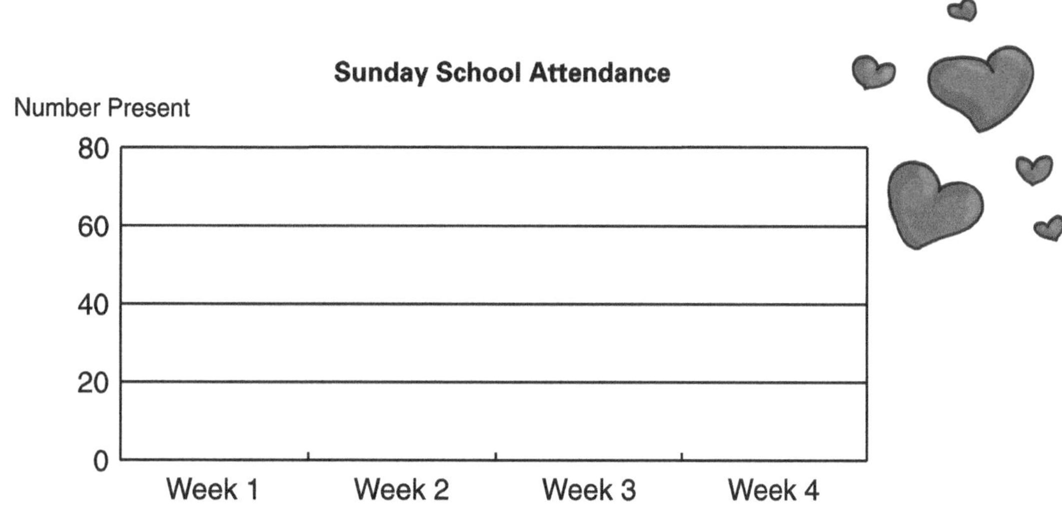

5 Average.

89, 93, 56, 90

56, 58, 75

12, 15, 17, 20, 1

6 Divide.

$7\overline{)65}$ $9\overline{)69}$ $6\overline{)46}$ $5\overline{)29}$

7 Solve. Reduce the answer to lowest terms.

$n + \frac{3}{4} = \frac{4}{4}$ $\frac{5}{11} + n = \frac{9}{11}$ $n - \frac{6}{14} = \frac{1}{14}$ $n - \frac{1}{32} = \frac{1}{32}$

Graphs

A coordinate graph uses a **grid** and **ordered pairs** to locate points. A **grid** is a chart of intersecting lines. Each point of intersection has a corresponding name called an **ordered pair**. Look at the example below.

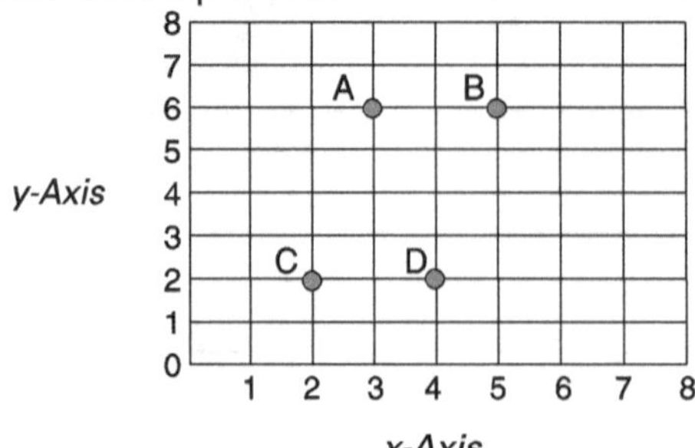

Point A is located at (3, 6). To get to this ordered pair start at 0 on the bottom row, or x-Axis, and move right to line number 3. Then move up line 3 until it intersects with line 6 on the side axis, or y-Axis. When reading an ordered pair, the first number will always be on the x-Axis (bottom row) and the second number will always be on the y-Axis (side row).

Move to the right
↓
(3, 6)
↑
Move up

Which letter is located at (5, 6)? Move to the right along the x-Axis until you get to the 5 line. Move up the 5 line until it intersects with line 6 on the y-Axis. Letter B is located at ordered pair (5, 6).

What is the ordered pair for letter C? To get to letter C move over 2 and up 2. (2, 2) is the ordered pair for letter C.

1 Find the point. Write the letter below for each ordered pair below to spell a word.

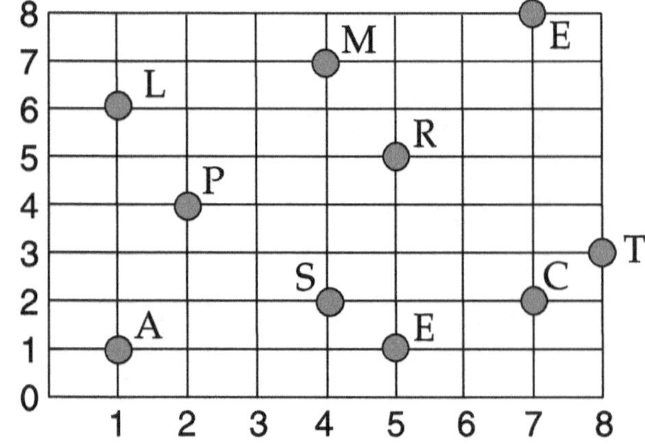

(2, 4) ____
(7, 8) ____
(1, 1) ____ John 14:27
(7, 2) ____
(5, 1) ____

2 Complete the graph.
Electronic Equipment sold in one day.
Televisions-50; Tablets-25; Computers-15; Printers-10

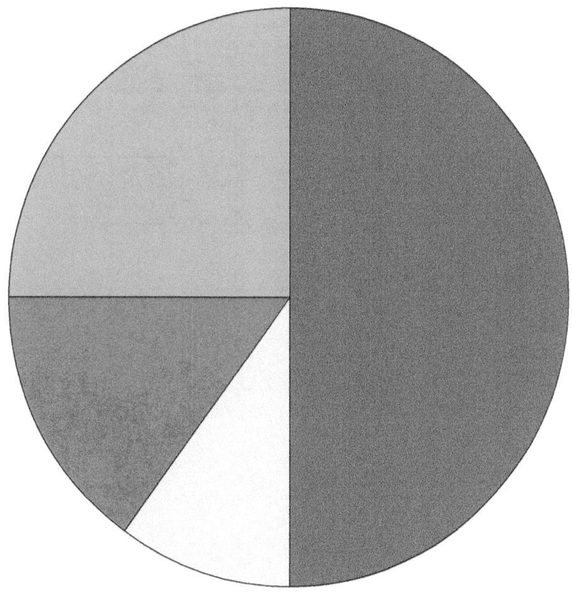

3 Complete the pictograph about cellphone sales. Use the data in the table.

Monday	Tuesday	Wednesday	Thursday	Friday	Saturday
30	25	30	35	60	75

Monday-
Tuesday-
Wednesday-
Thursday-
Friday-
Saturday-

= 10 cellphones

4 Draw a line graph for the following information.
Total number of preschool students enrolled over a 5-year period.
2011-32 students; 2012-50 students; 2013-74 students; 2014-95 students; 2015 -110 students

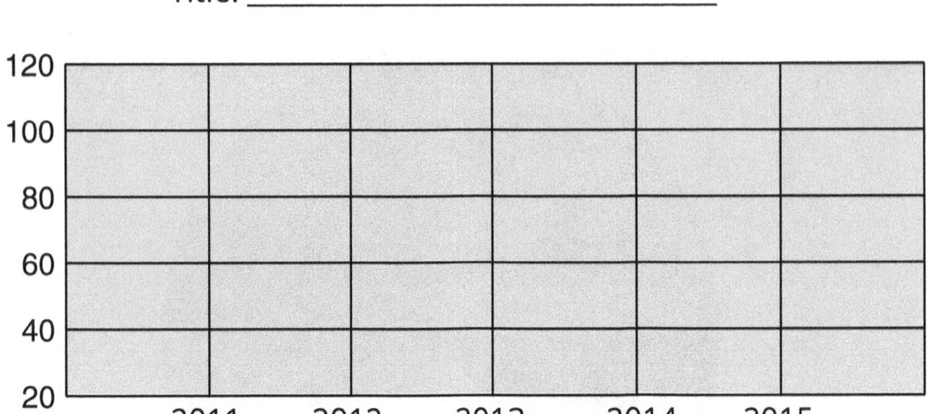

5 Solve.

$n = (12 \div 3) + 6$ $7 + n = 13 + 2$ $9 + 3 = n + 6$

6 Divide.

48)311 66)235 72)420 57)428 73)500

7 Use these digits to write 3 different numbers with a 6 in the tenths' place: 1; 4; 6; 0; 9.

______ ______ ______

8 Write the missing numbers.

$1\frac{4}{8} + 2\frac{1}{\square} = 3\frac{\square}{8}$

$5\frac{3}{\square} - 2\frac{1}{5} = 3\frac{\square}{5}$

$1\frac{1}{12} + 9\frac{5}{12} = 10\frac{6}{\square}$

Ratio

In the Bible there are 27 books in the New Testament to 39 books in the Old Testament. We can write this number as a **ratio**. A **ratio** is used to compare two quantities. The ratio of New Testament books to Old Testament books is 27 to 39. We can also write this ratio as the fraction $\frac{27}{39}$.

The ratio of Old Testament books (39) to New Testament books (27) would be 39 to 27 or $\frac{39}{27}$. When writing a ratio, the first number given is the numerator and the second number given is the denominator.

Look at the pictures below.

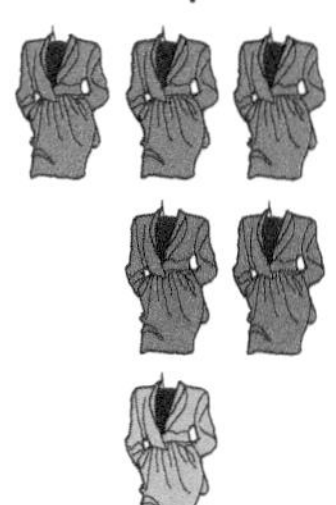

What is the ratio of blue dresses to the red dresses? There are 3 blue dresses and 2 red dresses so the ratio is 3 to 2 or $\frac{3}{2}$.

What is the ratio of red dresses to green dresses? There are 2 red dresses and 1 green dress so the ratio is 2 to 1 or $\frac{2}{1}$.

Kyle and Paige went to the county fair. Kyle saw the sign when he went to purchase tickets for the rides. What was the ratio of tickets to dollars?

Five Tickets
for
$3.00

Kyle can purchase 5 tickets for $3.00. The ratio of tickets to dollars is 5 to 3 or $\frac{5}{3}$.

1 Write each ratio as a fraction.

Movie tickets were on sale 2 for $10.00
The ratio of tickets to dollars is: _______

There are 3 adults at the fair for every 5 children.
The ratio of adults to children at the fair is: _______

4 out of every 6 shirts sold at the souvenir stand are black.
The ratio of black shirts to all shirts: ______

7 out of every 10 horses in the rodeo were brown.
Brown horses → __
All horses →

The Ferris wheel goes completely around 10 times in 2 minutes.
times around → ___
minutes →

2 Plot the following coordinates. Each set of coordinates draws a separate picture. Connect the coordinates in the order they are written to draw each individual picture.

Figure 1		Figure 2			Figure 3	
(2, 0)	(3, 5)	(7, 0)	(6, 5)	(10, 5)	(12, 0)	(13, 5)
(2, 1)	(3, 4)	(7, 1)	(7, 5)	(10, 4)	(12, 1)	(13, 4)
(2, 2)	(4, 4)	(7, 2)	(7, 6)	(9, 4)	(12, 2)	(14, 4)
(2, 3)	(4, 3)	(7, 3)	(7, 7)	(8, 4)	(12, 3)	(14, 3)
(1, 3)	(3, 3)	(7, 4)	(8, 7)	(8, 3)	(11, 3)	(13, 3)
(1, 4)	(3, 2)	(6, 4)	(8, 6)	(8, 2)	(11, 4)	(13, 2)
(2, 4)	(3, 1)	(5, 4)	(8, 5)	(8, 1)	(12, 4)	(13, 1)
(2, 5)	(3, 0)	(5, 5)	(9, 5)	(8, 0)	(12, 5)	(13, 0)

8 7 6 5 4 3 2 1 0

1 2 3 4 5 6 7 8 9 10 11 12 13 14 15 16

"But God demonstrates his own love for us in this: While we were still sinners, Christ died for us." Romans 5:8

3 Find the errors in the circle graph. Correct the errors when they are found.

Graph Data

Time Used for an 8-Hour School Day.
6 hours of instruction
30 minutes for lunch
1 hour for Art
30 minutes for recess

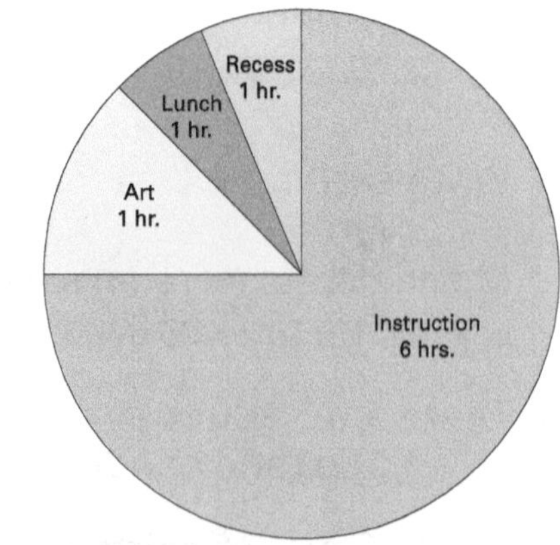

4 Fill in the graph.

Graph Data:
Number of Sunny Days in a Year

Jan.	14	April	10	July	30	Oct.	20
Feb.	17	May	23	Aug.	29	Nov.	18
March	12	June	26	Sept.	25	Dec.	14

= 2 Days

Title: ____________________________

Jan.
Feb.
March
April
May
June
July
Aug.
Sept.
Oct.
Nov.
Dec.

5 Solve.

$5 + n = 15$ $80 + n = 92$ $50 + 3 = 45 + n$ $13 - 4 = 3 + n$

6 Count the change. Use the fewest coins and bills possible. Write the total amount due.

Price	Paid	Change Due
Example: $1.55	$2.00	2 dimes, 1 quarter = $.45
$3.64	$5.00	
$8.19	$10.00	
$13.36	$20.00	
$37.15	$50.00	
$255.50	$260.00	

7 Order from smallest to largest.

$\frac{1}{2}$ $\frac{3}{4}$ $\frac{1}{12}$ $\frac{8}{8}$

________ ________ ________ ________

Ratio

Brett was making an individual bowl of pudding. The instructions called for 1 scoop of pudding mix to $\frac{1}{2}$ cup of milk. If Brett wants to make enough pudding for 3 people how much pudding and how much milk will he need?

We can make ratio tables by finding equivalent fractions. Look at the table below.

Think:	2 x 1 = 2	2 x 2 = 4	2 x 3 = 6	2 x 4 = 8	2 x 5 = 10	2 x 6 = 12	2 x 7 = 14
Scoops of Mix	2	4	6	8	10	12	14
Cups of Milk	1	2	3	4	5		
Think:	1 x 1 = 1	1 x 2 = 2	1 x 3 = 3	1 x 4 = 4	1 x 5 = 5	1 x 6 = ?	1 x 7 = ?

Can you complete the table? 12 scoops of mix would need 6 cups of milk.
14 scoops of mix would require 7 cups of milk.

The ratios in this table are called equal ratios. Look at the table below.
How many eggs would be needed to make 32 pancakes?

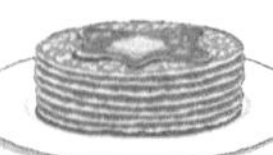

Pancakes	8	16	24	32
Eggs	2	4		

6 eggs would be needed to make 24 pancakes and 8 eggs would be needed to make 32.

1. Complete the table.

How many books can be purchased with $40.00?

Books	3	6	9	12
Dollars	10	20		

How many movie videos can be rented with $20.00?

Movies	2	4	6	8	10
Dollars	4	8			

How many tickets can be purchased with $5.00?

Tickets	3	6	9	12	15
Dollars	1				

2. Write a ratio and fraction for each.

The baker needs 5 bananas for every 2 loaves of bread.

____ to ____ = ____

The baker needs 12 apples for every pan of apple crisp.

_____ to _____ = _____

The baker needs 10 slices of bread for every 6 eggs when making the breakfast soufflé.

_____ to _____ = _____

3 Write the ordered pair for each letter shown

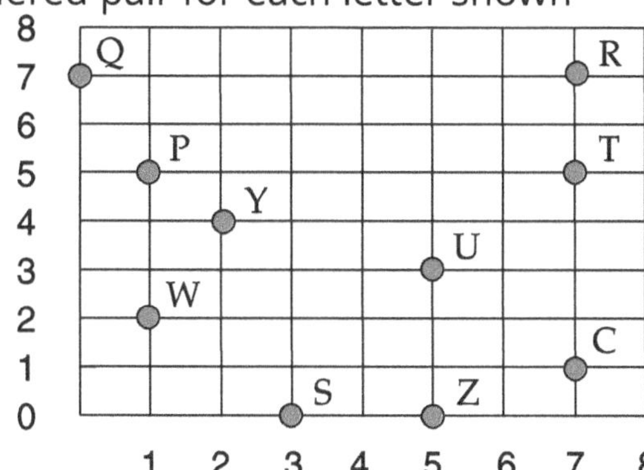

W = _______ R = _______

S = _______ Y = _______

C = _______ Q = _______

Z = _______ U = _______

T = _______ P = _______

4 Write the numbers.

There are 40 pair of shorts on the clearance table at Freeman's Department Store. These shorts come in 5 different colors. The graph below shows how many of each color are left. Use the fraction in each section of the pie chart to determine the exact number of shorts left in each color.

Black = ____________

White = ____________

Green = ____________

Blue = ____________

Red = ____________

Number of Colored Shorts on Clearance Table

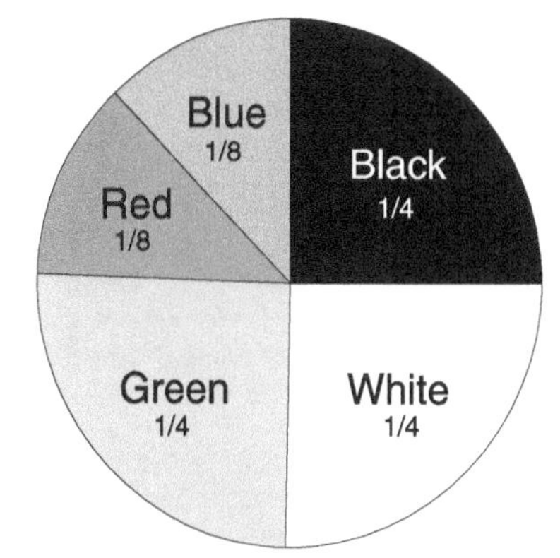

5 Divide.

$22\overline{)880}$ $38\overline{)570}$ $24\overline{)312}$ $44\overline{)1,320}$

6 Write the amount shown.

= ________________

= ________________

= ________________

= ________________

7 Write <, >, or =.

$\frac{1}{5}$ ___ $\frac{1}{2}$

$\frac{7}{8}$ ___ $\frac{3}{9}$

$\frac{1}{4}$ ___ $\frac{1}{2}$

Ratio

You can find an equal ratio by multiplying both the top (numerator) and the bottom (denominator) numbers of the ratio by the same number. This is just like finding equivalent fractions!

If the store is selling 2 drinks for 50¢, an equal ratio will tell you how many drinks you can purchase for $1.50.
You know that the top and bottom of the ratio have to be multiplied by the same number in order to get an equal ratio. If 50 x 3 = 150 then 2 should also be multiplied by 3.

Think: 2 x 3 = 6

$\frac{2}{50} = \frac{n}{150}$ $\frac{2}{50} = \frac{6}{150}$ For $1.50 you could purchase 6 drinks.

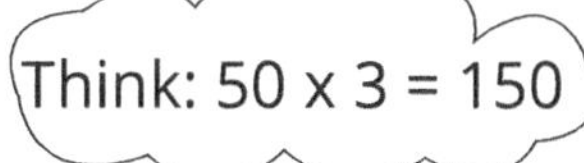

If the same store was selling 7 pieces of candy for 25¢, then how much would it cost to purchase 21 pieces of candy?

$\frac{7}{25} = \frac{21}{n}$ Think: 7 x 3 = 21. The top has been multiplied by 3.
Think: I need to multiply the bottom by 3 to get an equal ratio.
25 x 3 = 75

$\frac{7}{25} = \frac{21}{75}$ To get 21 pieces of candy you would have to pay 75¢.

1 Find the equal ratio by multiplying.

$\frac{3}{2} = \frac{n}{8}$ $\frac{2}{5} = \frac{14}{n}$ $\frac{2}{15} = \frac{n}{30}$ $\frac{3}{7} = \frac{18}{n}$

2 Complete the chart with equivalent ratios and answer the questions.

	1 Pitcher	2 Pitchers	3 Pitchers	4 Pitchers
Lemons	6	12		
Cups of sugar	1.5			
Cups of water	1.5		4.5	6

How many lemons are needed to make 4 pitchers of lemonade? ____________

How much sugar is needed to make 3 pitchers of lemonade? ____________

How much water is needed to make 2 pitchers of lemonade? ____________

3 Write the ratio as a fraction.

Above are 4 tree cookies, 6 star cookies, and 3 bell cookies.
Give the ratio:

Tree cookies to bell cookies ____________

Bell cookies to star cookies ____________

Star cookies to tree cookies ____________

Star to bell and tree ____________

4 Write the coordinates which draw the picture. Connect the coordinates in the order written.

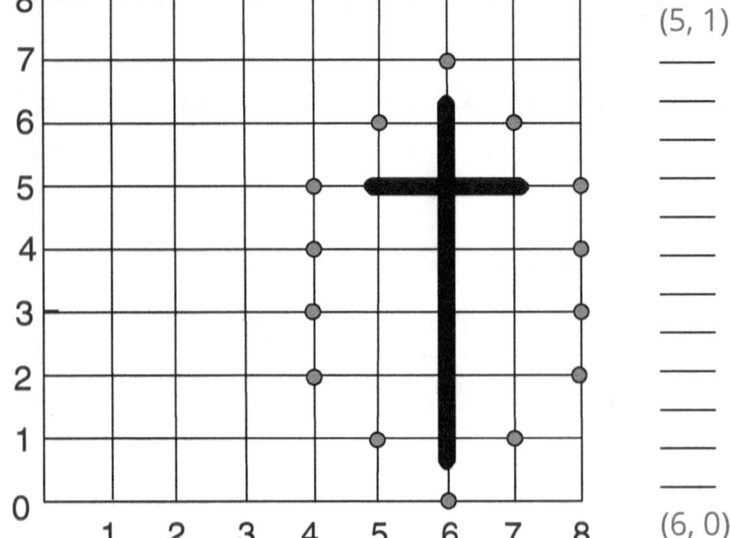

"In addition to all this, take up the shield of the faith, with which you can extinguish all the flaming arrows of the evil one."

Ephesians 6: 16

5 Divide

$27\overline{)726}$ $50\overline{)3,258}$ $44\overline{)523}$

6 Label each geometric figure or item from the Word Bank.

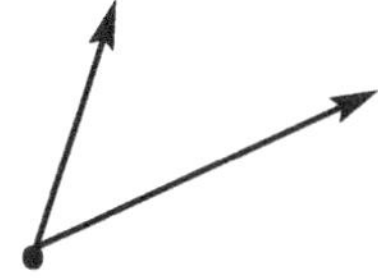

_________ _________ _________

WORD BANK: obtuse angle, right angle, ray, segment, line, acute angle

7 Write <, >, or =.

$\frac{4}{5}$ ______ $\frac{1}{9}$ $\frac{1}{3}$ ______ $\frac{1}{12}$ $\frac{3}{10}$ ______ $\frac{3}{4}$ $\frac{1}{2}$ ______ $\frac{2}{4}$

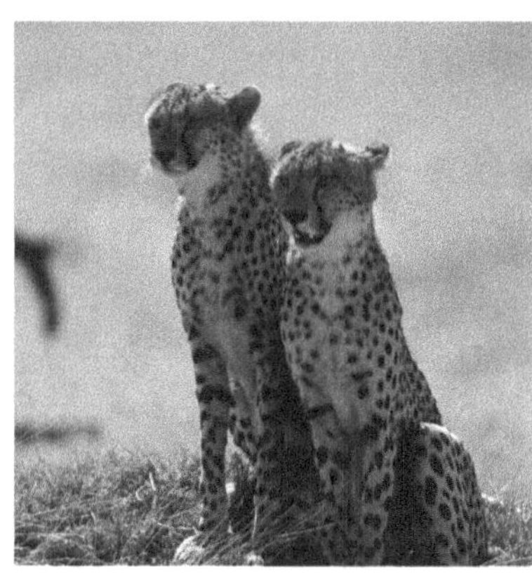

Ratio

Sally has to cook for the local Christian school. She is always preparing large amounts of food. Today she decided to make poppy seed muffins like she makes for the students. However, she only needs to make enough muffins for her family, not for a large number of people. If she needs 6 eggs for every 3 cups of milk to make 36 muffins, how many eggs will she need to make 12 muffins?

If we multiply a ratio by the same number on top and bottom to find an equal ratio, then we should be able to divide the top and bottom of a ratio by the same number and also get an equal ratio. Look below.

Think: 36 ÷ 3 = 12 so divide the numerator and denominator by 3.

Number of muffins	36	12
Number of eggs / Cups of milk	$\frac{6}{3}$	$\frac{2}{1}$

In the book store of Matthew's Christian School a student can purchase 12 pencils for $1.00. How much would a student have to pay for 3 pencils?

Ratio: $\frac{12}{100} = \frac{3}{?}$ Think: 12 ÷ 4 = 3, so divide the bottom number by 4.

100 ÷ 4 = 25

A student would pay 25¢ for 3 pencils.

1 Find the equal ratio by dividing.

$\frac{8}{36} = \frac{n}{9}$ $\frac{21}{28} = \frac{3}{n}$ $\frac{6}{15} = \frac{n}{5}$ $\frac{12}{24} = \frac{2}{n}$

2 Find an equal ratio.

$\frac{5}{6} = \frac{25}{n}$ $\frac{2}{5} = \frac{10}{n}$ $\frac{2}{6} = \frac{n}{18}$ $\frac{3}{5} = \frac{n}{20}$

3 Write the ratio.

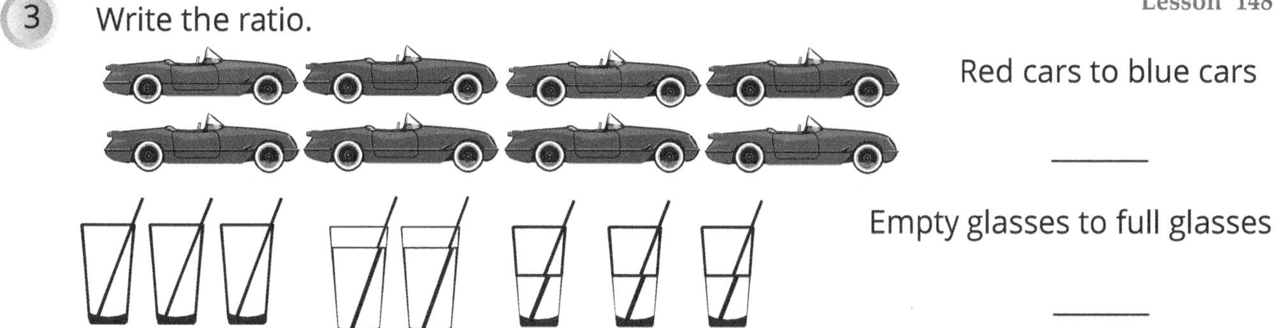

Red cars to blue cars

______

Empty glasses to full glasses

______

Full glasses to $\frac{1}{2}$ full glasses

______

4 Multiply.

$$\begin{array}{r} 818 \\ \times\ 70 \\ \hline \end{array} \qquad \begin{array}{r} 600 \\ \times\ 30 \\ \hline \end{array} \qquad \begin{array}{r} 273 \\ \times\ 20 \\ \hline \end{array} \qquad \begin{array}{r} 928 \\ \times\ 77 \\ \hline \end{array}$$

5 Match.

radius	A figure that can be folded so that the two halves match exactly.
diameter	Two angles with the same measurement.
congruent angles	A segment from the center of a circle to any point of the circle.
similar figures	Having the same shape, but not the same size.
symmetric figures	A segment containing two points of a circle and passing through the center of the circle.

6 Color an equivalent fraction. Write the fraction for each picture.

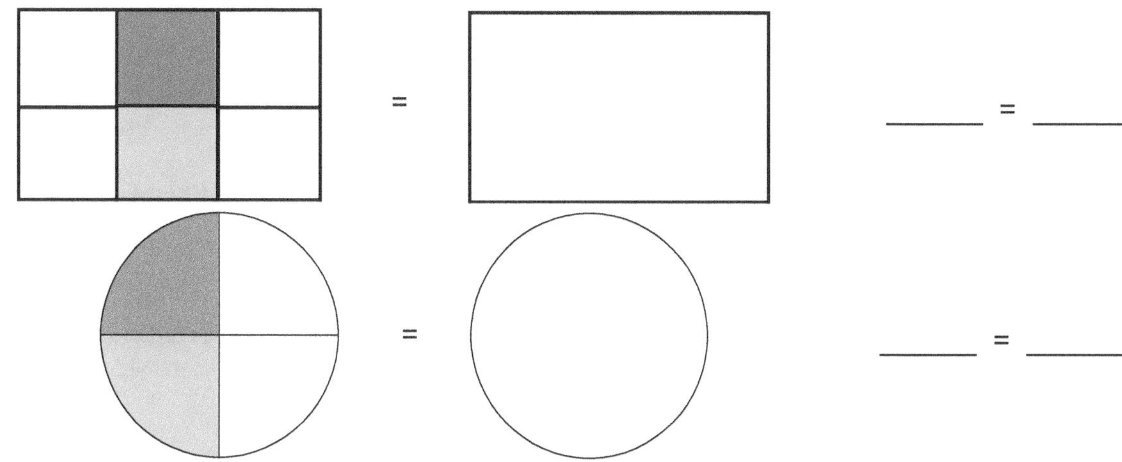

______ = ______

______ = ______

Graphs

The Loganville First Baptist Preschool has a Fall Festival each year to raise money for the school. The double graph below shows the amount of money made in several booths for the years 2015 and 2016. How do they compare?

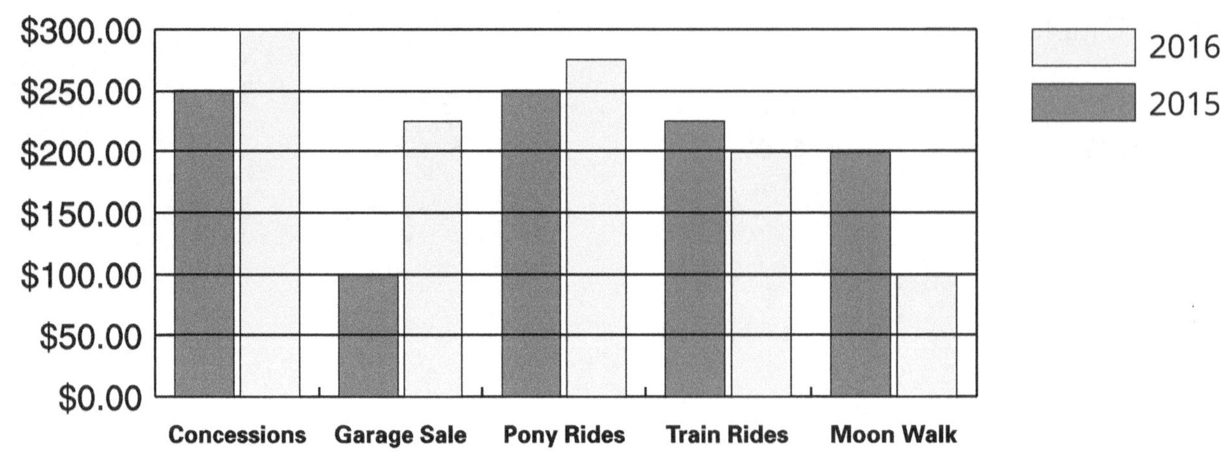

Double graphs are an excellent way to compare information.

Did the school make more off the Garage Sale booth in 2015 or 2016? Look at the graph bars for the garage sale booth. The yellow bar is taller than the purple bar. This means that more money was made off of this booth in 2016 (Hint: Remember to look at the graph key! The yellow bars represent 2016, the purple represent 2015)

How much more money was made off of the Moon Walk in 2015 than in 2016? The yellow bar for the Moon Walk reaches the $100 line. The purple bar for the Moon Walk reaches the $200.00 line. $200.00 - $100.00 = $100.00. There is a $100.00 difference in the 2015 and 2016 earnings.

1. Use the graph above to answer the questions.

   Which booths made more money in 2015 than 2016?

   How much more money did the Concessions stand make in 2016 than it did in 2015?

   How much money was made on the Pony Rides in both 2015 and 2016?

   Was more money made in 2015 or 2016 overall?

2. Solve.

   $\frac{4}{5} = \frac{n}{20}$ $\frac{45}{50} = \frac{n}{10}$ $\frac{8}{40} = \frac{n}{5}$ $\frac{n}{70} = \frac{1}{10}$

3. Write the ratio.

   6 Cokes cost \$2.00 4 tickets cost \$50 3 turns per minute

4. Solve.

   $n - 2 = 3$ $n - 4 = 7$ $n + 11 = 15$ $n - 20 = 6$

5. Multiply.

409	642	763	301
x 13	x 10	x 21	x 50

6. Solve.

   $\frac{15}{45} = \frac{1}{n}$ $\frac{n}{30} = \frac{3}{10}$ $\frac{14}{16} = \frac{n}{8}$

Ratios

1 Write the ratio.

1. 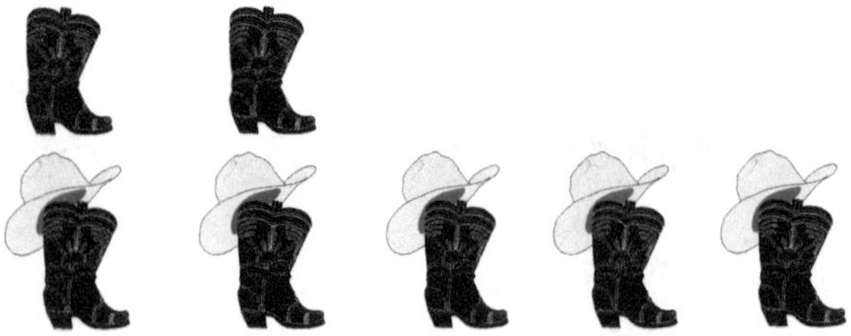 number of hats / number of boots

2.  number of helmets / number of footballs

3.  number of baseball caps / number of baseballs

4.  number of books / number of children

5.  number of saddles / number of horses

6. 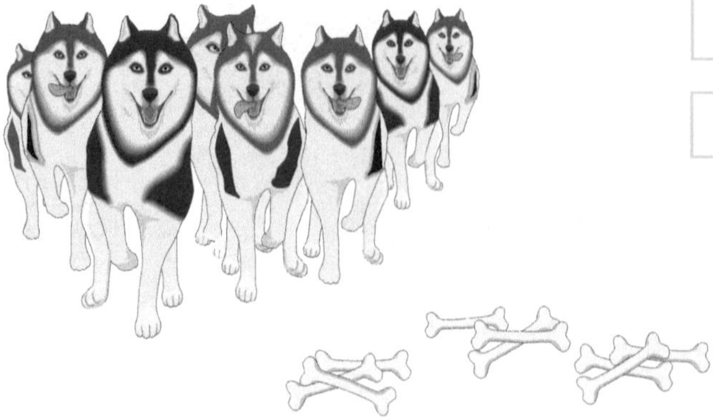 number of dog bones / number of dogs

2 Complete each chart with equivalent ratios.

cups of rice	2	3	4	5		7	
cups of water	4	6		10	12		16

cars	1	2		4	5		
wheels	4		12			24	28

3 Divide by 4 to find equal ratios.

$\frac{40}{80}$	
$\frac{20}{40}$	
$\frac{4}{16}$	
$\frac{8}{40}$	

$\frac{24}{28}$	
$\frac{4}{12}$	
$\frac{20}{32}$	
$\frac{4}{8}$	

$\frac{12}{16}$	
$\frac{16}{20}$	
$\frac{4}{24}$	
$\frac{8}{12}$	

4 Find each difference. Find the answer and letter in the solution box.
Place the letter beside the answer in the space provided to solve the riddle:
What bird can lift the heaviest weight?

258 R	135 A	96 C	52 E	465 N

$$\begin{array}{r} 890 \\ -\ 794 \\ \hline \end{array} \quad \begin{array}{r} 397 \\ -\ 139 \\ \hline \end{array} \quad \begin{array}{r} 402 \\ -\ 267 \\ \hline \end{array} \quad \begin{array}{r} 732 \\ -\ 267 \\ \hline \end{array} \quad \begin{array}{r} 401 \\ -\ 349 \\ \hline \end{array}$$

_____ __ _____ __ _____ __ _____ __ _____ __

5 Reduce fractions to lowest terms.

$\frac{5}{10}$ _____ $\frac{12}{16}$ _____ $\frac{15}{30}$ _____ $\frac{8}{32}$ _____

$\frac{7}{14}$ _____ $\frac{11}{22}$ _____ $\frac{12}{32}$ _____ $\frac{6}{36}$ _____

6 Find the sum or difference. Reduce to lowest terms if possible.

$\frac{1}{4} + \frac{3}{8} =$ $\frac{6}{12} + \frac{1}{6} =$ $\frac{3}{4} - \frac{1}{2} =$ $\frac{7}{10} - \frac{2}{5} =$

$\frac{1}{3} + \frac{2}{6} =$ $\frac{1}{2} + \frac{1}{4} =$ $\frac{1}{2} + \frac{1}{8} =$ $\frac{2}{3} - \frac{1}{6} =$

84 points total Lessons 136-145

1 Write each measurement in centimeters and millimeters. The first one has been done for you. 8 pts. total for this exercise.

4 cm 8 mm	7 cm 4mm	8cm 9mm	1 cm 5mm
4.8 ____ cm	______ cm	______ cm	______ cm
48 ____ mm	______ mm	______ mm	______ mm

2 Complete using the conversion chart. 6 pts. total for this exercise.

Kilo	Hecto	Deka	Basic Unit (Meter, Liter or Gram)	deci	centi	milli

195 mm = ______ cm

6,495 mm = ______ m

9.09 m = ______ mm

84.69 m = ______ cm

7.54 Km = ______ dm

3.01m = ______ cm

3 Complete using the conversion chart. 6 pts. total for this exercise.

Kilo	Hecto	Deka	Basic Unit (Meter, Liter or Gram)	deci	centi	milli

6,000 ml = ______ L

300 L = ______ ml

200 ml = ______ L

50 L = ______ ml

75 ml = ______ L

4 L = ______ ml

4 Complete using the conversion chart. 6 pts. total for this exercise.

Kilo	Hecto	Deka	Basic Unit (Meter, Liter or Gram)	deci	centi	milli

6 g = ______ kg

3 kg = ______ g

23 g = ______ kg

50 kg = ______ g

175 g = ______ kg

467 kg = ______ g

5

Favorite Sports

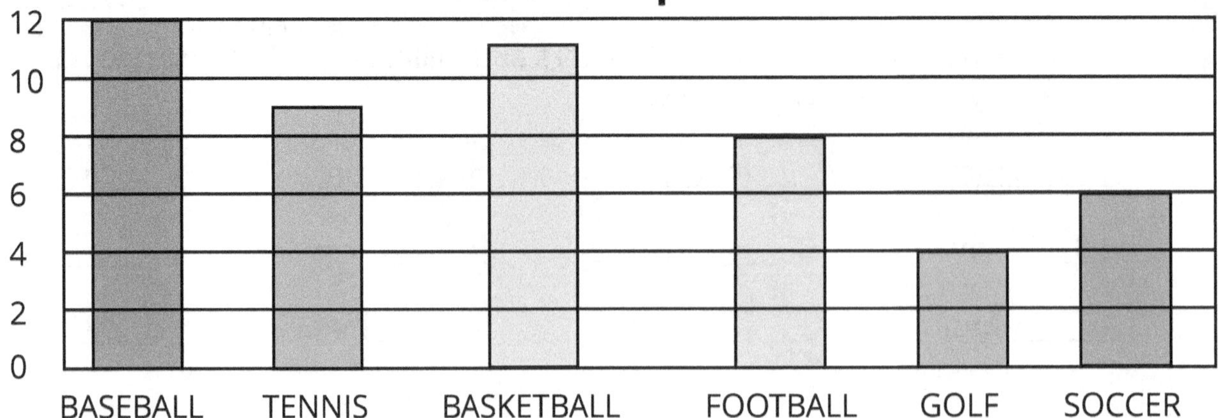

The fourth grade students at Hopkins Elementary completed a survey about their favorite sports. Mrs. Martin's class made a bar graph to display the data. Use the graph to answer the following questions. 4 pts. total for this exercise.

1. If each person voted for one favorite sport, how many people participated in the survey? ______________________
2. What was the favorite sport? ____________________
3. What was the least favorite sport? ______________________
4. Rank the sports from most liked to least liked. ____________________

____

6

Temp

Daily Temperatures-Phoenix

80°F
75°F
70°F
65°F
60°F
55°F
50°F
45°F

Mon. Tues. Wed. Thurs. Fri. Sat. Sun.

Days of the Week

✳ High daily temperature ✳ Low daily temperature

Record the information on the graph. The first ones have been done for you. Connect the red suns to see the daily high temperature change. Connect the blue suns to see the daily low temperature change. 16 pts. total for this exercise.

	High Temperature	Low Temperature
Monday	65°F	45°F
Tuesday	70°F	47°F
Wednesday	75°F	50°F
Thursday	80°F	50°F
Friday	80°F	52°F
Saturday	78°F	48°F
Sunday	80°F	47°F

7 Students from several cities in the United States recorded snowfall for the month of January. Each day that it snowed the students put a snowflake on a chart. Below is the data collected. 5 pts. total for this exercise.

Snowfall in January

✳✳✳✳✳	**Des Moines, Iowa**
✳✳✳	**Lincoln, Nebraska**
✳✳✳✳✳✳✳	**Orangeville, Utah**
✳✳	**Chicago, Illinois**
✳✳✳	**Dublin, Michigan**
✳	**Rochester, New York**

Use the pictograph to answer the questions. If the question cannot be answered with the data given, write no data available.

✳ = **Snowfall for one day**

1. How many cities participated in the data collection? ______________________
2. Which city had the most days in which it snowed? ______________________
3. Which city had the least days in which it snowed? ______________________
4. Which cities had the same number of days in which it snowed? ____________
5. Which city had the most inches of snow? ______________________________

8 Ben saved $200.00 for a trip to San Diego. He saved his money as follows: 50% Magazine Sales, 25% Allowance, 15% Can Collection, 10% Miscellaneous. Complete the circle graph with the information given. 4 pts. total for this exercise.

9

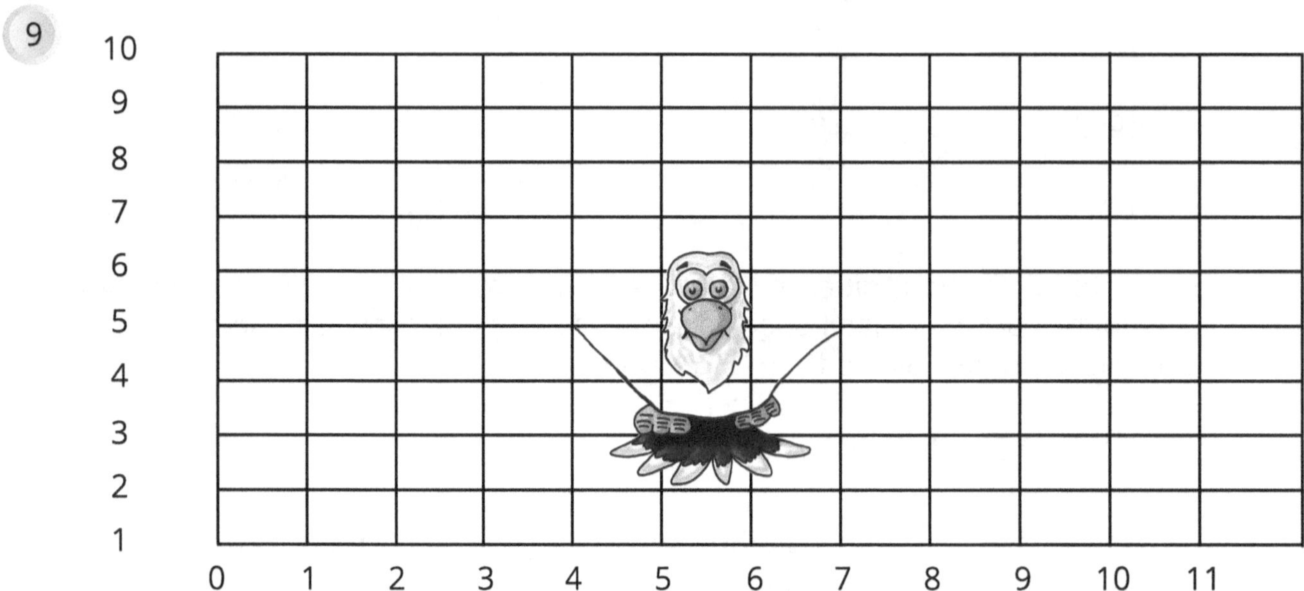

Plot the coordinates and connect them in the order they are written. 26 pts.

(4, 5)	(0, 6)	(1, 9)	(5, 7)	(9, 8)	(10, 7)	(8, 6)
(3, 6)	(1, 7)	(2, 8)	(6, 7)	(10, 9)	(11, 7)	(7, 5)
(2, 7)	(0, 8)	(3, 8)	(7, 8)	(10, 8)	(10, 6)	
(1, 6)	(1, 8)	(4, 8)	(8, 8)	(11, 8)	(9, 7)	

"They that wait on the Lord shall renew their strength; They shall mount up with wings as eagles; They shall run and not be weary, they shall walk and not faint." Isaiah 40:31

10 Write the ratio. 3 pts. total for this exercise.

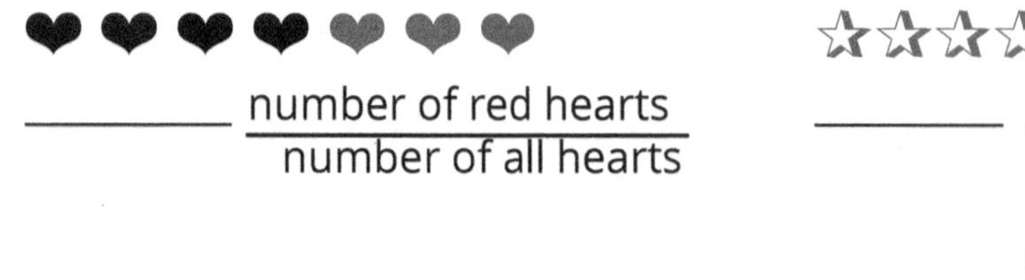

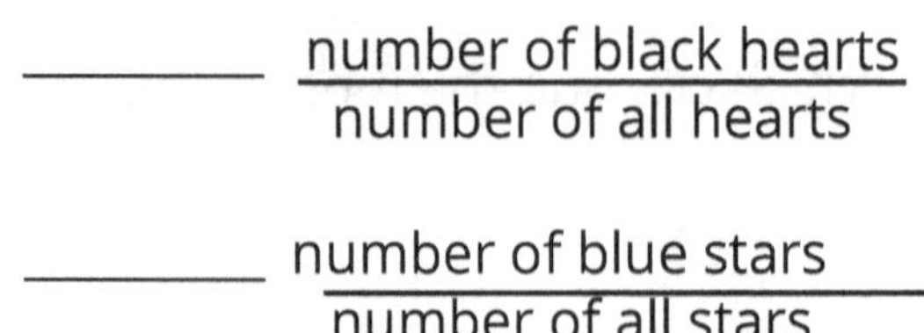

_______ $\frac{\text{number of red hearts}}{\text{number of all hearts}}$

_______ $\frac{\text{number of black hearts}}{\text{number of all hearts}}$

_______ $\frac{\text{number of blue stars}}{\text{number of all stars}}$

1 Shade the prime numbers and read the message.

37	8	3	16	17	19	29	60	11	5	3
41	10	5	28	7	12	35	40	7	36	48
4	11	6	30	11	2	25	45	13	17	19
20	2	9	50	23	14	15	25	100	4	31
24	13	12	10	5	3	7	80	37	47	43

2 Write A.M. or P.M. after each time.

1. Adam ate breakfast at 7:30 ________.

2. School was out at 3:30 ________.
3. The class went to an observatory to see the stars at 9:15 ________.
4. The family sat down for dinner at 6:30 ________.

5. Jeannine went to her gymnastics class after school at 4:00 ________.
6. Ben's piano lesson is Monday evening at 6:25 ________.

3 Solve the equations.

$n - 7 = 12 - (4 \times 2)$

$n - 4 = 4 + (3 \times 3)$

$n - 6 = 11 - (1 \times 8)$

4 Complete the charts with equivalent ratios and answer the questions.

milk	2 cups		6 cups	
pancake mix	3 cups	6 cups		

How many cups of milk are needed to make 12 cups of mix? ___________

sugar	1 cup			
lemonade	2 quarts		6 quarts	

How many cups of sugar are needed to make 8 quarts of lemonade? ___________

5 Complete the crossword puzzle.

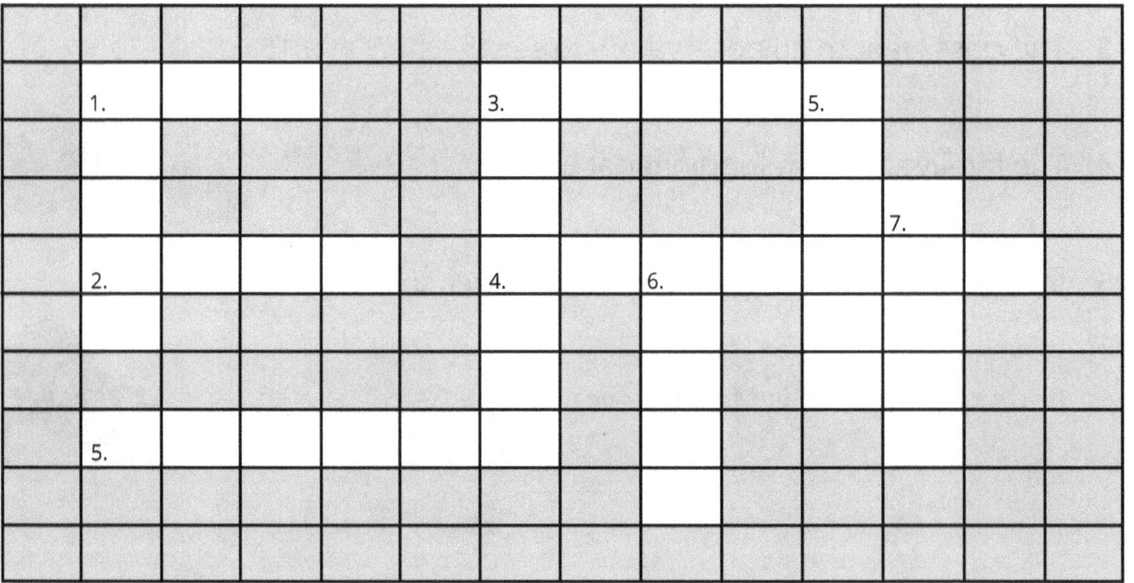

Across
1. 5,000 – 4,632 = ______________
2. 9,030 – 1,731 = ______________
3. 21,860 – 11,297 = ______________
4. 8,435.21 + 1,421.56 = ______________
5. 683.02 – 576.99 = ______________

Down
1. 12.46 + 20.29 = ______________
3. 3,768.50 – 2,689.47 = ______________
5. 164.43 + 169.02 = ______________
6. 18,372 + 36, 812 = ______________
7. 33,082 – 16,069 = ______________

6 Find the sum or difference. Write the answer in lowest terms.

$\frac{1}{4} + \frac{1}{2} =$ ______ $\frac{1}{3} + \frac{3}{6} =$ ______ $\frac{9}{12} - \frac{1}{3} =$ ______

$\frac{1}{8} + \frac{2}{4} =$ ______ $\frac{9}{10} - \frac{2}{5} =$ ______ $\frac{1}{10} + \frac{1}{5} =$ ______

$\frac{7}{8} - \frac{1}{4} =$ ______ $\frac{6}{6} - \frac{1}{3} =$ ______ $\frac{4}{12} + \frac{1}{6} =$ ______

7 Write each fraction in lowest terms.

$\frac{2}{10}$ ____ $\frac{6}{30}$ ____ $\frac{8}{12}$ ____ $\frac{17}{34}$ ____ $\frac{14}{20}$ ____ $\frac{100}{500}$ ____

$\frac{3}{18}$ ____ $\frac{30}{90}$ ____ $\frac{6}{40}$ ____ $\frac{15}{50}$ ____ $\frac{11}{77}$ ____ $\frac{20}{90}$ ____

1 Find the quotient. Write any remainders as whole numbers.

$4\overline{)36}$ $8\overline{)75}$ $8\overline{)65}$ $5\overline{)9}$ $4\overline{)8}$

$7\overline{)49}$ $4\overline{)5}$ $7\overline{)22}$ $7\overline{)50}$ $6\overline{)37}$

2 Solve the problems and find your answers below. Each time you see the answer, write the letter above it until you have found the solution to the riddle:
What is smarter than a cat who can count?

Find the sum or difference.

12.369 + 79.823 = __________ **E**

132.019 + 278.992 = __________ **A**

346.07 + 465.119 = __________ **G**

45.304 – 27.980 = __________ **N**

650.037 – 395.451 = __________ **L**

42.646 – 29.36 = __________ **P**

2.870 – 0.987 = __________ **I**

465.329 + 23.54 = __________ **B**

59.903 + 123.012 = __________ **S**

____
411.011

__________ __________ __________ __________ __________ __________ __________ __________
182.915 **13.286** **92.192** **254.586** **254.586** **1.883** **17.324** **811.189**

__________ __________ __________
488.869 **92.192** **92.192**

3 Write the temperature below each Fahrenheit thermometer.

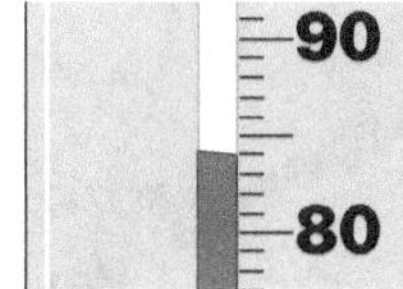

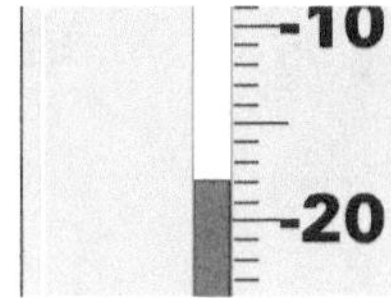

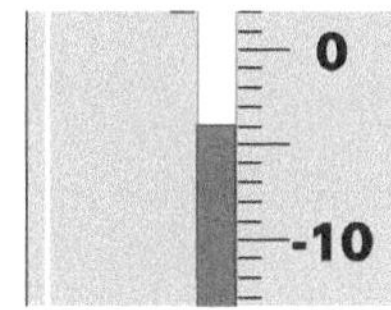

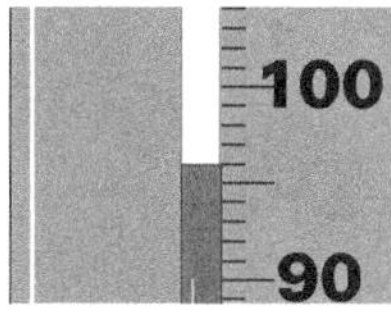

_____ _____ _____ _____ _____

4 Start at 12 A.M. Work your way through the times in the day connecting dots. When you get to 6 A.M., stop. Do you recognize the picture that you have drawn?

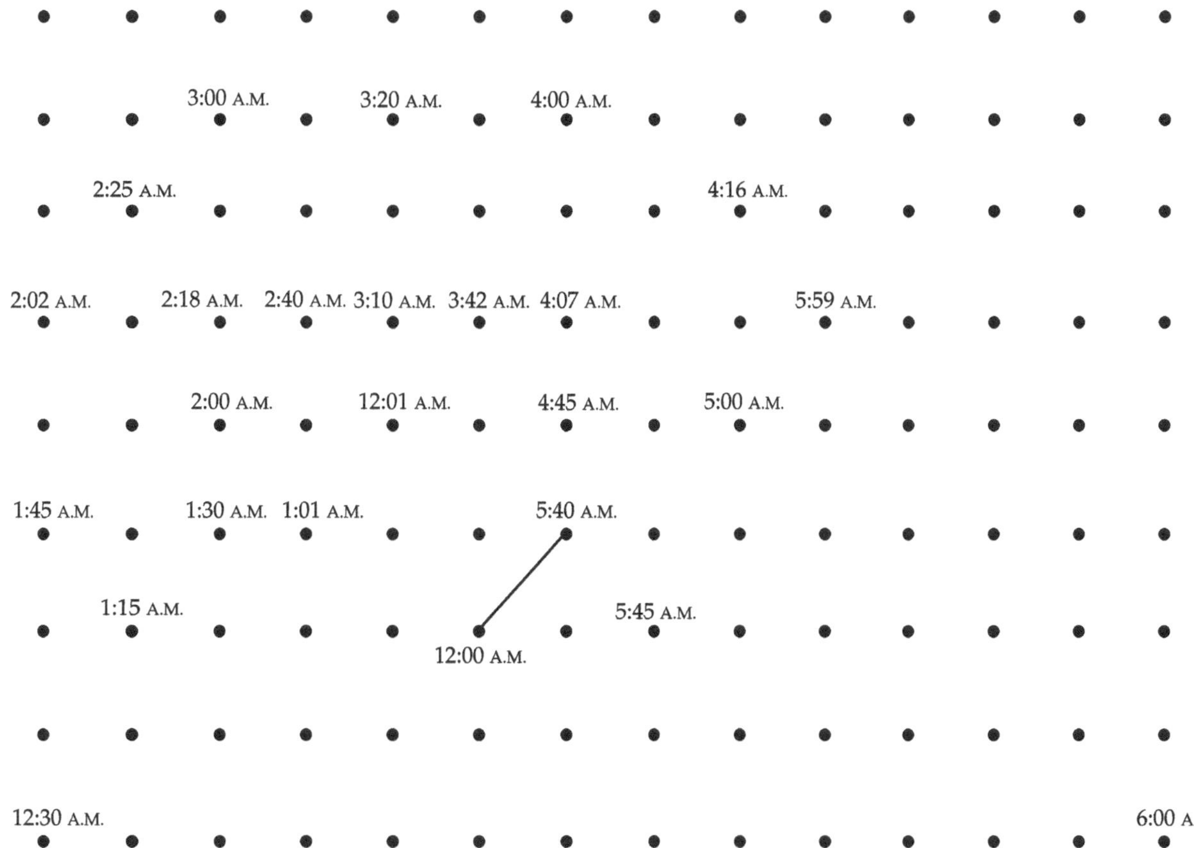

5 Find the average.

50, 40, 45, 45

75, 85, 65, 75

15, 20, 23, 27, 17, 18

157, 140, 180, 123

6 Find the sum or difference. Write the answer in lowest terms.

$\frac{4}{20} + \frac{6}{20} =$ ______

$\frac{3}{9} + \frac{6}{9} =$ ______

$\frac{8}{25} + \frac{7}{25} =$ ______

$\frac{2}{15} + \frac{4}{15} =$ ______

$\frac{12}{15} - \frac{3}{15} =$ ______

$\frac{10}{12} - \frac{8}{12} =$ ______

$\frac{4}{16} - \frac{2}{16} =$ ______

$\frac{28}{30} - \frac{8}{30} =$ ______

1 Write each fraction in decimal form. Find the decimals in the boxes below and shade them. The letters that remain in the unshaded boxes will spell out the hidden answer to the riddle: ***What would you call a stage performance by ponies?***

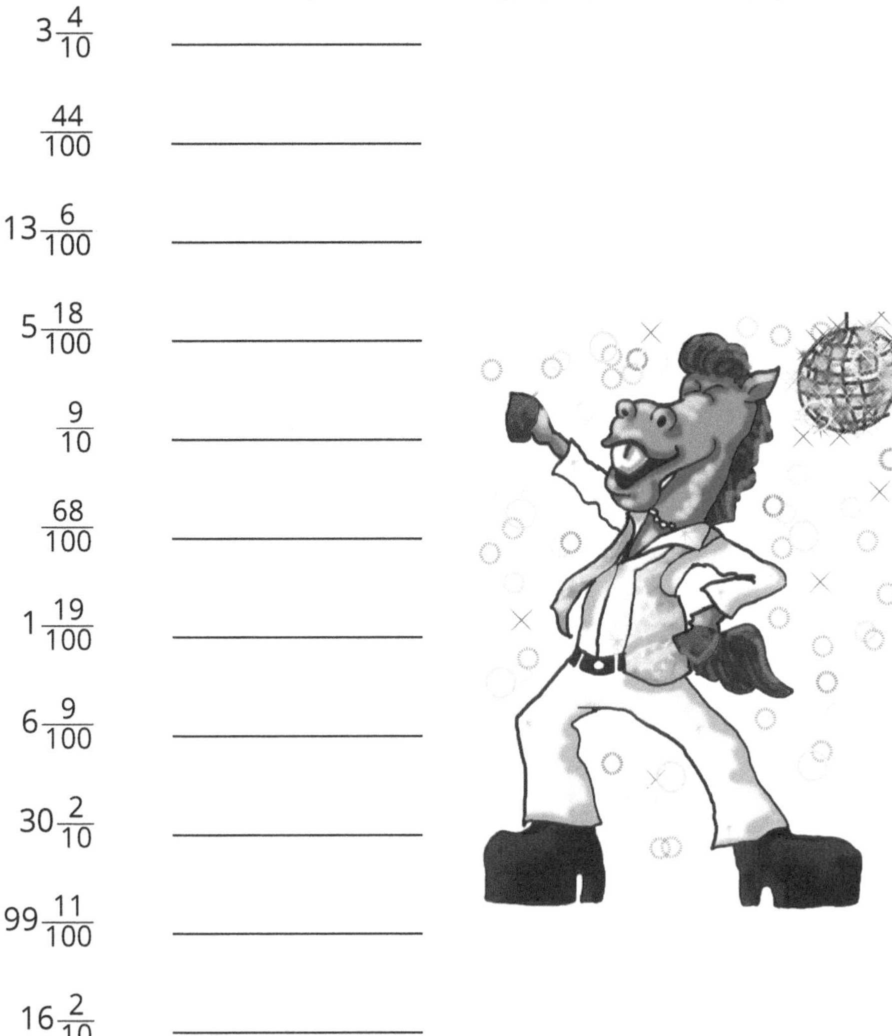

$3\frac{4}{10}$ ______________

$\frac{44}{100}$ ______________

$13\frac{6}{100}$ ______________

$5\frac{18}{100}$ ______________

$\frac{9}{10}$ ______________

$\frac{68}{100}$ ______________

$1\frac{19}{100}$ ______________

$6\frac{9}{100}$ ______________

$30\frac{2}{10}$ ______________

$99\frac{11}{100}$ ______________

$16\frac{2}{10}$ ______________

5.18 **T**	3.7 **H**	6.09 **L**	99.4 **O**	0.44 **A**	7.03 **R**	13.06 **K**	99.11 **M**	12.1 **S**	0.68 **S**
7.9 **E**	0.9 **N**	3.4 **A**	90.7 **P**	0.77 **L**	1.19 **D**	4.8 **A**	0.06 **Y**	30.2 **S**	16.2 **L**

2 Write the temperature below each Celsius thermometer.

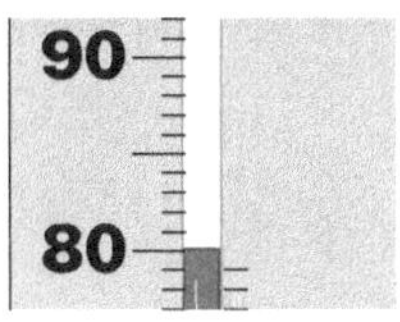

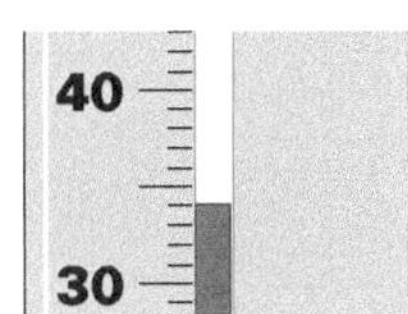

______________ ______________ ______________ ______________ ______________

3 Solve.

$n - 16 = 38 - (4 \times 6)$ $n - 4 = 7 + (7 \times 3)$ $n - 11 = 12 + (2 \times 8)$

4 Beside each date, write the century.

1911 ____________ 1712 ____________

211 ____________ 476 ____________

1512 ____________ 1156 ____________

2001 ____________ 704 ____________

1997 ____________ 1211 ____________

5 Find the sum or difference. Write the fractions in lowest terms.

$\frac{1}{8} + \frac{4}{8} =$ $\frac{17}{20} + \frac{3}{20} =$ $\frac{12}{16} - \frac{8}{16} =$

$\frac{4}{12} + \frac{4}{12} =$ $\frac{16}{18} - \frac{6}{18} =$ $\frac{10}{15} - \frac{5}{15} =$

$\frac{3}{4} - \frac{1}{4} =$ $\frac{10}{14} - \frac{3}{14} =$ $\frac{7}{10} + \frac{1}{10} =$

6 Find the quotient. Write the remainder as a fraction. Be sure it is in lowest terms.

$12\overline{)16}$ $48\overline{)79}$ $12\overline{)69}$ $27\overline{)156}$ $20\overline{)92}$ $31\overline{)127}$

7 Write the measure of each object.

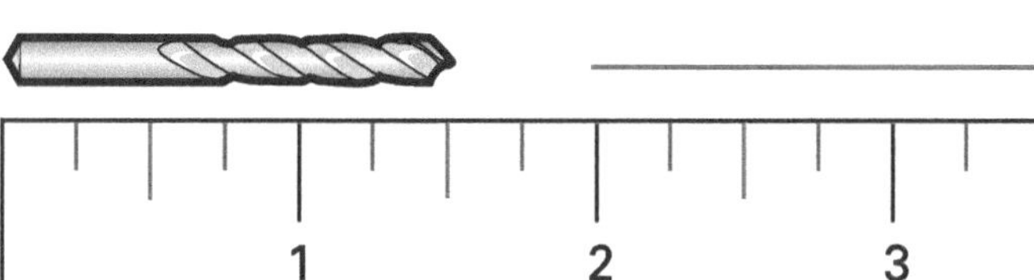

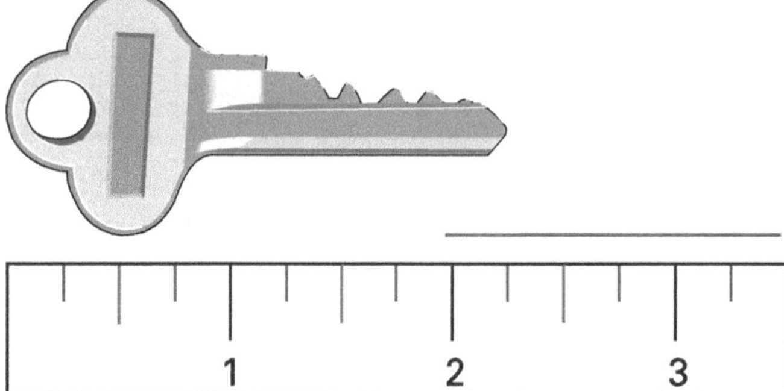

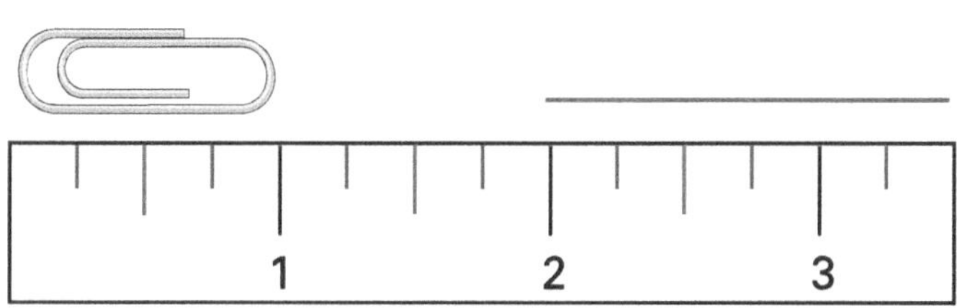

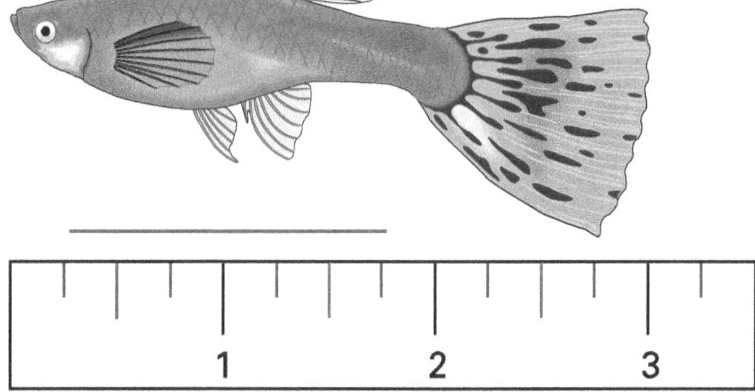

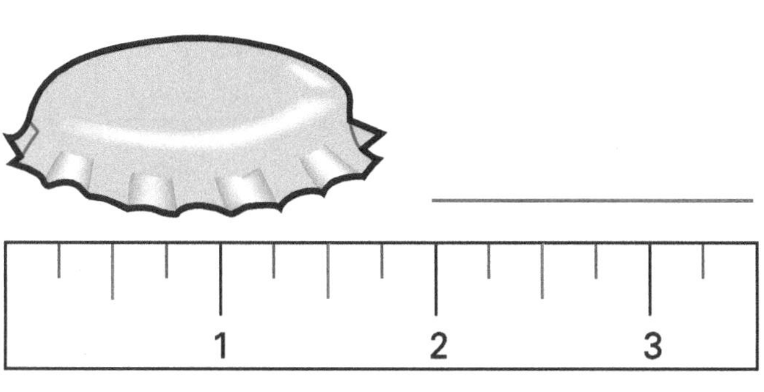

1 The numbers are written as decimals in the top nine boxes. The numbers are written as mixed numerals in the bottom nine boxes. Change any decimal in the top box into a mixed numeral, and find the mixed numeral in the bottom box. Write the word from the top box into the bottom box. You will spell out a message.

1.8	12.9	6.12	6.9	0.02	7.19	8.4	4.98	1.78
the	want	not	shall	shepherd	is	my	Lord	I

$1\frac{8}{10}$	$4\frac{98}{100}$	$7\frac{19}{100}$	$8\frac{4}{10}$	$\frac{2}{100}$	$1\frac{78}{100}$	$6\frac{9}{10}$	$6\frac{12}{100}$	$12\frac{9}{10}$
____	____	____	____	____	____	____	____	____

2 Write the dates in the answer box next to the correct century.

1812	2089	354	102
1999	1406	816	3

1st century ____________ 2nd century ____________

20th century ____________ 4th century ____________

9th century ____________ 21st century ____________

15th century ____________ 19th century ____________

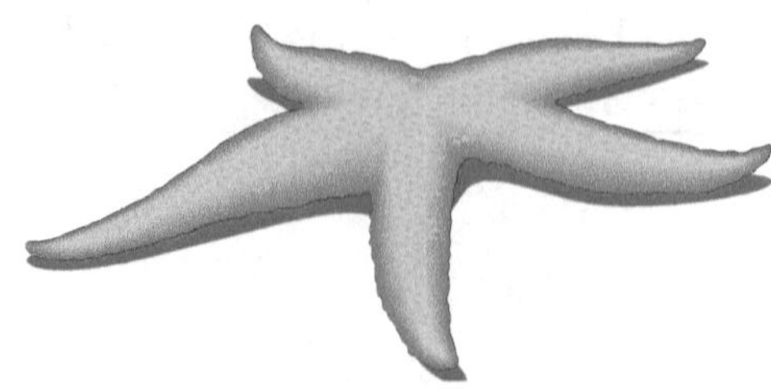

3 Use the table to help you make the following conversions.

1 foot = 12 inches
1 yard = 3 feet = 36 inches
1 mile = 1,760 yards = 5,280 feet

1. 6 yd = ______________ ft
2. 2 mi = ______________ yd
3. 36 in = ______________ ft
4. 36 in = ______________ yd
5. 3 mi = ______________ ft
6. 10 ft = ________________ in
7. 100 yd = ______________ ft
8. 24 ft = ________________ yd
9. 4 yd = ________________ ft
10. 2 yd = ________________ in

4 Work the division problems. Find the quotients below each dot. Connect the dots in the same order as the problems are numbered. Watch an object appear.

1. $12\overline{)942}$
2. $17\overline{)904}$
3. $62\overline{)981}$
4. $18\overline{)610}$
5. $12\overline{)257}$
6. $25\overline{)597}$

78 r 6 • 23 r 22

•
15 r 51

•
33 r 16

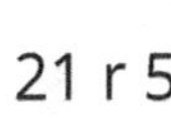
21 r 5

53 r 3

5 Find the product. Tell the exact change each customer will receive using the least number of coins.

Cost: 3 gumballs at $0.25 a piece. Customer paid $1.00.

____

Cost: 6 lemon drops at $0.05 a piece. Customer paid $0.50.

____

Cost: 8 sour balls at $0.12 a piece. Customer paid $1.00.

____

Cost: 2 Cinnamon Rockets at $0.45 a piece. Customer paid $1.00.

____

6 Solve.

$n - 6 = 30 - (4 \times 4)$	$n - 12 = 2 + (7 \times 7)$	$n - 13 = 18 + (2 \times 9)$

1 Use the table to help you make the following conversions.

16 ounces (oz) = 1 pound (lb)
2,000 pounds (lb) = 1 ton (T)

1. 32 oz = ___________ lb
2. 6,000 lb = ___________ T
3. 160 oz = ___________ lb
4. 5 T = ___________ lb
6. 6 lb = ___________ oz
7. 4 T = ___________ lb
8. 4 lb = ___________ oz
9. 12,000 lb = ___________ T

2 Tell the exact change each customer will receive using the least number of bills and coins.

Cost: 1 shirt at $8.95. Customer paid $10.00. ______________________________

____

Cost: 1 pkg. of blocks at $4.45. Customer paid 5.00.______________________________

____

Cost: 1 pkg. of socks at $5.99. Customer paid $10.00. ______________________________

____

Cost: 1 tube of toothpaste at $1.39 Customer paid $2.00.______________________________

____

3 Find the sum or difference. The problem marked with an asterisk (*) is more difficult to solve.

$$1\frac{2}{8} + 2\frac{3}{8}$$

$$4\frac{10}{12} - 2\frac{2}{12}$$

$$13\frac{6}{8} + 11\frac{1}{8}$$

$$9\frac{12}{15} - 7\frac{7}{15}$$

$$4\frac{7}{7} - 2\frac{5}{7}$$

$$25\frac{6}{8} + 13\frac{1}{8}$$

$$16\frac{14}{16} - 10\frac{2}{16}$$

* $$10\frac{6}{8} + 23\frac{6}{8}$$

4 Compare using <, >, =.

$\frac{2}{8}$ ___ $\frac{1}{4}$ $\frac{3}{7}$ ___ $\frac{12}{21}$ $\frac{10}{12}$ ___ $\frac{3}{4}$

$\frac{8}{9}$ ___ $\frac{16}{18}$ $\frac{3}{7}$ ___ $\frac{4}{8}$ $\frac{13}{16}$ ___ $\frac{7}{8}$

$\frac{1}{4}$ ___ $\frac{3}{8}$ $\frac{1}{9}$ ___ $\frac{9}{81}$ $\frac{20}{25}$ ___ $\frac{4}{5}$

5 Find each quotient. Shade the quotients that are even. Read the riddle left in the unshaded boxes: ***What school do you need a ladder to reach?***

21)693 **H**	12)168 **O**	19)152 **W**	12)564 **I**	10)310 **G**
5)495 **H**	21)231 **S**	18)360 **O**	27)243 **C**	15)225 **H**
41)533 **O**	19)456 **N**	28)168 **G**	45)315 **O**	12)204 **L**

Place each term beside the appropriate problem.

multiplicand	quotient	sum	multiplier	numerator
divisor	dividend	product	subtrahend	denominator
minuend	addend	difference	addend	

```
   1 __________
 x 8 __________
   8 __________
```

```
                12 __________
__________  2)24   __________
```

```
6 __________
-
8 __________
```

```
 72 __________
-10 __________
 62 __________
```

```
 47 __________
+23 __________
 70 __________
```

1 Compare using <, >, = .

$\frac{2}{6}$ ___ $\frac{1}{4}$	$\frac{3}{4}$ ___ $\frac{12}{16}$	$\frac{8}{12}$ ___ $\frac{3}{4}$
$\frac{8}{10}$ ___ $\frac{16}{20}$	$\frac{8}{9}$ ___ $\frac{4}{5}$	$\frac{2}{3}$ ___ $\frac{12}{16}$
$\frac{1}{4}$ ___ $\frac{25}{100}$	$\frac{5}{7}$ ___ $\frac{8}{9}$	$\frac{4}{8}$ ___ $\frac{5}{10}$

2 Use the table to help you make the following conversions.

1 kilogram (kg) = 1,000 grams (g)

5 kg = ______________ g

4,000 g = ______________ kg

27 kg = ______________ g

12,000 g = ______________ kg

Choose the more sensible answer.

Dime: 2 g 2 kg

Paperclip: 1 g 1 kg

Hardback book: 1 g 1 kg

Brick: 1 kg 1 g

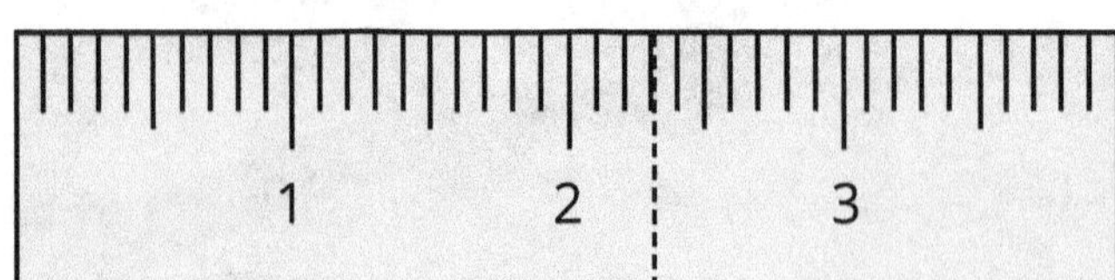

We can express this measurement in three ways:

2 cm 3 mm 23 mm, or 2.3 cm

3 Express the measurements below in all three ways.

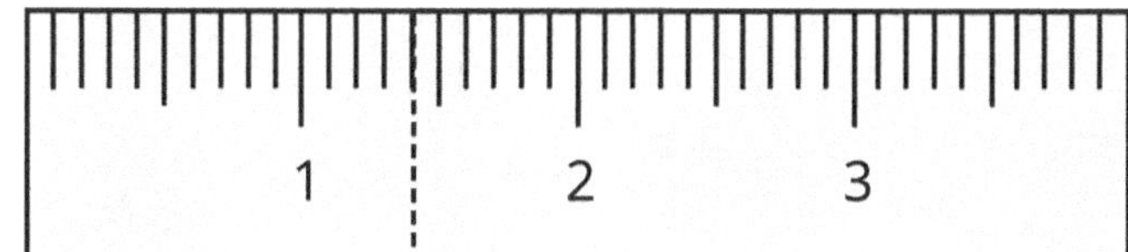

__________ __________ __________

__________ __________ __________

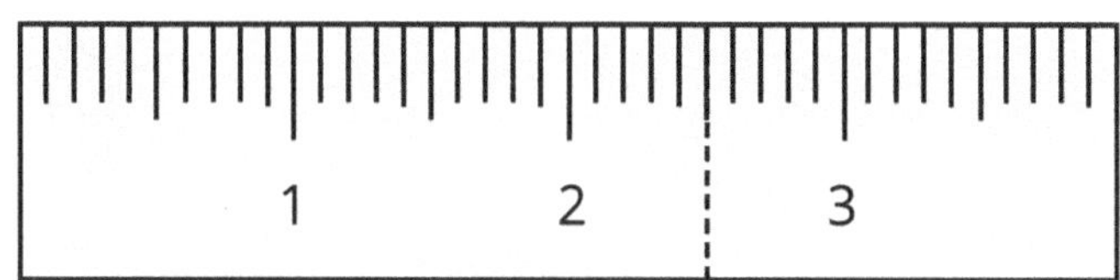

__________ __________ __________

4 Use the table to help you make the following conversions.

1 gallon (gal) = 4 quarts (qt)
1 quart (qt) = 2 pints (pt)
1 pint (pt) = 2 cups (c)

8 qt = __________ gal   4 c = __________ pt

8 pts = __________ qt   12 c = __________ pt

16 qt = __________ gal   12 pt = __________ qt

5 Solve each problem and fill in the boxes.

$\frac{3}{6}$	+	$\frac{1}{6}$	=					
				+				
				$\frac{1}{6}$				
				=				
$\frac{1}{6}$					–	$\frac{1}{3}$	=	
+								–
$\frac{5}{12}$								$\frac{1}{6}$
=								=
	–	$\frac{1}{12}$	=		–	$\frac{1}{6}$	=	

6 Find the sum or difference.

134.35 + 156.07	890.01 + 242.9	403.21 + 391.92	893.37 + 912.03	745.1 + 156.18
590.02 – 297.00	902.19 – 191.8	781.98 – 689.99	642.39 – 281.28	798.9 – 281.24

We can express this measurement in three ways:

3 cm, 6 mm ______ 36 mm ______ 3.6 cm ______

1 Express the measurements below in all three ways.

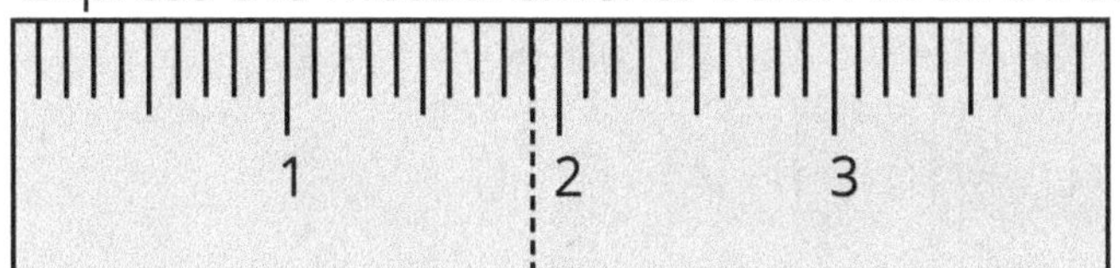

______ ______ ______

1 2 3

______ ______ ______

1 2 3

______ ______ ______

WORD BANK:	point	intersecting lines	line
	parallel	perpendicular lines	ray

2 Define each symbol using words from the Word Bank.

1. • D

____

2. 

____

3. ________________

4. ________________

5. ________________

6. ________________

3 Use the table to help you make the following conversions.

1 cm = 10 mm

3 cm = __________ mm　　60 mm = __________ cm

70 cm = __________ mm　　110 mm= __________ cm

450 cm = __________ mm　　470 mm = __________ cm

4 Find all the fractions that equal $\frac{1}{2}$ and color them blue. Find all the fractions that equal $\frac{1}{4}$ and color them red. Find all the fractions that equal $\frac{1}{3}$ and color yellow.

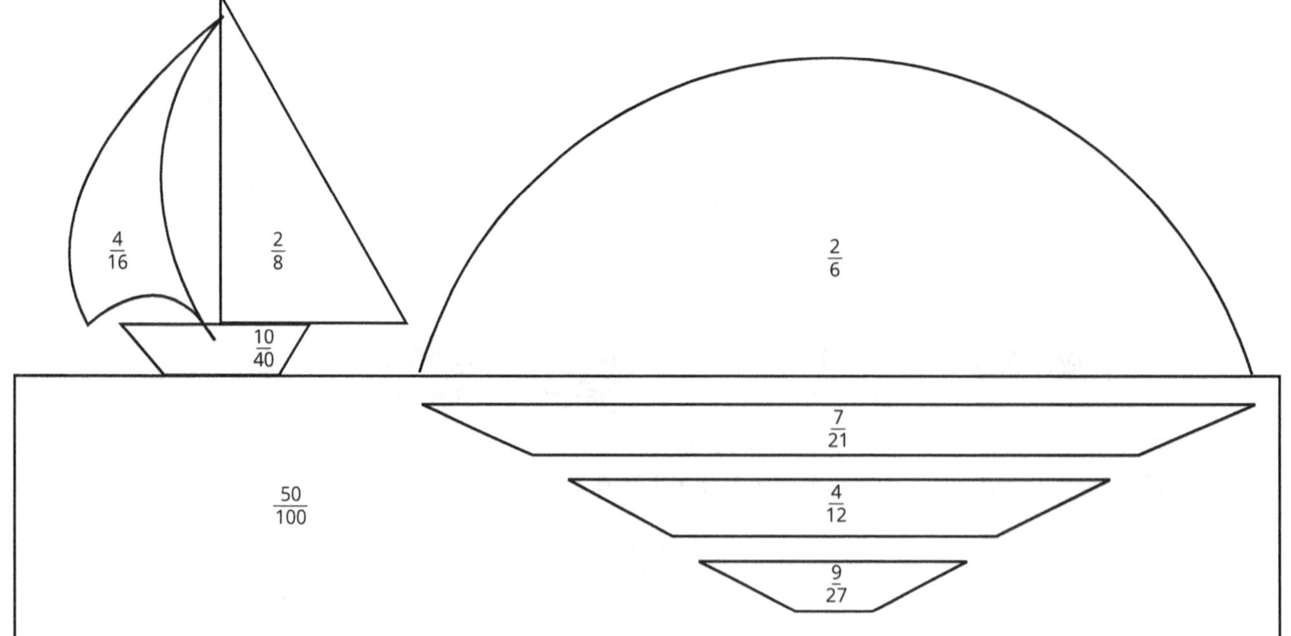

5 Find the sum.

```
  48        89        42
+ 89      + 29      + 78

  97        38        53
+ 34      + 79      + 57
```

Find the product.

```
  670       405       284
x  45     x  21     x  11

  209       365       196
x  37     x  41     x  23
```

6 Complete each chart by multiplying to find the ratios.

eggs	1		3	4	5
cups of batter	3	6	9		

cartons	1	2	3		
eggs	12	24		48	

1 Circle the ratio that does not belong.

1. $\frac{5}{6}$, $\frac{10}{12}$, $\frac{15}{18}$, $\frac{17}{19}$, $\frac{20}{24}$

2. $\frac{1}{2}$, $\frac{2}{4}$, $\frac{3}{6}$, $\frac{4}{20}$, $\frac{4}{8}$

3. $\frac{2}{3}$, $\frac{4}{6}$, $\frac{6}{15}$, $\frac{6}{9}$, $\frac{8}{12}$

4. $\frac{2}{5}$, $\frac{4}{10}$, $\frac{8}{20}$, $\frac{16}{40}$, $\frac{24}{50}$

2

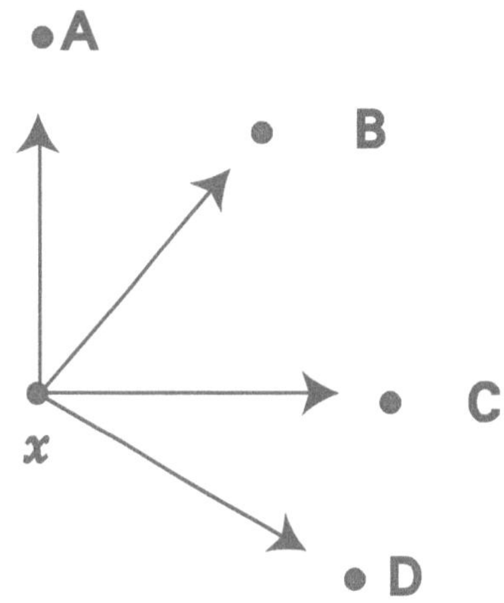

1. Name the right angle. ____________________
2. Name the obtuse angle. ____________________
3. What is the vertex of ∠ AXC ? ____________________
4. Name the sides of ∠ AXB. ____________________
5. Name at least two acute angles. ____________________

3 Find the value of n.

$\frac{5}{10} = \frac{n}{20}$ $\frac{6}{8} = \frac{n}{24}$ $\frac{3}{9} = \frac{27}{n}$ $\frac{1}{7} = \frac{4}{n}$

4 Find each product. Place the letter above the answer below to solve the riddle:
What always keeps its hands on its face?

$\begin{array}{r} 365 \\ \times\ 23 \\ \hline \end{array}$ = **L**

$\begin{array}{r} 209 \\ \times\ 83 \\ \hline \end{array}$ = **O**

$\begin{array}{r} 475 \\ \times\ 31 \\ \hline \end{array}$ = **A**

$\begin{array}{r} 275 \\ \times\ 40 \\ \hline \end{array}$ = **K**

$\begin{array}{r} 197 \\ \times\ 56 \\ \hline \end{array}$ = **C**

____	____	____	____	____	____
14,725	11,032	8,395	17,347	11,032	11,000

5 Shade the even numbers to read the message.

24	33	99	31	10	8	6	3	50	5	94	9	18	26	94
18	35	87	11	4	55	70	13	56	5	68	7	80	3	21
42	3	75	61	78	57	72	95	98	5	60	5	4	10	19
90	11	21	83	64	87	26	97	92	5	52	3	8	12	17
16	15	13	73	88	67	54	83	2	5	14	1	14	5	7
4	22	66	67	76	40	20	91	3	6	3	11	8	68	66

1 Corinthians 13:13: **"So faith, hope, love abide, these three; but the greatest of these is love."**

6 Find the sum.

$$\begin{array}{r} 354 \\ +\ 309 \\ \hline \end{array} \qquad \begin{array}{r} 870 \\ +\ 268 \\ \hline \end{array} \qquad \begin{array}{r} 295 \\ +\ 990 \\ \hline \end{array}$$

$$\begin{array}{r} 363 \\ +\ 879 \\ \hline \end{array} \qquad \begin{array}{r} 909 \\ +\ 287 \\ \hline \end{array}$$

1 Find the sum.

47	49	39	56	74
71	82	91	71	21
90	88	41	52	80
12	43	81	93	89
+ 21	+ 30	+ 27	+ 19	+ 26

2 Solve the equations.

$2 \times n = (2 \times 8) - 2$ $6 \times n = (4 \times 10) - 4$ $7 \times n = (8 \times 8) - 8$

3 Who Am I?

1. My three digits are all even.
2. The product of my first and third digits equals the second.
3. The first digit is less than the third digit.

I am __________

Who Am I?

1. I have four digits.
2. My first two digits are the product of 8 and 4 minus 1.
3. My last two digits are equal and even.
4. My last two digits are greater than 6.

I am __________

4 Match the temperatures. There is both a Celsius and Fahrenheit for each.

37°C	Boiling Point	32°F
0°C	Freezing Point	98.6°F
-20°C	Room Temperature (comfortable)	10°F
100°C	Inside a Freezer	212°F
25°C	Body Temperature (normal)	72°F

5 Use the words in the box to complete the sentences.

century	21st	decade	20th
millennium	B.C.	A.D.	

1. A ________________ is a period of 1,000 years.
2. A ________________ is a period of ten years.
3. A ________________ is a period of one hundred years.
4. ________________ stands for before Christ.
5. If I was born in 1987, I was born in the ________________ century.
6. In the year 2003, it will be the ________________ century.
7. ________________ stands for in the year of our Lord.

6 Write liquid, linear, or weight.

milligram	________	liter	________	kilogram	________
meter	________	centimeter	________	milliliter	________
kilometer	________	gram	________	millimeter	________
decimeter	________	kiloliter	________	decigram	________

7 Write each fraction in lowest terms.

$\frac{5}{10}$ ________	$\frac{4}{64}$ ________	$\frac{8}{32}$ ________
$\frac{6}{90}$ ________	$\frac{50}{100}$ ________	$\frac{11}{77}$ ________
$\frac{16}{32}$ ________	$\frac{18}{81}$ ________	$\frac{4}{48}$ ________
$\frac{15}{45}$ ________	$\frac{8}{24}$ ________	$\frac{10}{100}$ ________

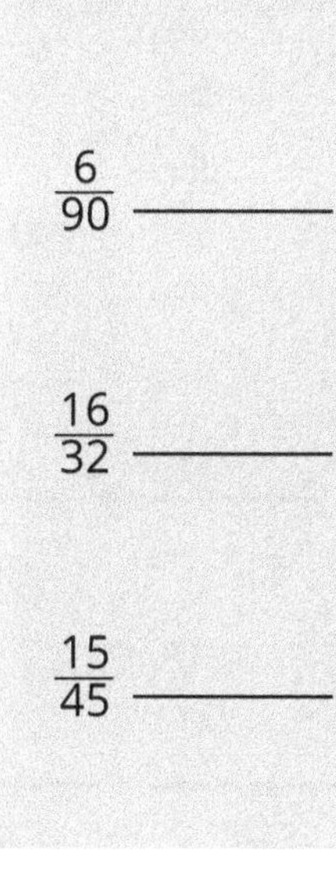

1 Write the missing numbers.

Word Number	Decimal	Fraction
nine tenths	0.9	$\frac{9}{10}$
one and twenty-one hundredths		
	57.04	
		$7\frac{3}{10}$
three and two hundredths		
		$61\frac{5}{10}$
	4.25	
forty-two and five tenths		
		$1\frac{2}{100}$
	8.13	

2 Find the difference. Place the letter above the answer to solve the riddle:
What are the biggest gems in the world?

$798 - 273$ = **S**

$403 - 374$ = **B**

$139 - 108$ = **M**

$482 - 395$ = **N**

$302 - 119$ = **I**

$465 - 364$ = **A**

$400 - 374$ = **E**

$317 - 232$ = **L**

$925 - 246$ = **D**

$641 - 298$ = **O**

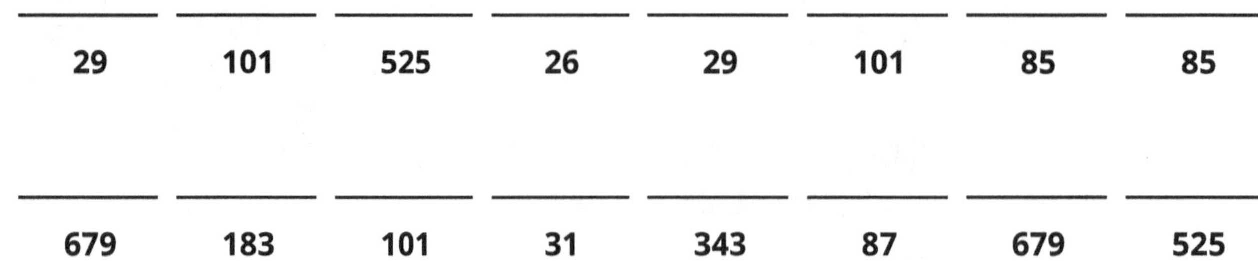

3 Match the equivalent fractions.

$\frac{1}{2}$	$\frac{4}{6}$
$\frac{2}{3}$	$\frac{33}{99}$
$\frac{1}{3}$	$\frac{12}{22}$
$\frac{4}{5}$	$\frac{10}{14}$
$\frac{5}{7}$	$\frac{12}{15}$
$\frac{2}{5}$	$\frac{4}{10}$
$\frac{6}{11}$	$\frac{50}{100}$

4 Solve the equations.

$n - 3 = 16 - (2 \times 3)$ $n - 8 = 3 + (4 \times 5)$ $n - 3 = 30 - (4 \times 4)$

5 Find the sum or difference. Make sure the answer is in lowest terms.

$\frac{1}{4} + \frac{1}{3} =$ $\frac{4}{5} - \frac{1}{10} =$ $\frac{2}{8} + \frac{1}{4} =$

$\frac{2}{6} + \frac{1}{3} =$ $\frac{8}{9} - \frac{2}{9} =$ $\frac{9}{10} - \frac{1}{2} =$

$\frac{5}{6} - \frac{1}{2} =$ $\frac{1}{8} + \frac{1}{4} =$ $\frac{1}{9} + \frac{1}{3} =$

6 Think it through.

$\frac{1}{6}$ of 36 = $\frac{1}{10}$ of 50 = $\frac{1}{8}$ of 64 = $\frac{1}{7}$ of 21 =

63 points total Lessons 146-155

1 Complete the chart with equivalent ratios. 7 pts. total for this exercise.

cups of pudding	5	10		20		30	
cups of milk	1	2				6	

2 Find the equal ratios by multiplying. 4 pts. total for this exercise.

$\frac{3}{12} = \frac{9}{n}$ $\frac{4}{5} = \frac{40}{n}$ $\frac{5}{8} = \frac{25}{n}$ $\frac{7}{8} = \frac{42}{n}$

3 Divide by 2 to find equal ratios. 12 pts. total for this exercise.

$\frac{4}{8}$		$\frac{30}{60}$		$\frac{12}{16}$		$\frac{2}{4}$	
$\frac{4}{10}$		$\frac{12}{14}$		$\frac{4}{16}$		$\frac{20}{30}$	
$\frac{4}{32}$		$\frac{6}{8}$		$\frac{6}{10}$		$\frac{8}{16}$	

4 Write in lowest terms. 5 pts. total for this exercise.

$\frac{4}{8} =$ $\frac{6}{24} =$ $\frac{18}{36} =$ $\frac{12}{48} =$ $\frac{21}{42} =$

5 Add. 6 pts. total for this exercise.

$\frac{6}{25} + \frac{19}{25} =$ ______ $\frac{3}{18} + \frac{1}{18} =$ ______ $\frac{5}{15} + \frac{5}{15} =$ ______

$\frac{4}{16} + \frac{2}{16} =$ ______ $\frac{4}{13} + \frac{2}{13} =$ ______ $\frac{2}{30} + \frac{2}{30} =$ ______

6 Find the difference. 5 pts. total for this exercise.

147	175	890	354	908
- 104	-90	-351	-162	- 512

7 **Temp** **Monthly Average Temperatures–Phoenix**

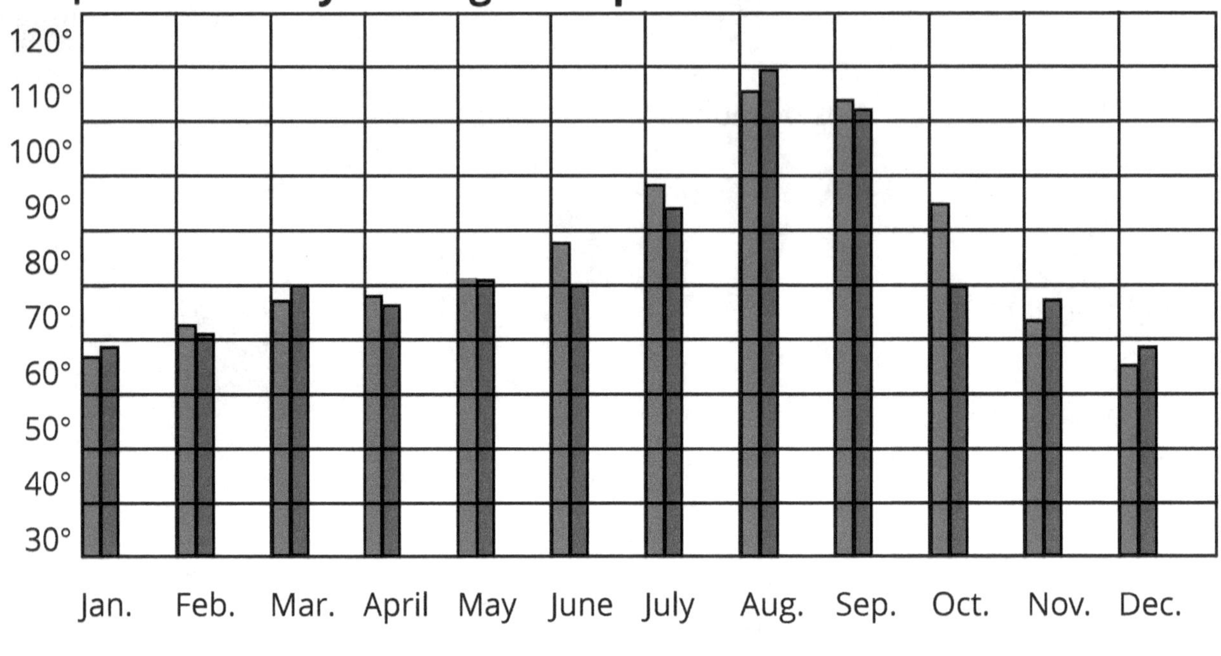

2009 2010 4 pts. total for this exercise.

1. What month had the coldest average monthly temperature in 2009? 2010?
2. What month had the warmest average monthly temperature in 2009? 2010?
3. What month was the temperature the same in 2009 and 2010?
4. What month showed the greatest difference in temperature between 2009 and 2010?

8 Find the product. 15 pts. total for this exercise.

x	3	6	8	2	9
2					
7					
9					

9 Label each shape (rhombus, parallelogram, rectangle, trapezoid, and square). 5 pts.

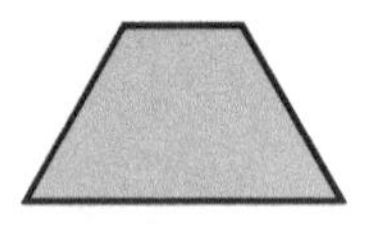

_______ _______ _______ _______ _______